NON-AXIOMATIC LOGIC
A Model of Intelligent Reasoning

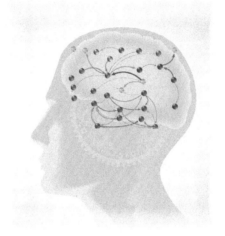

NON-AXIOMATIC LOGIC
A Model of Intelligent Reasoning

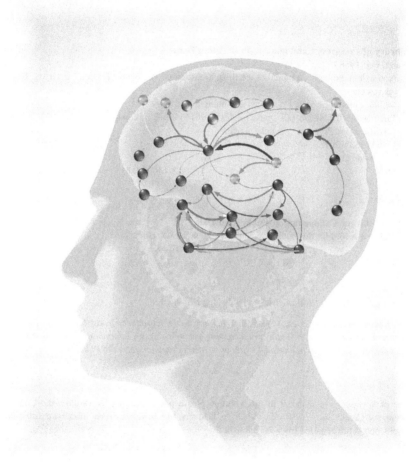

Pei Wang

Temple University, USA

 **World Scientific**

NEW JERSEY · LONDON · SINGAPORE · BEIJING · SHANGHAI · HONG KONG · TAIPEI · CHENNAI

Published by

World Scientific Publishing Co. Pte. Ltd.

5 Toh Tuck Link, Singapore 596224

USA office: 27 Warren Street, Suite 401-402, Hackensack, NJ 07601

UK office: 57 Shelton Street, Covent Garden, London WC2H 9HE

Library of Congress Cataloging-in-Publication Data
Wang, Pei, 1958–
   Non-axiomatic logic : a model of intelligent reasoning / Pei Wang, Temple University, USA.
   pages cm
   Includes bibliographical references and index.
   ISBN 978-9814440271 (alk. paper) -- ISBN 9814440272 (alk. paper)
   1. Artificial intelligence. 2. Logic. I. Title.
   Q335.W3535 2013
   511.3'6--dc23
                         2013007458

British Library Cataloguing-in-Publication Data
A catalogue record for this book is available from the British Library.

In-house Editor: Amanda Yun

Typeset by Stallion Press
Email: enquiries@stallionpress.com

Printed in Singapore

To my parents
Wang Zhizhong
and
Zhai Minghui

CONTENTS

PREFACE

This book provides a comprehensive, precise, and up-to-date description of Non-Axiomatic Logic, abbreviated as NAL.

This logic is designed for the creation of general-purpose Artificial Intelligence (AI) systems, by formulating the fundamental regularity of human thinking at a general level. Therefore, this work also belongs to Cognitive Science (CogSci), the interdisciplinary study of "mind" and "cognition". This book directly addresses many topics in logic, psychology, linguistics, philosophy, and computer science.

The distinctive feature of NAL is the "relative rationality" it exhibits when guiding the adaptation process of a system that has to work with *insufficient* knowledge and resources. NAL differs from ordinary logic systems in all of its major components: it uses *subject–predicate* (rather than *predicate–argument*) sentences, *experience-grounded* (rather than *model-theoretic*) semantics, and *syllogistic* (rather than *truth-functional*) inference rules. In fact, NAL is so different from the other logics that some logicians are reluctant to consider it a "logic". Though this reaction is understandable, and this system indeed can be described using other terminologies (such as a conceptual graph), in this book it is still presented as a *logic* system. Technically, this presentation is selected because NAL can be accurately specified as consisting of a formal language, a set of formal inference rules, and a semantic theory; conceptually, it is because that NAL is an attempt to capture the "laws of thought", that is, the patterns of valid inference in human thinking. For the latter reason, NAL is arguably closer to the general and original sense of "logic" than mathematical logic is.

NAL is the logical part of the AI system NARS (Non-Axiomatic Reasoning System). Since this book focuses on the logic, the other aspects of the system (such as memory and control) are mentioned only when necessary. Since NARS aims at a general-purpose "thinking machine", this project is related to almost all previous works in AI and CogSci. However, restricted by its length and focus, this book cannot compare my approach to all of the others, but only to the most relevant ones. Many of the aspects of NARS have been discussed in my previous publications, such as Wang (1995, 2006b), as well as many journal articles and conference papers that are cited in this book.

This book is written for readers with college-level knowledge of AI, computer science, and mathematical logic. It can be used as the textbook for a one-semester graduate or upper-level undergraduate course. The chapters should be read in the given order, with the appendices as references on the formal content of NAL.

NARS is an on-going project. For its latest development, documentations, demonstrations, and source code, see the project website (Currently at `http://sites.google.com/site/narswang/`, which is mostly mirrored at `http://www.cis.temple.edu/~wangp/`).

ACKNOWLEDGMENTS

It was the invitation of Dr. K. K. Phua, the Chairman and Editor-in-Chief of World Scientific, that initiated this writing project. His suggestion of presenting the materials as lecture notes is also very valuable.

Thanks to Temple University for rewarding me a sabbatical leave in the 2011–2012 academic year, which has given me the time to finish this book. Drafts of the book were used as teaching materials at Peking University (in Spring 2012) and Reykjavik University (in Summer 2012), and I thank the attendants of my lectures for their helpful feedback.

The comments and English corrections by Selmer Bringsjord, Ben Goertzel, Bill Hibbard, Ólafur Hlynsson, Brandon Rohrer, Lukasz Stafiniak, and Eugene Surowitz greatly helped in the revision of this book.

My research in recent years has benefited from many discussions with Lang Deng, Eric Nivel, Kris Thórisson, Xihong Wu, Yingjin Xu, and Beihai Zhou.

Last but not least, thanks to my dear wife Hongyuan Sun for her support for so many years.

Pei Wang

LIST OF TABLES

CHAPTER 1

INTRODUCTION

This chapter explains the theoretical considerations behind the logic to be described in this book.

1.1. Intelligence

This new logic is proposed as part of a normative theory of what we usually call "intelligence", "cognition", or "thinking". Its direct objective is to serve as a formal model to be implemented in computer systems to achieve "Artificial Intelligence" (AI). For that purpose, it must also specify the "laws of thought" followed by the human beings.

Like many basic concepts, "intelligence" has many different interpretations and understandings. In the context of AI, the majority opinion is to consider it as the ability to solve problems that are solvable by human beings only [McCarthy *et al.* (1955); Russell and Norvig (2010)]. Though this approach has contributed greatly to computer science and technology, it has not made much progress toward the original and ultimate objective of AI, that is, the building of "thinking machines" that have intellectual power comparable to that of human beings. Instead, the research results focus on special aspects of intelligence, and are hard to be either generalized to other tasks, or to be integrated together [Brachman (2006)]. On the contrary, the research project described in this book belongs to the emerging field of "Artificial General Intelligence" (AGI), which differs from the mainstream AI by emphasizing the general and holistic nature of intelligence [Goertzel and Pennachin (2007); Wang and Goertzel (2007)].

1

On the other hand, the study of intelligence in the context of Cognitive Science (CogSci) focuses on descriptive theories of the human mind and brain, where the objective of computer models is to simulate the human structure, activities, and behaviors as accurately as possible [Newell (1990)]. Though such research contributes greatly to neuroscience and psychology, it is not necessarily the best approach for AI. After all, a computer system is very different from the human brain at the low (hardware/wetware) level, so it may be neither necessary nor possible for a computer to work like a brain in all the details. In a sense, the very idea of AI is based on the assumption that what we call "intelligence" can be reproduced in artifacts that have different origins and details when compared to the human brain.

Therefore, though all AI projects aim at the common goal of building computer systems that are "similar to the human mind" in certain aspects, they are nevertheless very different from each other in *where* this similarity is or should be, which corresponds to different working definition of intelligence [Wang (2008)]. My working definition is:

> *Intelligence is the ability for a system to adapt to its environment and to work with insufficient knowledge and resources* [Wang (1994c, 2008)].

In this context, to *adapt* requires the system to decide on its actions according to its experience, so as to better achieve its goals when the environment is relatively stable. It can be considered as a principle of "relative rationality". Compared to the other theories of rationality, the most significant feature of this relative rationality is the *Assumption of Insufficient Knowledge and Resources*, or AIKR [Wang (1994c, 2011)], which is with respect to the problems to be solved by the system, and it demands the following three features of the system:

Finite: The system can work with constant information-processing capacity, in terms of processor speed and storage space.

Real-time: The system has to deal with problems that may appear at any moment and demand immediate response.

Open: The system must face input data and problems of any content, as far as they can be expressed in a format recognizable to the system.

It follows from AIKR that the system's behaviors are not absolutely optimal — for a given problem, usually the system could do better if it had more knowledge and resources. However, AIKR does not endorse *arbitrary* actions. The future is probably not identical to the past, but when we need to make predictions, we have nothing else to depend on but past experience. When facing a problem, we usually cannot consider all possibilities, but only consider the most important and relevant ones, judged according to our past experience, and we consider as many of them as allowed by the current resource supply.

Such an understanding of "intelligence" is in agreement with the opinions of some cognitive scientists. For instance, Piaget (1960) took intelligence as "the most highly developed form of mental adaptation"; Medin and Ross (1992) wrote that "Much of intelligent behavior can be understood in terms of strategies for coping with too little information and too many possibilities"; and my "relative rationality" is similar to Simon's "bounded rationality" [Simon (1957)]. Even so, in current AI research, few projects are aimed at such a goal [Russell and Norvig (2010)], or are designed under the restriction of AIKR.

Compared to the alternatives, my approach toward AI has the following major advantages [Wang (2008)]:

- It gives "intelligence" a coherent and compact description, from which all the concrete conclusions are implied. It is a preferred form of theorization, both in science and in engineering.
- It is less anthropocentric. Though human intelligence is indeed the best-known form of intelligence, the notion of "artificial intelligence" presumes a concept of "intelligence" that is more general than "human intelligence". Consequently, a computer system can be considered as intelligent without being similar to the human mind in all the details.

- It provides an explanation for why the conventional computer systems are not intelligent yet. That is, though such a system may have remarkable capability in dealing with certain practical problems, this capability comes from its design, and consequently it usually lacks creativity and flexibility.

- It gives the field of AI a proper identity, while the other approaches have the risk of reducing AI into an existing branch of science and engineering (such as neuroscience, cognitive psychology, computer science, or computer technology).

For these reasons, my research goal is *to design and build a computer system that can adapt to its environment while working with insufficient knowledge and resources.* The system may have other properties and applications, but they are derivative and secondary.

Since the above research goal is different from the goals of the mainstream AI systems, this research should not be evaluated according to the common standard of the AI field, i.e., in terms of a system's practical problem-solving ability. This research is not aimed at a system with given (domain-specific) *problem-solving skills*, but a system with a given (meta-level and general-purpose) *learning ability* that allows the system to acquire various problem-solving skills from its experience.

1.2.   Reasoning System

Since the objective of this research is to identify the "laws of thought", it is quite natural for the system to be designed in the framework of a reasoning system, following a formal logic. After all, in the general sense, logic is about the laws (or rules) of valid inference (or reasoning).[1]

At the conceptual level, a *reasoning system* consists of the following major components:

Grammar rules: These rules define the format of the representation language used in the system, by specifying how a legitimate sentence can be composed from words and phrases.

---

[1]In this book, *reasoning* and *inference* are treated as synonyms.

Inference rules: These rules define the pattern of valid reasoning in each inference step, where certain sentences are derived (as conclusions) from some given sentences (as premises).

Semantic theory: This theory specifies how the words and sentences of the language get their meaning, and explains why the inference rules are valid.

Memory structure: This structure is responsible for the storage and retrieval of the sentences involved in the inference processes of the system.

Control mechanism: This mechanism is responsible for the selection of premises and inference rules of each step in the inference processes.

Usually, the first three components are referred to as the "logic" implemented in the reasoning system.

At the present time, the study of reasoning systems is dominated by the tradition of "mathematical logic", which mainly consists of propositional calculus, predicate calculus, model theory, set theory, and computation theory. This tradition started as an attempt to provide a logical foundation for mathematics [Frege (1999); Whitehead and Russell (1910)], but it has been widely used in many other domains outside mathematics, including cognitive science [Allwood *et al.* (1977); Braine and O'Brien (1998)] and computer science [Halpern *et al.* (2001)]. To create AI as reasoning systems is not a new idea, and it has been promoted in theory by the "logicist AI" school [Hayes (1977); McCarthy (1988); Nilsson (1991)], and explored in practice by various "knowledge-based systems" [Lenat and Feigenbaum (1991)].

From the very beginning, it has been very clear that mathematical logic is not designed to be a *descriptive* model of human reasoning. However, even when considered as a *normative* model of reasoning, it is still quite limited. In the "classical" form (i.e., first-order predicate calculus), this type of logic only covers binary deduction in closed (axiomatic) systems. There have been many attempts (in logic, AI, and other related fields) to extend or revise it to get logic systems with certain properties that are considered as necessary for various reasons:

Uncertainty: In natural languages, a statement is usually neither absolutely true nor absolutely false, but somewhere in between. Furthermore, since an intelligent system should be able to compare different possibilities, a three-valued logic is not enough, and some type of numerical measurement is often needed. Proposed solutions to this issue include various forms of *probabilistic logic* [Nilsson (1986); Adams (1998)] and *fuzzy logic* [Zadeh (1983)].

Openness: In realistic situations, the system cannot evaluate the truth-value of statements according to a constant set of axioms, but has to depend on assumptions, and to be open to new evidence. To work in these situations, it is necessary to reason by "default rules", and to revise the tentative conclusions when counter-evidence show up. This is what *non-monotonic logics* attempt to handle [McCarthy (1989); Reiter (1987)].

Ampliation: Classical logic only covers deduction, but there are also induction, abduction, analogy, and other types of inference that play crucial roles in human thinking. These types of inference are often called "ampliative", since their conclusions seem to include knowledge that is not in the premises. Consequently, they are not "truth-preserving" in the traditional sense. The validity of these types of inference has been a controversial topic, and many different solutions have been proposed, including various forms of *inductive logic* [Kyburg (1970); Flach and Kakas (2000)].

Relevance: Classical logic suffers from the notorious "paradoxes of material implication" — the "implication" defined in the logic does not match the intuitive meaning of "if–then", and it leads to various "logically correct" but intuitively problematic inference, where the premises and conclusions are unrelated in content. This issue triggered the development of *relevance logic* [Anderson and Belnap (1975)], and is also important for AI, because no system can afford resources to generate many "true-but-useless" conclusions.

In both logic and AI, the above issues are usually addressed separately, and a new logic is typically built by extending or revising a single aspect of classical logic, while leaving the other aspects unchanged [Haack (1996); Gabbay (2007); Russell and Norvig (2010)]. Though each non-classical logic has its applicable situations, and can be used to solve some practical problems, none of them is powerful enough to support a general-purpose reasoning system. Furthermore, it looks implausible to "integrate" these non-classical logics together into a coherent logic, since they are based on quite different assumptions.

What makes my approach different is the belief that the above issues have a common root at a deeper level, so may be resolved together in a new system that fundamentally differs from the classical logic.

When designing or selecting a reasoning system, two types of situation can be distinguished:

Idealized, where the system has *sufficient knowledge and resources*, with respect to the problems to be solved. All the knowledge needed is available to the system at the very beginning with guaranteed correctness and consistency, and all the required conclusions are implied by them. The system has enough processing time and storage space to carry out the required inference activity, so the resource expense can be ignored.

Realistic, where the system has *insufficient knowledge and resources*, with respect to the problems to be solved. The knowledge comes to the system from time to time, without guaranteed correctness and consistency. New problems may show up at any moment, with required response time. The solution of a problem often requires knowledge that is not available to the system at the moment, and the system cannot simply reject the problem without a try. The system usually cannot afford the time–space resource to consider all possibilities when solving a given problem.

It is not hard to recognize that classical logic is designed for reasoning in this *idealized* situation, while the human mind and many (if not all) AI systems need to work in this *realistic* situation. Even so, the traditional opinion is that a "logic" must be designed for the idealized situation. When reasoning activities have to be carried out in the realistic situation, idealized situation is *approximated* as closely as possible.

I have been advocating the opinion that these two types of situations require two types of logic:

Axiomatic logic is suitable for an idealized situation. The initial knowledge is represented as axioms, and all solutions to the problems are provided by the theorems derived by deduction. Since all the inference rules are truth-preserving, the truth of the theorems is guaranteed by the truth of the axioms.[2]

Non-axiomatic logic is suitable for a realistic situation. Since all knowledge may be challenged by new evidence, there is no axiom in the system that has guaranteed truth. Since the problem may fall outside the current knowledge scope of the system, ampliative reasoning becomes necessary, although it does not have the traditional validity. Since the computational resources are in short supply, a conclusion may not be based on all the relevant knowledge in the system, but only on part of it.

From this description, it is obvious that these two types of logic are fundamentally different, and we cannot use one to approximate the other. As analyzed in Wang (2006b), the problems in logic-based AI are not caused by notions like "reasoning", "logic", or "formalization", but by the type of logic and reasoning system that has been used in AI. Especially, the root of the problems is in the notion of "axiomatization". Though such a reasoning system is favored in mathematics, it is improper for AI, since it disobeys the previously introduced AIKR.

For the purpose of AI, what is needed is a reasoning system that is adaptive to its environment, and works under AIKR. Such a system is still a "reasoning system", since it consists of the same

---

[2]In logic literature, "axiomatic logic" is sometimes used to refer to a logic system whose inference rules can be derived from a set of axioms. This is not how this name (as well as its opposite, *non-axiomatic logic*) is used in this book. Here the "axiomatic versus non-axiomatic" difference is at the object-level (where domain knowledge is represented), not the meta-level (where the inference rules are represented), of the reasoning system.

five major components listed above; however, it is not "axiomatic", since none of the beliefs in the system can be considered as axioms or theorems. Instead, they are merely summarized past experience, and can be modified by future experience or further deliberation. Similarly, the inference rules are "valid" not in the sense of "deriving truth from truth", but "faithfully summarizing experience". It is in this sense that the reasoning system and its logic to be introduced in this book are referred to as "non-axiomatic". Such a system can still have fixed grammar and inference rules that cannot be modified by the system itself, but they are not axioms among the system's beliefs, since they are at the meta-level of the system, while the beliefs are on the object-level.

1.3.   NAL Overview

Now the objective of this book can be clearly specified as: to define a logic named *NAL*, short for *Non-Axiomatic Logic*.

NAL is a *logic* since it includes a set of symbolic grammar rules specifying the system's representation language, a set of symbolic inference rules specifying the system's reasoning competence, and a semantic theory containing the definitions of "meaning" (so as to explain the usage of the representation language) and "truth" (so as to justify the validity of the inference rules).

NAL is "non-axiomatic" in the sense that it is based on AIKR, so that the truth-value of a conclusion in the system does not indicate how much the sentence agrees with the "state of affair" in the world, or with a constant set of assumptions (the axioms), but how much it is supported by the evidence provided by the past experience of the system. Therefore, no sentence in its representation language can be taken as an "axiom" (or a "theorem") with a truth-value that will never be challenged by the future experience. Similarly, the meaning of words in the representation language does not denote "objects" in the world, but stable patterns in the system's experience. The inference rules are *valid*, not because their conclusions are guaranteed to agree with future experience, but that they properly summarized past experience, so can be used to predict the future by an adaptive system, even though the predictions can be wrong when compared with future experience.

For such a logic to be used by a reasoning system, the rules need to be coded in a programming language, and the system also needs a memory–control part. NARS is such a *non-axiomatic reasoning system*, which, in its various stages of development, has been described in Wang (1995, 2006b) and many other publications. Since this book focuses on NAL, the other components and aspects of NARS are only mentioned briefly.

The representation language of NARS is called "Narsese", which serves both the roles of internal representation and external communication for NARS. That is, the language is used to represent beliefs and tasks within the system, as well as to exchange knowledge and problems with other (computer or human) systems in the outside world. It is important to distinguish Narsese from the other two languages used in the NARS project. As far as NARS is considered as an inference system, Narsese is on the *object-level* and is used to represent the *system's* knowledge about its environment and itself. When we talk about the design of NARS and NAL in this book, the language (English for this book) is at the *meta-level* and used to represent *our* knowledge about the system. Finally, when NARS is implemented in a computer system, it is coded in a programming language (currently Java and Prolog). These three types of language have different properties, and do not include one another as subsets.

To provide a more accurate description of the system, the meta-level description of NAL also uses other formal theories, including set theory, first-order predicate logic, the theory of formal languages, etc., but once again, these theories are parts of our knowledge about NARS, rather than part of the knowledge of NARS.

In the following, NAL will be introduced in multiple "layers". Each of them extends the sets of grammar and inference rules of the "lower" layers, so as to increase the expressive and inferential powers of the system, and consequently to make it more intelligent. The semantic theory and the memory–control parts also become more complicated with more layers in the system. Since the current design include nine layers, in the following chapters the corresponding logic will be named as NAL-1 to NAL-9, respectively. Additionally, there is a chapter that provides an introduction, and another one a summary. Given this arrangement, the chapters should be read in the given order.

CHAPTER 2

IL-1: IDEALIZED SITUATION

Since the existing logic systems are mostly designed for axiomatic systems, establishing NAL on AIKR is not a trivial job. We will see in the following that none of the major components of classical logic can be accepted into NAL in its current form. To simplify the design and analysis of NAL, we start from an idealized situation, where AIKR can be temporarily ignored.

In this chapter, we introduce an *Inheritance Logic*, or IL [Wang (1994b)]. IL is an *idealized version* of NAL, in the sense that it is similar to NAL in grammar, semantics, and inference rules, though it assumes *sufficient* knowledge and resources. Therefore, IL is not a "non-axiomatic" logic, but a step in building such a logic. Just like NAL, IL is also built with layers. For each layer i ($1 \leq i \leq 9$), the corresponding IL-i is defined first, then the effect of insufficient knowledge and resources is introduced, to turn IL-i into NAL-i. This chapter defines IL-1, the simplest inheritance logic.[1]

In the history of logic, there are two major traditions: a "term logic" tradition exemplified by Aristotle (1882) and Sommers (1982), and a "predicate logic" tradition exemplified by Frege (1999) and Whitehead and Russell (1910). Though at the present time the latter is the dominating paradigm, NAL and IL belong to the former. The reasons of this important decision will be gradually explained in the following chapters.

---

[1] IL-1 was called "IL" in Wang (1994b), and "NAL-0" in Wang (2006b).

2.1.   Categorical Language

The simplest sentence in a predicate logic has a *"predicate-arguments"* format, such as $P(a_1, \ldots, a_n)$, where P is the *predicate symbol*, while each a_i $(1 \leq i \leq n)$ is an *argument* of the predicate. On the contrary, the simplest sentence in a term logic has a *"subject-copula-predicate"* format, which is often called a "categorical sentence", and a language consisting of such sentences is called a "categorical language". Since term logic uses this type of language, it is sometimes called "categorical logic" [Smith (2012)].

Narsese is a categorical language, and IL uses a version of it. The smallest component of the language is a "term", which, in its simplest form, is an identifier used in the logic.[2]

Definition 2.1. The basic form of a *term* is a *word*, that is, a string of characters from a finite alphabet.

There is no additional requirement on the alphabet. In this book, the alphabet includes English letters, digits 0 to 9, and a few special signs, such as hyphen ('-'). In the examples, we often use common English nouns for terms, such as *bird* and *animal*, just to make the examples easy to understand. There is no problem to do the same in a different natural language, such as Chinese. On the other hand, it is also fine to use terms that are meaningless to human beings, such as *drib* and *aminal*.

Definition 2.2. The basic form of a *statement* is an *inheritance statement*, "$S \rightarrow P$", where S is the *subject term*, P is the *predicate term*, and '$\rightarrow$' is the *inheritance copula*, defined as being a *reflexive and transitive* relation from one term to another term.

Graphically, an inheritance statement can be represented as two vertices connected by a directed edge. Its direction is purely conventional, though usually it is taken to be from the subject to the predicate.

---

[2]In NARS, a (normal) term is the name of a concept. See [Wang (2006b)].

The intuitive meaning of "$S \rightarrow P$" is "S is a special case of P" or "P is a general case of S". For example, "Bird is a type of animal" can be represented in Narsese as

$$bird \rightarrow animal.$$

Now we begin to see the difference between IL, as a term logic, and a predicate logic, like FOPL (First-Order Predicate Logic). The same example is typically represented in FOPL as a proposition

$$(\forall x)(Bird(x) \Longrightarrow Animal(x)),$$

where predicates *Bird* and *Animal* both take variable x as argument, and '$\Longrightarrow$' is the implication operator defined in propositional logic.[3] Though the IL statement and the FOPL proposition have similar meanings, they are based on different ontological presumptions. FOPL presumes objects (represented by *arguments*) with properties and relations (represented by *predicates*), while IL presumes categories (represented by *terms*) within a generalization hierarchy (established by *inheritance*). One consequence of this difference is that in FOPL "predicates" and "arguments" are disjoint sets, while in IL (and NAL) "subject term" and "predicate term" are defined *relatively*, with respect to a certain statement, in the sense that the subject term of a statement (like the "*bird*" in "*bird* → *animal*") can be the predicate term of another statement (like "*dove* → *bird*"), which is also the case in other term logics, such as Aristotle's Syllogistic. Therefore, the "predicate symbol" in FOPL and the "predicate term" in IL are not the same, though they are intuitively related to each other.

We can also compare IL with set theory, where the above example can be represented as "*Bird* $\subseteq$ *Animal*" with *Bird* and *Animal* being sets. Since the *subset* relation is both reflexive and transitive,

---

[3]In this book, we use a short single arrow '→' for the *inheritance* relation in NAL, and a long double arrow '$\Longrightarrow$' for the *implication* relation in FOPL. They are related in meaning, though should not be confused with each other.

Table 2.1. The grammar rules of IL-1.

$\langle statement \rangle ::= \langle term \rangle \langle copula \rangle \langle term \rangle$
$\langle copula \rangle ::= \rightarrow$
$\langle term \rangle ::= \langle word \rangle$

it is just like the *inheritance* relation. Here the difference is that *inheritance* is defined between two *terms*, which are not sets in general. For example, "Water is a type of liquid" that can be similarly represented in IL as *"water → liquid"*, though the two terms cannot be naturally considered as sets. More differences between term and set will be introduced later.

The representation language used in IL-1 contains inheritance statements as sentences, as defined by the grammar rules in Table 2.1. All grammar rules in this book are represented using a variant of the Backus Naur Form (BNF) specified in Appendix A.

2.2.   Experience-Grounded Semantics

The semantic theory of IL-1 defines the truth-value of a statement, as well as the meaning of a term.

Definition 2.3. The *truth-value* of a statement in IL is either *true* or *false.*

Therefore, IL is a binary logic, like most of the existing logic systems.

From the relevant definitions, some theorems can be proved, as conclusions about IL.[4] The proofs of the theorems in this book are collected in Appendix D. The following theorems directly come from the reflexivity and transitivity of the *inheritance* copula.

Theorem 2.1. *For any term X, statement "$X \rightarrow X$" is true.*

Following the tradition of logic, such a statement is called a *tautology.*

---

[4]Since NAL is non-axiomatic, there is no "theorem", but its ideal version, IL, is still binary and axiomatic. We can prove theorems in IL, though not in NAL.

Theorem 2.2. *For any term X, Y, and Z, if both "$X \to Y$" and "$Y \to Z$" are true, so is "$X \to Z$".*

Treating an IL statement as a proposition, the above theorems can be expressed in FOPL as

$$(\forall x) Inheritance(x, x)$$

$$(\forall x)(\forall y)(\forall z)((Inheritance(x, y) \land Inheritance(y, z))$$

$$\implies Inheritance(x, z)).$$

The inheritance relation is neither symmetric nor anti-symmetric. That is, for different X and Y, given "$X \to Y$" alone, the truth-value of "$Y \to X$" cannot be determined.

An inference process needs to start from some initial knowledge. In IL, the initial knowledge of the system is defined as its "ideal experience".

Definition 2.4. For a reasoning system implementing IL-1, its *ideal experience*, K, is a non-empty and finite set of statements in IL-1, which does not include any tautology.

For example, K can be $\{robin \to bird, bird \to animal, water \to liquid\}$.

Definition 2.5. Given ideal experience K, the system's *knowledge*, K^*, is the transitive closure of K, excluding any tautology.

Therefore, K^* is also a non-empty and finite set of sentences in IL-1, which includes K, as well as the sentences derived from K according to the transitivity of the inheritance relation. For example, given the above K, $K^* = \{robin \to bird, bird \to animal, robin \to animal, water \to liquid\}$. In the following, K^* is also referred to as the "beliefs" of the system.

Graphically, both K and K^* can be represented as directed graphs, with terms as vertices and statements as edges.

Definition 2.6. Given ideal experience K, the truth-value of a statement is *true* if it is in K^*, or it is a tautology, otherwise it is *false*.

Therefore IL-1 can represent two types of true statement: *empirical* and *literal*, or *synthetic* and *analytic*, respectively. The former is "true according to experience", and the latter is "true by definition". Similar distinctions are often made in the literature [Haack (1978)]. Statements in these two categories have no overlap, since K^* contains no tautology.

When X and Y are different terms, "$X \to Y$" is a statement in the language of IL-1, but "$X \to Y$ is true" and "$X \to Y$ is false" are not — they are sentences in the meta-language of IL-1. These sentences may be either *positive* (on what is *true*) or *negative* (on what is *false*). Within IL-1, negative sentences are implicitly represented: they are the statements that are *not known to be true*. They are not represented by statements in IL-1, but sentences in its meta-language. In this way, IL-1 accepts the "Closed-World Assumption" [Russell and Norvig (2010)], by treating "unknown" as "false".

Therefore, in IL-1 the truth-values of empirical statements are decided with respect to a given experience, which is a set of empirical statements themselves. The meanings of terms are decided similarly, as explained in the following definitions.

Definition 2.7. Given ideal experience K, the set of all terms appearing in K is the *vocabulary* of the system, V_K.

When K is represented as a graph, V_K is the set of its vertices. For the previous K, $V_K = \{robin, bird, animal, water, liquid\}$.

Definition 2.8. Given ideal experience K, the *extension* of a term T is the set of terms $T^E = \{x \mid (x \in V_K) \land (x \to T)\}$. The *intension* of T is the set of terms $T^I = \{x \mid (x \in V_K) \land (T \to x)\}$.

Obviously, both T^E and T^I are determined with respect to K, so they should be written as T_K^E and T_K^I. In the following, the simpler notions are used, with the experience K implicitly assumed.

Intuitively, the *extension* of a term in V_K contains its *known specializations* (plus itself); the *intension* of a term contains its *known generalizations* (plus itself). When the system's knowledge is represented as a graph, the extension of a term is given by its *incoming* edges, and the intension its *outgoing* edges.

The above definition is different from the common usage of the two words in most of the current logic literature, where the "extension" of a term is taken to be the set of concrete instances denoted by the term, while its "intension" to be the abstract properties connoted by the term. In the history of logic, "extension" and "intension" have been given different definitions, though the intuitive meaning remains, that is, they are for "instances" and "properties", respectively [Stebbing (1950)]. In IL (and NAL), the above intuitive properties are kept, though these notions are not assumed to be about something *outside* the language, but *inside* the language. The significance of this difference will be explained later.

Since "extension" and "intension" are defined in a symmetric way in IL, for any result about one of them, there is a dual result about the other. Each statement in the knowledge of the system reveals part of the intension for the subject term and part of the extension for the predicate term.

Theorem 2.3. *For any term* $T \in V_K$, $T \in (T^E \cap T^I)$. *If* T *is not in* V_K, $T^E = T^I = \{\}$.

Here $\{\}$ is the empty set, somethimes written as $\emptyset$. So the extension and intension of a term are not empty, if and only if the term appears in the system's experience.

Definition 2.9. Given experience K, the *meaning* of a term T consists of T^E and T^I.

Therefore, the meaning of a term is its relation with other terms, according to the experience of the system. A term T is "meaningless" to the system, if it has never got into the experience of the system, otherwise it is "meaningful". The larger the extension and intension of a term are, the "richer" its meaning is.[5]

---

[5]The *richness* of a concept named by a term will be taken into consideration by the inference control mechanism of NARS.

For the above example, there are only five meaningful terms to the system, whose meaning is specified in the following:

Term	Extension	Intension
robin	$\{robin\}$	$\{robin, bird, animal\}$
bird	$\{bird, robin\}$	$\{bird, animal\}$
animal	$\{animal, robin, bird\}$	$\{animal\}$
water	$\{water\}$	$\{water, liquid\}$
liquid	$\{water, liquid\}$	$\{liquid\}$

According to the above definitions, the meaning of a term is *defined by its relations with other terms*, rather than *reduced into the meaning of other terms*, so this practice should not be considered as giving circular definitions. Furthermore, these relations come from the system's experience, which is the only perceivable information exchange between the system and its environment, so this practice should not be considered as "dictionary-go-round" [Harnad (1990)].[6]

Theorem 2.4. *If both S and P are in V_K, then*

$$(S \rightarrow P) \Longleftrightarrow (S^E \subseteq P^E) \Longleftrightarrow (P^I \subseteq S^I).$$

Here "$\Longleftrightarrow$" is the "equivalence" ("if and only if") connective in propositional logic.

The above theorem says that there is an inheritance relation from S to P, if and only if the extension of S is inherited by P, and, equivalently, the intension of P is inherited by S. This is why the copula is named "inheritance".

If "$S \rightarrow P$" is false, it means that the inheritance is incomplete — either $(S^E - P^E)$ or $(P^I - S^I)$ is not empty. However, it does not mean that S and P share no extension or intension.

Theorem 2.5. $(S^E = P^E) \Longleftrightarrow (S^I = P^I)$.

---

[6]In the following chapters, we will see how to extend this definition to include other contents, such as those provided by sensorimotor mechanisms.

This means that in IL-1, terms with the same extension have the same intension, and *vice versa*. Therefore, the extension and intension of a term are mutually determined, and one of the two uniquely determines the meaning of a term. This result partially explains why in a binary logic like IL it is usually enough to process extension alone. However, it will not be the case in NAL, as we will see in the coming chapters.

In summary, IL-1 has an "Experience-Grounded Semantics", or EGS [Wang (2005)], since the truth-values of its statements and the meanings of its terms are all determined by the experience of the system, except in trivial cases (such as analytical statements and meaningless terms).

EGS is similar to approaches like "Proof-Theoretic Semantics" and "Inferentializing Semantics" [Peregrin (2010)], while is fundamentally different from the "Model-Theoretic Semantics", or MTS, used by most of the logic systems at the current time. MTS assumes the existence of a "model", consisting of entities with properties and relations described in a meta-language, and an "interpretation" mapping the terms and statements (or call them other names) onto the entities, properties, and relations. Then, the meaning of a term is the entity it mapped onto, and the truth-value of a statement indicates whether it is mapped into an existing relation in the model [Barwise and Etchemendy (1989)]. A detailed comparison between these two types of semantics can be found in Wang (2005), and here it is enough to remember that for terms to get meaning and for statements to get truth-value, in IL (and NAL) what is required is *experience*, rather than *interpretation*. Other related issues will be gradually addressed later.

2.3. Syllogistic Inference Rules

IL-1 has a single inference rule that derives *knowledge* from *experience*, justified by the transitivity of the inheritance copula. It is a special type of "deduction", in the common sense of the notion.

The rule is shown in Table 2.2, where the premises are the *inheritance* statements from M to P, and from S to M, respectively. The derivable conclusion is an inheritance statement from S to P.

Table 2.2. The inference rules of IL-1.

$premise_1$	$premise_2$	$conclusion$
$M \rightarrow P$	$S \rightarrow M$	$S \rightarrow P$

The inference rule in Table 2.2 can also be written as:

$$\{M \rightarrow P,\ S \rightarrow M\} \vdash S \rightarrow P.$$

This rule is "syllogistic", in the sense that the two premises share one common term, and the rule derives a conclusion between the other two terms. Here the word "syllogistic" is used in a broad sense, with Aristotle's Syllogistic [Aristotle (1882)] as a special case. The usage of syllogistic inference rules is another character that distinguishes a term logic from a predicate logic, so a term logic is called a "syllogistic logic" [Smith (2012)].

Inference rules in predicate logic are not syllogistic, since their premises are not categorical sentences, and there is no requirement for the premises to contain common terms. Though it is possible to represent the inheritance copula of IL as a predicate name in FOPL, this predicate is not directly recognized and processed by the inference rules of FOPL, which are "truth-functional only", that is, depending on the truth-values of the premises, rather than on the nature of their conceptual relations.

In IL (and NAL), inference in general is seen as the process in which one term "is used as", or "is replaced by", another one. For example, the rule in Table 2.2 says that for a given inheritance statement, the subject term can be replaced by another term in its extension, and the predicate term can be replaced by another term in its intension. Such a term (concept) substitution naturally corresponds to the conceptual hierarchy observed in human cognition, and is considered by some researchers as playing a central role in intelligence and cognition [Hofstadter (1995)].

The syllogistic rules in IL also have the desired property that in every inference step, the two premises are *semantically related*, and so do the conclusion and each premise, guaranteed by the shared term. On the contrary, there is no such requirement in propositional and predicate logic, and that is the root of the "paradoxes of material implication" — "$P \implies Q$" is true if P is false or Q is true, even when the two are semantically irrelevant. Various "relevance logics" have been proposed to solve this problem [Read (1989)], though they are almost all in the propositional and predicate logic framework. Few people have noticed that such paradox does not appear in syllogistic logics.

Though the inference rules in IL-1 are very simple when compared to the inference rules of FOPL, all inference rules in IL (and NAL), to be introduced in the following chapters, require the semantical relevance between the premises, and guarantee the semantical relevance between every conclusion and the promises that produce it.

Given ideal experience K, knowledge K^* can be produced by repeatedly applying the above rule on every possible pair of premises. This rule only derives *positive* conclusions directly, since from positive knowledge "$S \to M$ is *true*" and negative knowledge "$M \to P$ is *false*", the truth-value of "$S \to P$" cannot be decided — it can be either *true* or *false*. Instead, negative conclusions are derived implicitly, as statements that cannot be proved to be *true*.

Beside deriving new knowledge, IL-1 also has a *matching rule* to answer questions according to available knowledge.

Definition 2.10. For different terms S and P, knowledge "$S \to P$" is an answer to any *question* that has one of the following three forms: (1) "$S \to P$?", (2) "$S \to$?", and (3) "? $\to P$", where the '?' in the last two is a "query variable" to be instantiated. If no such answer can be found in K^*, "NO" is answered.

The first form of question asks for an *evaluation* of a given statement, while the other two ask for a *selection* of a term for a given relation with another term. If there are multiple answers to (2) and (3), they are considered as equally good. Tautology "$X \to X$" is a trivial answer to such a question, so it is not allowed.

The matching rule is shown in Table 2.3.

Similar to negative knowledge, in IL-1 questions are not represented as sentences in the object language, but in the meta-language

Table 2.3. The matching rules of IL-1.

Knowledge	Matching questions
$S \rightarrow P$	$S \rightarrow P?$ $S \rightarrow ?$ $? \rightarrow P$

only. Also, IL-1 does not accept the question "What is not T?", since an arbitrary term outside V_K can be used to answer such a question.

It is easy to prove that IL-1 has several desired properties of reasoning system, including consistency, soundness, completeness, and decidability.

CHAPTER 3

NAL-1: BASIC SYNTAX AND SEMANTICS

IL-1 has included the simplest form of the major components of NAL: a categorical language, an experience-grounded semantics, and a syllogistic rule. However, these components are defined in IL-1 under the assumption of sufficient knowledge and resources. It is assumed in IL that

- all object-level knowledge is summarized in the system's idealized experience K, which is given to the system at the beginning and remains unchanged;
- the system has the time and space resources to generate K^*, the transitive closure of K;
- the system can answer all questions by searching K^* for a matching statement.

NAL-1 is the simplest non-axiomatic logic. It moves the components defined in IL-1 onto a new foundation, that is, under AIKR. Consequently, all the above three assumptions cannot be made anymore, and the components need to be modified accordingly.

NAL-1 is described in two chapters. This chapter covers its language and semantics, and leaves the inference rules to the next chapter.

3.1. Evidence and its Measurement

IL-1 is still an *axiomatic* logic, with the *ideal experience* in set K as "axioms", the *derived knowledge* in set $(K^* - K)$ as "theorems", and the resource restriction is ignored. Each piece of knowledge is an

25

inheritance statement from one term to another, which is "perfect" in the sense that there is no, and will not be any, counter-evidence for the stated relation between the two terms.

As soon as AIKR is accepted, the relationship between a statement and an experience cannot be properly captured by a binary truth-value anymore. Since the system has to open to novel questions, it cannot just remember the statements in its past experience or only derive their deductive conclusions. Instead, it has to *generalize* and *summarize* the experienced statements, so as to efficiently apply them to novel situations. In this process, it cannot simply reject the conclusions that have counterevidence, as suggested by Popper (1959), since plausible, heuristic, and statistical knowledge all have great value in adaptation. After all, the system's ultimate objective is not "to describe the world as it is" but "to achieve its goals as much as possible". We could hardly do anything in the real world by only following knowledge that is absolutely true.

Not only are binary truth-values not enough, even a multi-value logic may not be enough for adaptation if the truth-values are *qualitative*, rather than *quantitative*. Since the system is open to unexpected future events, many predictions are "possibly true", and if their truth-values only tell the system that, there will not be any general rule for the choices among competing answers. To be "adaptive" means the system should be able to *quantitatively* compare different predictions, to see *how much* each of them is supported by available evidence.

Therefore, the first task in designing NAL-1 is to define and measure *evidence* for a statement, given the system's experience. Here "evidence" refers to the information that contributes to the truth-value of a statement, even though it cannot decide the truth-value once for all, under AIKR — the system does not have all the relevant information at once, and nor can it afford the resources to consider all available information.

In IL-1, the (binary) truth-value of the statement "$S \rightarrow P$" is determined by whether the statement is included in, or can be derived from, the system's experience K. Now we want this *inheritance* relation to be "true to a degree", but what does that mean exactly?

As shown by Theorem 2.4, inheritance relation "$S \to P$" is equivalent to subset relations "$S^E \subseteq P^E$" and "$P^I \subseteq S^I$", so when the former becomes a matter of degree, so does the latter, and the other way around. It is not hard to extend the subset relation from binary into graded, and to distinguish positive and negative evidence: If A and B are sets, for the subset relation "$A \subseteq B$", the elements in set $(A \cap B)$ are positive evidence, and the elements in set $(A - B)$ are negative evidence. Here '$\cap$' and '$-$' are the *intersection* and *difference* of sets, respectively, as defined in set theory.

Definition 3.1. For an inheritance statement "$S \to P$", its *evidence* are terms in its *evidential scope*, S^E and P^I. Among them, terms in $(S^E \cap P^E)$ and $(P^I \cap S^I)$ are *positive evidence*, and terms in $(S^E - P^E)$ and $(P^I - S^I)$ are *negative evidence*.

In other words, as far as a term in positive evidence is concerned, the inheritance statement is correct; as far as a term in negative evidence is concerned, the inheritance statement is incorrect. For example, to decide to what extent the statement "*bird* $\to$ *animal*" is correct, we can check the instances of *bird* and the properties of *animal*. If a (known) instance of *bird*, say *robin*, is also known to be an instance of *animal*, it is positive evidence for "*bird* $\to$ *animal*", otherwise it is negative evidence. Similarly, if a (known) property of *animal*, say being an *organism*, is also known to be a property of *bird*, it is positive evidence for "*bird* $\to$ *animal*", otherwise it is negative evidence. At this stage, the experience of the system is still defined as containing binary statements (as in IL-1). It is the *conclusions* derived from them that have positive and negative evidence, provided by the experience.

For each statement, if we only need to qualitatively distinguish situations like "all evidences are positive", "all evidences are negative", "some evidences are positive", and "some evidences are negative", as well as to concentrate on extension, we can get an extension of IL-1 that is functionally equivalent to Aristotle's logic [Aristotle (1882)], as shown in Wang (1994b). However, as argued previously, for the purpose of AI, a quantitative measurement is required. Since evidence is defined by sets, its "amount" can be naturally measured by the size (*cardinality*) of the corresponding sets.

Definition 3.2. For statement "$S \to P$", the amount of positive, negative, and total evidence is, respectively,

$$w^+ = |S^E \cap P^E| + |P^I \cap S^I|,$$
$$w^- = |S^E - P^E| + |P^I - S^I|,$$
$$w = w^+ + w^-$$
$$= |S^E| + |P^I|.$$

An important design decision made here is not to distinguish the "extensional" factor and the "intensional" factor in the above measurements. As argued in Wang (2006b), it is often either impossible to clearly separate the two factors, or necessary to mix them. Human beings routinely use extensional information to make intensional judgments, and *vice versa*. For instance, "representativeness" (which is intensional) is often used as "probability" (which is usually used as extensional) [Tversky and Kahneman (1974)], and this practice is defended in Wang (1996a, 2006b).[1]

A major reason for NAL to be designed within the term logic framework is the relative naturalness for the notion of "evidence" to be introduced. For a proposition in FOPL in the form of $P(a_1, \ldots, a_n)$, it is not easy to say what should be counted as its positive or negative evidence. Wang (2009d) contains a detailed discussion about the formalization of evidence in NAL, and as well as a comparison between this approach and some other approaches.

3.2. Two-Dimensional Truth-Value

In principle, the evidential support for a statement can be measured by any two of the three amounts introduced above: w^+, w^-, and

---

[1]When necessary, it is still possible to separately represent and process extensional evidence and intensional evidence in NAL. The method will be introduced in NAL-6, covered in Chapter 10.

w, each of which is a non-negative integer, and the range can be extended into real numbers in $[0, \infty)$ to include partial evidence.

Even so, when comparing competing beliefs and deriving new conclusions, *relative* measurements are usually preferred over *absolute* measurements, because the evidence of a premise normally cannot be directly used as evidence for the conclusion. Also, it is often more convenient for the measurements to take values from a finite range, while the amount of evidence has no upper bound. Finally, it is desired to use the binary truth-values, traditionally represented as 0 and 1, as limits of the continuous truth-value. These considerations lead to the following definition of truth-value in NAL.

Definition 3.3. The truth-value of a statement consists of a pair of real numbers in $[0, 1]$. One of the two is called *frequency*, defined as $f = w^+/w$; the other is called *confidence*, defined as $c = w/(w + k)$, where k is a positive constant, which is the system parameter for "evidential horizon".

In this definition, *frequency* is the proportion (percentage) of positive evidence among all evidences, which is the most common measurement of uncertainty used in everyday life. It is closely related to the *probability* defined in probability theory and statistics [Dekking *et al.* (2007)]. In the context of NAL, we can associate each statement S to the event E_S that the statement is confirmed when it is checked. In that way, the corresponding probability $P(E_S) = \lim_{w \to \infty}(w^+/w)$, that is, the *frequency* of a statement will converge to the *probability* of the corresponding event, if the latter exists. However, under AIKR, the system does not know if a given frequency has a limit or not, not to mention where the limit is. Therefore, in general the *frequency* in NAL should not be taken as a *probability*, nor even as an estimation or approximation of it.

Since *frequency* is defined by amounts of evidence in the system's experience, it changes as the experience unfolds in time. Therefore, as a measurement of uncertainty, *frequency* is uncertain in itself. While the uncertainty *within frequency* is caused by *negative evidence*, the uncertainty *about frequency* is caused by *future evidence*. The second measurement, *confidence*, is introduced for the latter. Here the issue is that if the *finite* amount of *past* evidence is compared to the *infinite* amount of *future* evidence, the ratio will be zero. On the other hand, to limit the future by setting a fixed lifespan for the system sounds arbitrary. The solution used in NAL is to compare the evidence in the *past* to that of a *near future*, defined by a *constant* evidential horizon. Since in competing conclusions the same evidential horizon is used, the ones supported by more evidence will have higher confidence value, which is consistent with the everyday usage of the word "confidence", though this definition makes the measurement completely different from the definition of "confidence interval" in statistics [Dekking *et al.* (2007)].

This *evidential horizon* k is a "personality parameter" of the system, in the sense that though it is a constant in a system, in different NAL-based systems it can take different values, and in general it is hard (if not impossible) to find an optimal value. A natural choice is $k = 1$, which means to compare the available evidence with new evidence of a unit amount. This parameter value will be used in the examples given in this book. The impact of this parameter on the system will be discussed later in the book.

NAL needs a "two-dimensional" truth-value, because the two values represent different types of uncertainty. *Frequency* indicates the system's "degree of belief" on the statement, which can be "belief" or "disbelief" to various degrees, and *confidence* indicates how strong or stable this degree of belief is, that is, how easy it is for the system to change its mind on this matter. Defined as above, the *frequency* value and the *confidence* value of a statement are *independent* of each other, in the sense that given the value of one, the value of the other cannot be determined, or even bounded, except the trivial case that *frequency* is undefined if and only if *confidence* is zero.

NAL needs to consider future evidence, exactly because of AIKR. Though similar problems are analyzed in probability theory and statistics, the usual assumptions are that (1) all relevant evidences are available to the system at the same time, and (2) the system can afford the time to take all of them into consideration when evaluating the certainty of a statement. Therefore, it is unnecessary to indicate the amount of evidence behind each individual statement. On the contrary, in NAL neither of the two assumptions can be made, and each statement has its own evidential basis, so it is necessary to be measured one by one.

A higher confidence value does not mean that the *frequency* is closer to the "objective probability", but that the *frequency* is harder to be changed by new evidence. Though *confidence* is about the stability of *frequency*, so is at a higher-order than the latter, it should not be considered as a "higher-order probability". Under AIKR, *frequency* is neither a probability, nor a random variable. The *frequency* of a statement may change its value when new evidence is taken into consideration, though its possible values do not necessarily follow a fixed probability distribution. Furthermore, when *confidence* is near its minimum value, it does not mean that the current *frequency* value is *improbable*, but that the system actually knows little about this matter to have an opinion at all. The definition of *confidence* is one of the most unique features of NAL. For more detailed discussions about it, as well as comparisons with other approaches, see Wang (2001b).

Fuzzy logic also treats categorical relations and truth as matters of degree [Zadeh (1965, 1975)]. Even though it has similar intuitions and motivations as NAL, fuzzy logic does not define its "grade of membership" as a function of available evidence, nor does it specify how the grades should be changed. In NAL, fuzziness typically comes from the diversity in the *intension* of a term. For example, "Penguins are birds" is true to a degree, because penguins do not have all the common properties of birds, but only some of them. On the other hand, randomness typically comes from the diversity in the *extension* of a term. For example, "birds fly" is true to a degree, because some birds fly, and some do not. These two types of uncertainty are uniformly represented and processed in NAL. For further comparisons between fuzzy logic and NAL, see Wang (1996b).

3.3. Representations of Uncertainty

Beside amount of evidence and truth-value, the uncertainty of a statement can be represented in a few other ways in NAL.

Within a fixed evidential horizon (i.e., until the amount of new evidence reaches a constant k), the *frequency* value of a statement will be restricted in an interval.

Definition 3.4. The *frequency interval* $[l, u]$ of a statement contains its *frequency* value from the current moment to the moment when the new evidence has amount k. The two end-points of the interval are called *lower frequency* and *upper frequency*, respectively.

The lower frequency l equals $w^+/(w + k)$, and the upper frequency u equals $(w^+ + k)/(w + k)$. It is the case because the current amount of evidence is w, including positive evidence of amount w^+. For the new evidence of amount k, if it is pure positive, the new *frequency* will be $(w^+ + k)/(w + k)$; if it is pure negative, the new *frequency* will be $w^+/(w + k)$; and all the other situation will be in between these two extreme values.

Definition 3.5. The *ignorance* of a statement is measured by the *width* of the frequency interval, i.e., $i = u - l$.

Here the "ignorance" is not about the "true value" of *frequency*, but about "where it will be" in the near future. For a statement, its *confidence* and *ignorance* are complement to each other, that is, $c + i = 1$. This result is in agreement with the everyday usage of the two words.

This *frequency interval* is not the lower/upper bound of *frequency*, which can be obtained only at the *infinite future*, while the interval only holds for the *near future*. In NARS, *frequency* does not necessarily converge to a limit. Even if it does, the limit is not necessarily in the *frequency interval* at every previous moment. No matter where a *frequency* value is in $(0, 1)$ at a given moment, it can be anywhere in that range after a unspecified period of time, given proper future evidence. When *frequency* values have limited accuracy, the above conclusion also applies to the range of $[0, 1]$.

For comparisons between *frequency interval* and other "interval" measurements of uncertainty, such as Dempster–Shafer Theory [Dempster (1967); Shafer (1976)] and Walley's theory on Imprecise Probabilities [Walley (1991)], see Wang (1994a, 2001b, 2009d).

The interval representation of uncertainty also provides a mapping between the above "continuous representations" and certain "discrete representations" of uncertainty, because "discrete" corresponds to a willingness to change a value within a certain range.

If in a situation there are only N words that can be used to specify the uncertainty of a statement, and the uncertainty can be anywhere in $[0, 1]$ with the same chance, the most informative way to communicate is to evenly divide the $[0, 1]$ range into N intervals: $[0, 1/N]$, $(1/N, 2/N]$, ..., $((N - 1)/N, 1]$, and to use a label for each section.[2]

For instance, if we have to use three labels (such as "wrong", "unsure", and "right") to roughly indicate the correctness of statements, they can be mapped into $[0, 1/3]$, $(1/3, 2/3]$, and $(2/3, 1]$, respectively. Since the width of the intervals is $1/N$, the larger N is, the smaller the *ignorance* is (and the higher the *confidence* is). On the other hand, to distinguish N different situations, the amount of evidence should be at least $w = N - 1$ (so w^+, if restricted into integers, has N possible values from 0 to $N - 1$), which leads to the same *frequency interval* assignments to the situations (with $k = 1$).

A variation of this approach is to use a single number, with its accuracy, to represent uncertainty. For example, if the uncertainty of a statement is represented by a single number 0.6, it will be mapped into *frequency interval* $[0.55, 0.65)$, while another statement with uncertainty 0.60 will be mapped into $[0.595, 0.605)$. These two statements have similar *frequency*, but very different *confidence*. Here a higher accuracy corresponds to a lower *ignorance* (and therefore a higher *confidence*).

In summary, NAL uses three functionally equivalent representations for the uncertainty (or degree of belief) of a statement:

Amounts of evidence: $\{w^+, w\}$, where $0 \leq w^+ \leq w$, or using $w^- = w - w^+$ to replace one of the two;

---

[2]When the numerical value is continuous, whether to include a boundary value into its left-side interval or its right-side interval does not matter much, as far as a consistent convention is followed. For example, we can change the above intervals into frequency intervals $[0, 1/N)$, $[1/N, 2/N)$, ..., $[(N - 1)/N, 1]$, respectively.

Truth-value: $\langle f, c \rangle$, where both f and c are real numbers in $[0, 1]$, and are independent of each other;

Frequency interval: $[l, u]$, where $0 \leq l \leq u \leq 1$, or using $i = u - l$ to replace one of the two.

The last one has variants where a single label (from a given sequence of labels) or number (with accuracy) is taken as an interval.

When necessary, these representations can be used together in a mixture. As discussed in Wang (2006b), to allow multiple representations of uncertainty makes the design and usage easier. This will become more clear in the following chapters.

Among all possible values of the measurements, there are normal cases that actually happen in NAL, and two extreme cases that only appear in the meta-level descriptions of NAL:

Normal evidence: This is indicated by $w \in (0, \infty)$, $c \in (0, 1)$, or $i \in (0, 1)$. It means the statement is supported by finite amount of evidence, which is the case for every statement that is actually involved in inference in NAL.

Null evidence: This is indicated by $w = 0$, $c = 0$, or $i = 1$. It means the system knows nothing at all about the statement, so the statement does not need to be actually stored or processed in the system.

Full evidence: This is indicated by $w \to \infty$, $c = 1$, or $i = 0$. It means the system already knows everything about the statement, which cannot occur in a NAL.

In an implementation of NARS, if an input or derived sentence has a truth-value corresponding to null or full evidence, the sentence is simply ignored, and will not be accepted into the system.

Though the extreme cases never appear in the sentences to be processed, they can be discussed in the meta-language of NAL as limit cases, and play important roles in system design. This is why IL can be considered as an idealized version of NAL, while still being a meta-logic of it. In IL, the *ideal experience* provides all evidence the system can have — the system is not open to new evidence, and accepts Closed World Assumption (whatever cannot be proved

Table 3.1. The mappings among measurements of uncertainty.

to\from	$\{w^+, w\}$	$\langle f, c \rangle$	$[l, u]$ (and i)
$\{w^+, w\}$		$w^+ = k \times f \times c/(1-c)$ $w = k \times c/(1-c)$	$w^+ = k \times l/i$ $w = k \times (1-i)/i$
$\langle f, c \rangle$	$f = w^+/w$ $c = w/(w+k)$		$f = l/(1-i)$ $c = 1-i$
$[l, u]$	$l = w^+/(w+k)$ $u = (w^+ + k)/(w+k)$	$l = f \times c$ $u = 1 - c \times (1-f)$	

to be true is considered false). Given the definition of evidence and Theorem 2.4 (which states that "inheritance" means subset relation between extensions and intensions), every empirical belief in IL is absolutely true, because there is no negative evidence, nor will there be future evidence.

On the other hand, in NAL each belief may have both *positive* and *negative* evidence, and the impact of *future* evidence must be considered, too. In this case, "absolutely true" is mapped into truth-value $\langle 1, 1 \rangle$ of NAL, since there is neither negative evidence (so *frequency* is 1) nor future evidence (so *confidence* is 1). Similarly, if the probability of a statement is p, it can be seen as an extreme case of the truth-value of NAL, $\langle p, 1 \rangle$, where the statement has infinite amount of evidence (i.e., $w \to \infty$). In other words, the probability of a statement is the limit of its frequency, if such a limit exists. With insufficient knowledge, in NAL it is not assumed that the frequency of every statement has a limit, and nor is the truth-value handled as an approximation of such a limit.

For the normal case, formulas for inter-conversion among the three forms of uncertainty are summarized in Table 3.1, which can be extended to include $w^- = w - w^+$ and $i = u - l$.

3.4. Experience and Belief

The grammar rules of Narsese used in NAL-1, given in Table 3.2, are the same as for IL-1, except that a binary "statement" plus a truth-value becomes a multi-valued "judgment". In communications

Table 3.2. The grammar rules of NAL-1.

⟨*sentence*⟩ ::= ⟨*judgment*⟩ | ⟨*question*⟩
⟨*judgment*⟩ ::= ⟨*statement*⟩ ⟨*truth-value*⟩
⟨*question*⟩ ::= ⟨*statement*⟩ | ? ⟨*copula*⟩ ⟨*term*⟩ | ⟨*term*⟩ ⟨*copula*⟩ ?
⟨*statement*⟩ ::= ⟨*term*⟩ ⟨*copula*⟩ ⟨*term*⟩
⟨*copula*⟩ ::= →
⟨*term*⟩ ::= ⟨*word*⟩

between the system and its environment, the other two types of uncertainty representation can also be used instead of the truth-value of a judgment, though within the system they will be translated to (or from) truth-value. Also, a "question" is included in the object-level of the language, as a statement (without a truth-value), and may contain a variable to be instantiated.

In NAL-1 the truth-value of a statement, as well as the other uncertainty measurements, are defined with respect to K, an *ideal experience* consisting of binary inheritance statements. However, NARS cannot know such a K, nor can it afford the resources to produce a K^*, so as to calculate the truth-values of all the relevant statements — in NAL-1, we have to accept AIKR.

Definition 3.6. The *actual experience* of a system implementing NAL-1 is a stream of Narsese sentences, as defined in Table 3.2.

What differs *ideal experience* from *actual experience* is:

(1) The former contains *true* statements only, while the latter contains questions and *multi-valued* judgments.
(2) The former is a *set* (without internal order or duplicated elements), while the latter is a *stream* (where order matters, and duplicate elements are possible).
(3) The former is available to the system at the very beginning, and remains unchanged (that is why the Closed-World Assumption can be made in IL — whatever unknown at a moment cannot become true in the future), while the latter comes one piece at a time, and there is always future experience.

In summary, all these differences come from the common root that *ideal experience* is used in an axiomatic system that assumes the sufficiency of knowledge and resources, while *actual experience* is used in a non-axiomatic system that assumes the opposite. Nevertheless, since the binary truth-value *true* corresponds to a limit of normal truth-value $\langle f, c \rangle$, it is possible to take the former as an idealized version of the latter.

To introduce NAL-1, IL-1 is established first, then it is used to define the uncertainty measurements in NAL-1, so as to break an apparent "circular definition" in experience-grounded semantics. According to EGS, the truth-value of a statement is determined according to the system's experience, but if the experience is nothing but a stream of statements, each with a truth-value of its own, is it not a circular definition? The NAL solution of this problem is an example of "bootstrapping": to *define* the semantic notions (truth-value, meaning, etc.) in NAL according to an *ideal experience*, then use this semantic theory to guide the system design and usage.

For example, if there is a judgment *"penguin → bird* $\langle 0.75, 0.80 \rangle$*"* in the memory of the system, then according to the relation between truth-value and amount of evidence, we see that it corresponds to $w = 4$ and $w^+ = 3$, which means the system believes the statement *to the extent as if* it has four pieces of perfect evidence, and three of them are positive, and one negative. However, we know that it is not how the truth-value is actually produced — under AIKR, the system cannot get such perfect evidence. It may have tested the statement more than four times, but in imperfect situations so each result cannot be counted as having a unit amount; or maybe the system has not directly tested the statement at all (by comparing the extension or intension of the two terms), but reached the conclusion using an inference rule from other beliefs. Later, we will see that in NAL there are infinite numbers of ways for *"penguin → bird* $\langle 0.75, 0.80 \rangle$*"* to come into existence, though we can always *understand* a truth-value *as if* it comes from an ideal experience. In this way, when we communicate with a NAL-based system, we can decide the truth-value of an input judgment and interpret that of an output judgment according to the "equivalent ideal experience"; when we design and verify an inference rule, we can focus on the extreme situations, where the related measurements take special values — we will see that in the next chapter.

In AI history, a major objection to numerical truth-value (or degree of belief) is "where are the numbers coming from?" [McCarthy and Hayes (1969)]. Indeed, in most situations human knowledge is expressed as qualitative judgments, without numerical truth-values. However, it does not mean that numerical measurements are impossible or undesired. The NAL approach takes the position that:

- For internal representation, the system uses a numerical truth-value (which consists of two numbers) for every judgment, so as to use generally applicable rules for inference, decision making, and so on.
- For external communication, the system allows multiple approaches for uncertainty representation, as well as the usage of various verbal labels or default values.

For example, in the current implementation, the truth-value of an input judgment is optional. When no truth-value is specified, the system will assign $\langle 1.0, 0.9 \rangle$ to it. Here the default *confidence* value 0.9 is a system parameter, which reflects the system's "habit" in communication. As other such parameters, there is no "correct" or "optimal" value for it, so different systems can have different values (which lead to different "personality"). However, in a system the value should remain constant (for the system to have a coherent semantics), and it should be within a rough range (for the system to behave "normally" in communication).

Here, the advantage of numerical truth-value is not its accuracy, but its generality. As far as a proper semantic definition is provided, a numerical measurement can also be natural to the human users.

Now we have defined the *actual experience* in NAL-1 on the basis of the *ideal experience* in IL, by treating each judgment in the former as equivalent to a set of statements in the latter. In the following, we will continue to refer to the *experience* of a system as K, to cover both cases.

In IL, the system's *knowledge*, or *beliefs*, is K^*, the transitive closure of K. In other words, it is derived from K by exhaustively applying its single inference rule. In NAL-1, the same cannot be done, under the restriction of AIKR. Therefore, the system's belief set K^* starts from the judgments in the actual experience K, then the set is modified by the inference rules of NAL-1 (to be introduced in the next chapter), under the restriction of available resources. We can still represent either K or K^* as a directed graph, as in IL-1, except that in NAL-1 the graph is *weighted*, and the weight is measured by a pair of numbers. Furthermore, K^* changes over time, and does not include *all* conclusions derivable from K, but just some of them.

Definition 3.7. A *belief* in the system is a judgment in its memory that is either an element of experience K, or derived from some elements of K. At a given moment, the collection of all beliefs is called the system's *knowledge* K^*. The *evidential base* of a belief B is the set of beliefs in K from which B is derived.

An evidential base records the reasons for the statement to have its current truth-value, similar to a truth maintenance system [Doyle (1979)]. In NARS, the evidential base of an input judgment is a set containing itself, while the evidential base of a derived conclusion is the union of the evidential bases of the premises deriving the conclusion. If the same judgment appears multiple times in experience, each occurrence corresponds to a separate evidential base.

This definition reveals another important difference between NAL and other probabilistic logics. In reasoning systems based on probability theory, the system's degree of belief is usually represented by a (consistent) probability distribution defined on the belief space [Pearl (1988)]. Here all the degrees of belief are based on the same evidence, usually called background knowledge. When the Bayesian Rule is used to carry out conditioning, all the degrees of belief are reevaluated (in theory, though not necessarily in implementation) to take the effect of new evidence into account. On the contrary, in NAL each belief has its own evidential base, which usually does not include all relevant evidence in the experience. This result is directly implied by AIKR, and is a major reason for NAL to stay outside of probability theory — NAL does not even obey the axioms of probability theory [Kolmogorov (1950)], which, when applied to reasoning systems, would require each statement to have a unique probability, as well as a consistent probability distribution among the statements. Neither of the two requirements can be satisfied under AIKR, so in this situation probability theory is inapplicable.[3]

Similar to "truth-value", the definition of "meaning" of NAL-1 is also extended from that of IL-1. While the meaning of a term still consists of its *extension* and *intension*, these two are no longer classical sets, but sets with graded membership, like fuzzy sets [Zadeh (1965)].

Definition 3.8. A belief "$S \rightarrow P \langle f, c \rangle$" indicates that S is in the extension of P and that P is in the intension of S, with the truth-value of the judgment specifying their grades of membership.

In other words, whether a term has a generalization (property) or specialization (instance) is a matter of degree, measured by the two-dimensional truth-value of NAL. Even with this extension, the principle of the semantics of NAL is still "experience-grounded" as in IL, and the meaning of a term is fully determined by its *empirical relations* with other terms. However, some conclusions on IL do not hold in NAL anymore. For example, in NAL the extension and intension of a term do not fully determine each other. Also, a term is no longer in its own extension and intension. Some other implications of this semantics are discussed in Wang (2005).

---

[3]This is the root of the differences between NAL and Probabilistic Logic Network (PLN) [Goertzel *et al.* (2008)], which is partially based on NAL and partially based on probability theory. Such a mixture is a meta-level inconsistency not allowed in NAL — to me, it is invalid to treat a measurement as probability in some places of the system, while in other places to process the same measurement using methods that violate the axioms of probability theory.

CHAPTER 4

NAL-1: BASIC INFERENCE RULES

In this chapter, the inference rules of NAL-1 are described and justified based on the grammar rules and semantic theory introduced in Chapter 3.

In terms of the content of conclusion, there are three types of inference rules in NAL-1:

- *Local* rules that do not produce new statement,
- *Forward* rules that produce new statements as judgments,
- *Backward* rules that produce new statements as questions,

and they will be introduced in that order.

4.1. Local Inference Rules

In NAL, "local" inference rules are the rules whose conclusions have the same content as a premise; therefore, no new statement is introduced into the system in such an inference step. In NAL-1, there are two such rules: the *revision rule* merges its premises into its conclusion, and the *choice rule* picks one of its premises as its conclusion.

Revision

One direct implication of AIKR is the existence of *inconsistent beliefs*, in the sense that at a given moment, there may be two (or more) beliefs that have the same content (i.e., statement), but different truth-values. This happens because the system is open to new experience of any content, including incoming judgments that are inconsistent with the existing ones. Furthermore, since each belief is derived from a certain evidential base, beliefs with different evidential bases may also be inconsistent. Consequently, this type of inconsistency is inevitable in an open system.

Given the binary truth-value in traditional propositional logic, an "inconsistency" or "contradiction" means the coexistence of a proposition P and its negation $\neg P$. Following the widely accepted Principle of Contradiction, inconsistency is strictly prohibited in traditional logics. According to the definition of material implication, $(P \wedge (\neg P)) \Longrightarrow Q$ is always true for arbitrary propositions P and Q. Therefore, as soon as the system's beliefs contain an inconsistency, the system may derive any proposition as conclusion, which is clearly unacceptable. In certain situations, it is desired for a logic system to have some tolerance to inconsistency, which leads to the study of "paraconsistent logic" [Priest *et al.* (1989)] and "belief revision" [Alchourrón *et al.* (1985)], which are still carried out in the binary logic framework.

In a multi-valued logic, such as probabilistic logic and fuzzy logic, inconsistency means a statement gets two or more truth-values (probability or degree of membership), even though the values are merely different, not necessarily opposite. Such a situation is usually prohibited, since the truth-value (or whatever it is called in the logic) is supposed to be a property of the statement, so should have a unique value.

For example, in a probabilistic logic, the probability of a given hypothesis H cannot be both 0.91 and 0.92, though the two values are close, so do not really form a contradiction. This requirement is implied by the axioms of probability theory, where each event or statement can only have a single probability value, no matter how this value is determined. It is fine for H to have different *conditional* probabilities $P(H|C_1)$ and $P(H|C_2)$, under different conditions that are explicitly specified in the statements. The requirement for probabilistic consistency or coherence is often justified by the "Dutch Book argument", that is, if a system's degrees of belief do not form a (consistent) probability distribution, then it may face sure loss in certain betting situations [Ramsey (1926)].

According to the semantics of NAL, for a statement st, an inconsistency happens between judgment J_1: "st $\langle f_1, c_1 \rangle$" and judgment J_2: "st $\langle f_2, c_2 \rangle$", and it is caused by their different evidential bases or derivation paths.[1] A "contradiction" is the extreme case of an inconsistency, where the two truth-values approach $\langle 1, 1 \rangle$ and $\langle 0, 1 \rangle$, respectively.

At the meta-level of NAL, the inconsistent beliefs correspond to meta-statements "According to evidential base B_1, the truth-value of statement st is $\langle f_1, c_1 \rangle$" and "According to evidential base B_2, the truth-value of statement st is $\langle f_2, c_2 \rangle$", respectively. Here, both meta-statements can be correct, and there is no inconsistency between the two, since they have different (meta-level) contents. At the object-level, when the system has to decide the truth-value of statement st, the situation cannot be handled by treating J_1 and J_2 as conditional statements (like in probability theory), since the evidential bases are implicitly represented, rather than explicitly included as part of the statement. The fundamental difference between these two situations has been analyzed in detail in Wang (1993, 2004b).

The consequence of an inconsistency in NAL is also very different from that in a binary logic. Since in NAL every conclusion is semantically related to the premises, an inconsistency in the system is a "local" issue that only has an impact on the beliefs that are semantically related to the inconsistency, rather than a "global" issue that implies an arbitrary conclusion. For example, if a system finds contradicting evidence on whether birds can swim, it may not be able to decide whether robin, as a special kind of bird, can swim or not. However, this problem should have no effect on the system's belief on whether water is liquid, which has no semantic relation with bird or swimming, as far as the system knows.

Since the existence of inconsistent judgments is inevitable for systems working under AIKR, NAL must have some tolerance to it. An inconsistency may indeed lead to sure loss when the system faces a

---

[1]In NAL-1, judgments have no temporal attribute, so an inconsistency is not caused by a change in the environment. Time-related belief change is handled in NAL-7, to be introduced in Chapter 11.

betting situation, but the Dutch Book argument only shows that the consistency among beliefs *is highly desired*, not that it *can always be achieved*. In a system completely open to novel and surprising observations, it is quite common for the beliefs coming from different sources to conflict with each other.

However, it does not mean that the system does not need to do anything when an inconsistency is found. Since each judgment is supported by some evidence, to resolve an inconsistency does not mean to remove one of the judgments involved, as in Alchourrón *et al.* (1985). Instead, an adaptive system like NARS should take all available evidence into consideration when judging the truth-value of a statement. Therefore, whenever distinct evidential bases for the same statement are found, the system should try to poll the evidence bases B_1 and B_2, and form a judgment based on the merged evidence $B_1 \cup B_2$.[2]

When B_1 and B_2 are disjoint sets, the amount of positive and total evidence of the conclusion are simply the sums of those of the premises ($\{w_1^+, w_1\}$ and $\{w_2^+, w_2\}$), respectively:

$$w^+ = w_1^+ + w_2^+,$$
$$w = w_1 + w_2.$$

This inference is formalized as the *revision rule* of NAL, given in Table 4.1. The truth-value of the conclusion of revision, in the form of $\langle f, c \rangle$, is calculated by the truth-value function, F_{rev}, from the truth-values of the two premises. The function is derived from the additivity of amount of evidence, and its relationship with truth-value.

Table 4.1. The revision rule with truth-value function.

$$\{st \langle f_1, c_1 \rangle, st \langle f_2, c_2 \rangle\} \vdash st \langle F_{\text{rev}} \rangle$$
$$f = [f_1 c_1 (1 - c_2) + f_2 c_2 (1 - c_1)] / [c_1 (1 - c_2) + c_2 (1 - c_1)]$$
$$c = [c_1 (1 - c_2) + c_2 (1 - c_1)] / [c_1 (1 - c_2) + c_2 (1 - c_1) + (1 - c_1)(1 - c_2)]$$

---

[2]This understanding of belief revision and evidence combination is different from the one proposed in Dempster–Shafer Theory [Dempster (1967); Shafer (1976)]. For detailed discussion on this topic, see Wang (1994a); Dezert *et al.* (2012).

The truth-value function shows that in *revision* the *frequency* value of the conclusion is a weighted average of the *frequency* values of the premises; the *confidence* value of the conclusion is higher than the *confidence* values of both premises. In practical applications, this rule can either accumulate evidence of the same (positive or negative) nature, or weigh evidence of opposite nature against each other.[3]

As mentioned above, this rule is applicable only when the two premises have distinct evidential bases. Since the evidential base of a conclusion is the union of those of the premises, it will contain more elements than that of either premise. Under AIKR, the storage space used by a statement and the processing time of an inference step must be limited to a constant, so the maximum size of evidential bases is fixed (as a system parameter). When a new evidential base is created, it is formed by merging those of its "parents" (i.e., the two premises used in the inference step), then removing some elements if its size exceeds the maximum size. Consequently, it is possible for the revision rule to be used to merge two premises that should not be merged, since their actual evidential bases were not fully remembered. However, this type of error will happen only when the common ancestor of the two premises is many generations away from them, because all recent ancestors are remembered in the evidential bases. Restricted by AIKR, we cannot expect the system to remember and process all relevant information on every issue, but the most important and relevant information.

Choice

For two inconsistent judgments J_1 and J_2, if their evidential bases B_1 and B_2 *overlap*, i.e., have common elements, some evidence has been involved in the evaluation of both judgments. If the above *revision rule* were still used with J_1 and J_2 as premises, there may

---

[3]After a pair of judgments are used by the *revision rule* to get a summary of evidence as conclusion, the premises are not immediately removed, because they are still valid, with respect to their evidential bases. However, due to its higher *confidence* value, the conclusion usually has a higher *priority*, which will be explained in the next chapter.

be evidence that is counted more than once. As a special case, this situation happens between the conclusion of the revision rule and one of the premises that produces this conclusion. Unless some restrictions are applied to the revision rule, the conclusion would be merged again and again with its premises, causing an infinite loop of "self-strengthening" of a belief.

On the other hand, it is difficult (if possible) to accurately separate the contribution of every element in the evidential base of a judgment to its truth-value, without additional information about its derivation history. This is especially true when the evidential base only contains *some*, but not *all*, input judgments that have made the contribution, due to the resource constraint mentioned previously.

Therefore, if NARS faces two inconsistent judgments J_1 and J_2 and their evidential bases B_1 and B_2 have common elements, they are not merged using the *revision rule*. Instead, the judgment with the higher *confidence* value is chosen, by the *choice rule* of NAL.[4]

Therefore the *choice rule* can be used to resolve an inconsistency when the two judgments cannot be merged, and the solution is to use the one with higher *confidence* value. This rule is justified by the semantics of NAL, because when an adaptive system faces inconsistent beliefs, the one supported by more evidence should be preferred.

Later we will see that even from the same given experience, different derivation paths may lead to different truth-values to be given to a statement. Obviously, such conclusions cannot be merged. Instead, the conclusion with the highest confidence will be chosen when they are compared to each other.

A major function of the *choice rule* is to choose between competing answers to a given question. Here it can be seen as an extension of the *matching rule* of IL-1 (defined in Table 2.3). As in IL-1, judgment "$S \rightarrow P \ \langle f, c \rangle$" provides a *matching answer*, as a

---

[4]This simple solution does not necessarily lead to a loss in the inferential power of the system. When $B_1 \cap B_2$ is not empty, the statement st may get a truth-value from evidential base $B_1 - B_2$ (or $B_2 - B_1$), then merge with B_2 (or B_1) to get a conclusion based on $B_1 \cup B_2$.

candidate, to evaluative question "$S \rightarrow P$", as well as to selective questions "$S \rightarrow$?" and "? $\rightarrow P$". However, unlike the situation of IL-1, in NAL-1 all candidates are not equally good anymore. The *choice rule* of NAL chooses the better answer between two candidates, and if there are more than two candidates, the rule is repeatedly applied to choose the best.

For an *evaluative question* "$S \rightarrow P$", both candidate answers contain the same statement "$S \rightarrow P$", though have different truth-values. The quantitative property used to choose the best one is the *confidence* value, as explained above.

For a *selective question* "$S \rightarrow$?" or "? $\rightarrow P$", if two candidate answers suggest different instantiations T_1 and T_2 for the query variable in the question, in NAL-1 the choice only depends on the truth-values of the two candidates, and does not consider the properties of the terms involved.[5] Ideally, the question should be answered by a perfect element in the intension of S or the extension of P, respectively. However, in NAL there is no such perfect answer, so what the system looks for is an answer that is "as true as possible". Since a truth-value contains two factors, here we need a way to combine them into a single number, so as to put all candidates into a total order with respect to their truthfulness.

For example, question "? $\rightarrow bird$" asks the system to find a (best) special case for the term *bird*, and the system at the moment only knows two candidates, *robin* and *penguin*, with beliefs "*robin* $\rightarrow$ *bird* $\langle 1.0, 0.8 \rangle$" and "*penguin* $\rightarrow$ *bird* $\langle 0.9, 0.9 \rangle$". The former has a higher *frequency* value, but the latter has a higher *confidence* value, so the choice is not trivial.

Some people might say that the two simply cannot and should not be compared, because *frequency* and *confidence* are defined in NAL as different dimensions. However, under AIKR, the system has to make a choice between the two, even when they are "incomparable" in the strict sense. This requirement may not sound that strange if

---

[5]Those properties, such as the *simplicity* of a term, will be taken into consideration in a higher layer of NAL.

Table 4.2. The expectation function.

frequency-interval version: $e = (l + u)/2$
evidence-amount version: $e = (w^+ + k/2)/(w + k)$
truth-value version: $e = c \times (f - 1/2) + 1/2$

we consider the decisions we make on a daily basis, many of which ask us to compare values on different dimensions.

In NAL, the *choice rule*, when used in this situation, chooses the candidate with the highest *expectation* value, which is a prediction of the *frequency* for the statement to be confirmed in the near future. According to the analysis in the previous chapter, we know for sure that it will be in the interval $[l, u]$. Under the openness assumption, all values in the interval are equally probable, so the expected value will be the middle point of the interval. This function can also be given in the truth-value form and the amount of evidence form, as listed in Table 4.2.

Therefore, e normally takes its value in $(0, 1)$. When using this function to predict, a strong positive prediction (i.e., close to 1) will be made when the system has a lot of positive evidence and little negative evidence, a strong negative prediction (i.e., close to 0) will be made when the system has a lot of negative evidence and little positive evidence. When the system either has "balanced" evidence, or knows very little about the statement, the prediction will be indecisive (i.e., close to 0.5). From the *expectation* value alone, the *frequency* factor and the *confidence* factor cannot be accurately separated, because the mapping from *truth-value* to *expectation* is many-to-one.

According to this function, "*robin* → *bird* $\langle 1.0, 0.8 \rangle$" is taken as a better answer to question "? → *bird*" than "*penguin* → *bird* $\langle 0.9, 0.9 \rangle$".

The expectation function, especially its evidence-amount version, is related to several important previous results, including Laplace's "Rule of succession" [Jaynes (2003)] (when $k = 2$) and the "λ-continuum" in Carnap (1952). What makes this function different from the previous works is that it is fully based on AIKR. For more discussions, see Wang (2006b).

Table 4.3. The choice rule.

$$\{st_1 \langle f_1, c_1 \rangle, \ st_2 \langle f_2, c_2 \rangle\} \vdash st \langle F_{\text{cho}} \rangle$$

Let us take this chance to see the impact of the parameter k. Assume there are two competing answers for the same question, where the first one has been tested 20 times, with 19 success and 1 failure, and the second one has been tested n times without any failure yet. Which one is more likely to be true in the next testing? Intuitively, people will prefer the first answer when n is small, but switch to the second one when n becomes large enough. However, different people may "switch" at different values of n. For NAL, if $k = 1$, then the second answer catches up with the first one when n reaches 6; if $k = 2$, that happens when n reaches 9. Without any assumption about the distribution of future experience, it is hard to say which value is optimal. The systems show different "personalities" when predicting the future, and larger k corresponds to more conservative and risk-averse behavior.

In summary, the *choice rule* of NAL is formally defined in Table 4.3, where "$st_1 \langle f_1, c_1 \rangle$" and "$st_2 \langle f_2, c_2 \rangle$" are two candidate answers to a question (according to the *matching rule* of IL), and "$st \langle F_{\text{cho}} \rangle$" is the chosen answer. When st_1 and st_2 are the same statement, the candidate with a higher *confidence* value is chosen, otherwise the one with a higher *expectation* value is chosen.

4.2.   Forward Inference Rules

Forward inference is a process that derives *judgments* from given judgments. A typical forward inference rule in NAL takes two judgments as premise, and derives a judgment as conclusion. An example of a forward inference looks like:

$$\{premise_1 \langle f_1, c_1 \rangle, \ premise_2 \langle f_2, c_2 \rangle\} \vdash conclusion \langle f, c \rangle,$$

where $\langle f, c \rangle$ is calculated from $\langle f_1, c_1 \rangle$ and $\langle f_2, c_2 \rangle$ by a truth-value function associated with the rule.

Unlike the local rules, in a forward inference rule the two premises and the conclusion each has a different statement, and therefore a different evidential scope (as defined by the extension of its subject and the intension of its predicate). Consequently, the evidence of a premise cannot be directly used as evidence of the conclusion. On the other hand, the evidence of the conclusion comes from nowhere but the premises. To establish the truth-value functions in such a situation, we need a new calculus of uncertainty. This calculus is different from the existing theories (like probability theory and fuzzy set theory), because the measurements of uncertainty in NAL cannot be defined in those theories (though may be similar to them here or there), as explained in the previous chapter.

To solve this problem, in NAL the involved uncertainty measurements are taken to be extended Boolean variables, so the truth-value functions are defined as extended Boolean functions. To define a truth-value function, the involved variables are first treated as binary, and their relationships are established as Boolean functions, according to the semantic theory of NAL. If there are multiple functions satisfying the semantic condition, the mathematically and conceptually simplest function is used. After that, the variables and the functions are extended from binary to real-number [Wang (2006b)].

Definition 4.1. An *extended Boolean variable* takes its value in $[0, 1]$. Extended Boolean variables $x_1, \ldots, x_n$ are *mutually independent* if the value of any of them cannot been bounded to a subrange of $[0, 1]$ according to the values of the others. There are three *extended Boolean operators* defined among independent extended Boolean variables:

$$not(x) = 1 - x$$
$$and(x_1, \ldots, x_n) = x_1 \times \cdots \times x_n$$
$$or(x_1, \ldots, x_n) = 1 - (1 - x_1) \times \cdots \times (1 - x_n).$$

Clearly, the traditional Boolean variables and the three logical operators defined among them are extreme cases of the above definition. In literatures, the *and* and *or* operators satisfying this condition are called "Triangular Norm" ("T-norm") and "Triangular Conorm" ("T-conorm"), respectively [Bonissone (1987)]. In the context of NAL, they are used for functions that are *conjunctively* and *disjunctively* determined by the variables, respectively, and the above definition is chosen for its simplicity and smoothness [Wang (2006b)]. Though this definition is in agreement with probability theory, it is not derived from the theory, and nor are the variables interpreted as probability values.

According to the definitions of uncertainty measurements in Chapter 3, the two components in truth-value (*frequency* and *confidence*) and those in frequency interval (*lower frequency* and *upper frequency*) are extended Boolean variables, and so are the amounts of evidence when $w \leq 1$. The mutual independence requirement of the *and* and *or* operators is satisfied by measurements in different judgments, as far as they have distinct evidential bases. As for the measurements of the same judgments, they need to be analyzed pair by pair. For instance, *frequency* and *confidence* are mutually independent, but *lower frequency* and *upper frequency* are not.

Therefore, in every forward inference step of NAL-1, the premises must have distinct evidential bases, so as to avoid circular reasoning and repeated usage of evidence, as well as to allow the extended Boolean operators to be applied.

In the context of NAL, the word "syllogistic" is used in a broad sense, to mean rules where the two premises share exactly one common term, and the conclusion is between the other two terms. In the following, let us assume that the shared term is M, the first premise J_1 is between M and term P, and the second premise J_2 is between M and term S. Like in IL-1, all these syllogistic rules are about the transitivity of the *inheritance* copula, except that in NAL-1 the statements are not binary, but multi-valued, and the two terms may be in either order. There are four possible combinations of J_1 and J_2, and each combination can produce a pair of conclusions, as listed in Table 4.4. In each case, the subscript x of the truth-value function F_x indicates the inference type, and F'_x is F_x with the order of the two premises switched.

In the following, we are going to analyze the four rules one-by-one, where the first three inference types are named using the categories introduced in Peirce (1931).

Table 4.4. The basic syllogistic rules.

$J_2 \backslash J_1$	$M \to P \ \langle f_1, c_1 \rangle$	$P \to M \ \langle f_1, c_1 \rangle$
$S \to M \ \langle f_2, c_2 \rangle$	$S \to P \ \langle F_{\text{ded}} \rangle$ $P \to S \ \langle F'_{\text{exe}} \rangle$	$S \to P \ \langle F_{\text{abd}} \rangle$ $P \to S \ \langle F'_{\text{abd}} \rangle$
$M \to S \ \langle f_2, c_2 \rangle$	$S \to P \ \langle F_{\text{ind}} \rangle$ $P \to S \ \langle F'_{\text{ind}} \rangle$	$S \to P \ \langle F_{\text{exe}} \rangle$ $P \to S \ \langle F'_{\text{ded}} \rangle$

Deduction

In NAL-1, the *deduction rule* has the following form:

$$\{M \to P \ \langle f_1, c_1 \rangle, \ S \to M \ \langle f_2, c_2 \rangle\} \vdash S \to P \ \langle F_{\text{ded}} \rangle.$$

Obviously, this rule is an extended version of the inference rule in IL-1, justified by the transitivity of the *inheritance* copula.

Here the *frequency* and *confidence* in all the truth-values (of the premises and the conclusion) are treated as extended Boolean variables. As analyzed in IL-1, this rule derives positive conclusion when both premises are positive. This means that the *frequency* of the conclusion, f, is conjunctively determined by f_1 and f_2, and do not depend on c_1 and c_2. This is because whether the premise is confident or not has no impact on the *ratio* between positive and negative evidences of the conclusion. On the other hand, the *confidence* of the conclusion, c, is conjunctively determined by c_1 and c_2, as well as f, since this rule only derives positive conclusion. Therefore, the truth-value function F_{ded} is uniquely determined by the following extended Boolean equations:

$$f = and(f_1, f_2),$$
$$c = and(f_1, f_2, c_1, c_2).$$

For example, from two judgments with the default truth-value, a conclusion can be derived, which is positive, though has a slightly lower *confidence* value (compared to the premises):

$$\{bird \to animal \ \langle 1, \ 0.9 \rangle, \ robin \to bird \ \langle 1, \ 0.9 \rangle\} \vdash$$
$$robin \to animal \ \langle 1, 0.81 \rangle.$$

On the contrary, if a premise is purely negative, no conclusion can be derived by this rule[6]:

$$\{bird \rightarrow animal \,\langle 1,\, 0.9\rangle,\ tiger \rightarrow bird \,\langle 0,\, 0.9\rangle\} \vdash$$

$$tiger \rightarrow animal \,\langle 0, 0\rangle.$$

A chain of deduction can be formed by more than two judgments. For example, from given premises $\{a \rightarrow b \,\langle f_1,\, c_1\rangle,\ b \rightarrow c \,\langle f_2,\, c_2\rangle,\ c \rightarrow d \,\langle f_3,\, c_3\rangle\}$, a judgment on "$a \rightarrow d$" can be formed by applying the *deduction rule* twice. Here, like in many other places in NAL, the order of inference matters — the final conclusion may have different *confidence* (though the same *frequency* for this case), depending on weither "$a \rightarrow c$" or "$b \rightarrow d$" is derived as the intermediate conclusion. When both paths are followed, the choice rule will pick the more confident conclusion whenever the statement is queried.

This *deduction rule* captures one of the several inference patterns that are often labeled as "deduction", and the other forms of deduction will be introduced in the upper layers of NAL. It is important to remember that the variables in the truth-value function are not probability values, and the truth-value function is not established according to probability theory, though it shows some similarity with certain probabilistic calculations.

Induction

In NAL-1, the *induction rule* has the following form:

$$\{M \rightarrow P \,\langle f_1,\, c_1\rangle,\ M \rightarrow S \,\langle f_2,\, c_2\rangle\} \vdash S \rightarrow P \,\langle F_{\text{ind}}\rangle$$

In this inference step, the common term M is the subject of both premises, so it cannot be directly associated with the transitivity of the *inheritance* copula. Instead, M can be used as a piece of potential evidence. According to the definition of (extensional) evidence given in the previous chapter, M is a piece of purely positive evidence for "$S \rightarrow P$" if it is fully in $(S^E \cap P^E)$, and a piece of purely negative evidence for the statement if it is fully in $(S^E - P^E)$.

---

[6]How to derive a negative conclusion deductively is covered in NAL-5 (Chapter 9).

Expressed as equations among extended Boolean variables, the truth-value function F_{ind} is uniquely determined by

$$w^+ = and(f_2, c_2, f_1, c_1),$$
$$w^- = and(f_2, c_2, not(f_1), c_1).$$

It follows that $w = and(f_2, c_2, c_1)$, and from the amount of evidence, the truth-value of the conclusion can be calculated according to the relations given in Table 3.1.

For example, given a common instance of *animal* and *bird*, an *inheritance* statement will be made from one to the other:

$$\{robin \to animal \, \langle 1, \, 0.9 \rangle, \; robin \to bird \, \langle 1, \, 0.9 \rangle\} \vdash$$

$$bird \to animal \, \langle 1, 0.45 \rangle.$$

Switching the order of the premises, the same rule produces the symmetric conclusion "$animal \to bird \, \langle 1, 0.45 \rangle$", since positive evidence supports *inheritance* in both directions. On the contrary, negative evidence only supports inductive conclusion in one direction, not the other:

$$\{tiger \to animal \, \langle 1, \, 0.9 \rangle, \; tiger \to bird \, \langle 0, \, 0.9 \rangle\} \vdash$$

$$animal \to bird \, \langle 0, 0.45 \rangle$$
$$bird \to animal \, \langle 1, 0 \rangle.$$

Since the amount of evidence for a conclusion produced by the *induction rule* is at most 1 (a unit amount), the *confidence* has an upper bound $1/(1 + k)$, which is 0.5 when the evidential-horizon parameter k equals to 1.

It is crucial to remember that in this inference step, the common term (*robin* and *tiger* in the above examples) is taken as *one piece* of evidence, rather than as *a set of pieces* of evidence. This is the case, because a term is not a set in general, and the truth-values of the premises are not necessarily determined extensionally. A conclusion like "$bird \to animal \, \langle 1, 0.45 \rangle$" should be understood as indicating the extent to which the subject term is a special case of the predicate term (as well as the extent to which the predicate term is a general case of the subject term), rather than the percent of *birds* that are also *animals* (otherwise the amount of evidence may be more than one).

Like the deduction rule, the rule above only handles one form of induction, and NAL contains other rules for induction to be introduced later. We will see that all these forms have something in common, which is why they are classified as belonging to the same inference type.

The treatment of induction (and other non-deductive inference) is one of the most unique and distinguishing feature of NAL. Since "induction" is usually associated with "generalization", where the conclusion covers situations that are not covered by the premises, the validity of induction cannot be justified in the same way as deduction, as concluded by Hume (1748) and Popper (1959). Consequently, most of the "inductive logics" have been based on probability theory, with the hope that though inductive conclusions cannot be "true" in the traditional logical sense, their probability values can be evaluated, according to certain assumptions about the environment [Kyburg (1983)].

Because NAL is designed under AIKR, it cannot assume that the events or statements in the environment follow a (known or unknown) probability distribution. Instead, the truth-value of a judgment is defined as a function of the evidence collected from the (past) experience of the system. Such a truth-value is used by the system to make decisions in the present situation and predictions about the future, not because the system believes that the present and the future are the same as the past (that is, a "Uniformity Principle" embedded in object-level beliefs and postulates), but because the system is *adaptive*. Adaptation means to behave *as if* the present and the future are the same as the past (that is, a "Uniformity Principle" embedded in meta-level rules and procedures), even though such behaviors may lead to mistakes from time to time, and the system knows that in general the future is different from the past.

A forward inference rule in NAL is *valid*, as far as the conclusion correctly summarizes the information provided by the premises alone, without considering the other information not available at the moment (though such information will be taken into account later when it becomes available). Therefore, the judgment "$bird \rightarrow animal \langle 1, 0.45 \rangle$" is not about how much "$bird \rightarrow animal$" is the case *in the real world*, but how much it is the case *as far as the system knows.* In this way, "non-deductive" inference and "deductive" inference are justified in NAL according to the same semantics, though it is not the justification expected by people who still believe in objective truth [Wang (2005)].

Non-deductive rules, including the induction just introduced, is "truth-preserving" in the sense that the truth-value of the conclusion claims no more "truth" than what is actually provided by the premises. If the uncertainty of the premises is ignored, then from "Robin is a type of animal" and "Robin is a type of bird", it is invalid to derive "Bird is a type of animal", but valid to derive "There is a piece of evidence supporting that bird is a type of animal", which is exactly what the *induction rule* provides.

Abduction

In NAL-1, the *abduction rule* has the following form:

$$\{P \rightarrow M \langle f_1, c_1 \rangle,\ S \rightarrow M \langle f_2, c_2 \rangle\} \vdash S \rightarrow P \langle F_{abd} \rangle.$$

This rule is symmetric to the *induction rule*, just like how intension is to extension — while induction is based on extensional evidence, abduction is based on intensional evidence. As defined in IL-1, for a term M in the intension of P, if it is also in the intension of S, it is positive evidence, otherwise it is negative evidence. Expressed as Boolean equations, it means

$$w^+ = and(f_1, c_1, f_2, c_2)$$
$$w^- = and(f_1, c_1, not(f_2), c_2).$$

It follows that $w = and(f_1, c_1, c_2)$. The symmetry between abduction and induction also holds for the truth-value functions — F_{abd} is the same as F'_{ind}, and F_{ind} as F'_{abd}.

For example, given a common property of *robin* and *bird*, an *inheritance* will be made from one to the other:

$$\{bird \rightarrow animal \langle 1,\ 0.9 \rangle,\ robin \rightarrow animal \langle 1,\ 0.9 \rangle\} \vdash$$
$$robin \rightarrow bird \langle 1, 0.45 \rangle.$$

Table 4.5. Deduction–abduction–induction in NAL (1).

Deduction	Abduction	Induction
$bird \rightarrow animal$	$bird \rightarrow animal$	$robin \rightarrow animal$
$robin \rightarrow bird$	$robin \rightarrow animal$	$robin \rightarrow bird$
$robin \rightarrow animal$	$robin \rightarrow bird$	$bird \rightarrow animal$

The same holds for abduction as for induction, in abduction positive evidence supports *inheritance* in both directions, while negative evidence only supports the conclusion in a single direction.

It was Peirce who suggested that induction and abduction can both be obtained from deduction by switching a (different) premise and the conclusion [Peirce (1931)], as shown in Table 4.5 (in Narsese, truth-values omitted):

However, in his later works, Peirce moved away from the formal features of the three types of inference, and emphasized their functions, for demonstration, explanation, and generalization, respectively [Peirce (1931)]. Since then, there have been different descriptions and formalization of the three types of inference. In the current AI research, these types are usually defined by their functions, and formalized in the framework of propositional or predicate logic [Flach and Kakas (2000)], which looks different from the form above.

In NAL, all three types of inference are formalized in an extended syllogistic form, so it is closer to the "early Peirce". This treatment has the advantage of clarity and elegance, as argued in Wang (2001a).[7]

Conversion

When M and S are the same term, the *abduction rule* takes the following special form:

$$\{P \rightarrow S \langle f_1, c_1 \rangle, \ S \rightarrow S \langle f_2, c_2 \rangle\} \vdash S \rightarrow P \langle F_{\text{abd}} \rangle.$$

---

[7]In NAL, the trio of deduction–induction–abduction appears in several related forms. The other forms will be introduced in later chapters.

Table 4.6. The conversion rule of NAL-1.

$$\{P \rightarrow S \langle f_1, c_1 \rangle\} \vdash S \rightarrow P \langle F_{\text{cvn}} \rangle$$
$$F_{\text{cvn}} : f = 1, \ c = f_1 \times c_1 / (f_1 \times c_1 + k)$$

Here the second premise is a tautology, which, according to the previous chapter, has truth-value $\langle 1, 1 \rangle$, so the truth-value function restrictions are simplified into $w^+ = w = and(f_1, c_1)$. Since the tautology is always true, it can be omitted from the premises, and the inference is from a single premise to a conclusion, which is traditionally called "immediate inference". In the current situation, the conclusion is obtained from the premise by switching the subject term and the predicate term, which is an inference traditionally called "conversion" [Stebbing (1950)]. In NAL, this rule has the form as given in Table 4.6, which also includes the definition of the truth-value function F_{cvn}.

The same rule and function can be derived from the *induction rule* by letting M be P.

Since only one premise is used, in any rule of immediate inference the evidential base of the conclusion is the same as that of the premise.

According to the definition of evidence given in Chapter 3, statements "$S \rightarrow P$" and "$P \rightarrow S$" have the same positive evidence, but different negative evidence. However, to directly use this definition in the *conversion rule* would lead to the truth-value function restriction $w^+ = w = w_1^+$, which means when the *frequency* of the premise is 1, the conclusion will have the same *confidence* as the premise, so as a limit, "$S \rightarrow P \langle 1, 1 \rangle$" would be derived from "$P \rightarrow S \langle 1, 1 \rangle$" alone, which could not be allowed.

To prevent this type of problem, in the immediate inference rules of NAL, the evidence of a premise cannot be used directly as the evidence of the conclusion, which is the same as in syllogistic rules, as discussed before. Therefore, the positive evidence of "$P \rightarrow S$" is still counted as positive evidence "$S \rightarrow P$", though it is the term P (or S) that is counted as a single piece of evidence, rather than as a set of evidences. Consequently, F_{cvn} corresponds to the Boolean equation $w^+ = w = and(f_1, c_1)$, which is equivalent to the above F_{cvn}.

Since the *conversion rule* switches the order of the two terms in a statement, it seems that we can replace the *induction rule* and the *abduction rule* by a conversion followed by a deduction. For example, instead of directly using the *induction rule* on $M \to P \langle f_1, c_1 \rangle$ and $M \to S \langle f_2, c_2 \rangle$ to get $S \to P \langle f_1, \frac{f_2 \times c_1 \times c_2}{f_2 \times c_1 \times c_2 + k} \rangle$, we first apply the *conversion rule* to the second premise to turn it into $S \to M$ $\langle 1, \frac{f_2 \times c_2}{f_2 \times c_2 + k} \rangle$. Then this intermediate result and the first premise can be used by the *deduction rule* to derive $S \to P \langle f_1, \frac{f_1 \times f_2 \times c_1 \times c_2}{f_2 \times c_2 + k} \rangle$, which has the same frequency as the inductive conclusion, but cannot have a higher confidence value. Therefore, though this is a valid inference path, its result will not be chosen by the *choice rule* when competing with the inductive conclusion, nor to be merged with it by the *revision rule*, since they have the same evidential base. The same is true for abduction: though it can be replaced by conversion-then-deduction, there will be a confidence loss.

The above example shows a form of inconsistency in NAL: even from the same evidential base, different inference paths may lead to conclusions of the same content but different truth-values. This type of inconsistency is "milder" than the one caused by different evidence, since here the *frequency* values are usually the same, and the difference is in the confidence values. Since the *choice rule* always picks the most confident one (which is usually produced by the shortest inference path), and the *revision rule* will not merge them, this situation does not require special treatment.

Exemplification

In NAL-1, the *exemplification rule* has the following form:

$$\{P \to M \langle f_1, c_1 \rangle, \ M \to S \langle f_2, c_2 \rangle\} \vdash S \to P \langle F_{\text{exe}} \rangle.$$

This rule uses the same premises as the *deduction rule*, but derives an inheritance judgment in the opposite direction of deduction, so it can also be considered as a "reversed deduction", though in a different sense than induction and abduction. It is called "exemplification" in NAL, because it uses the most specific term of the three in the premises as a generalization of the most general term in the premises, for example:

$$\{robin \rightarrow bird \langle 1,\ 0.9 \rangle,\ bird \rightarrow animal \langle 1,\ 0.9 \rangle\} \vdash$$

$$animal \rightarrow robin \langle 1, 0.45 \rangle.$$

Here, the premises provide some (though not much) evidence for *robin* to be considered as an "example" of *animal*, so that in the following reasoning processes the properties of the former will be used as the properties of the latter. Similar to conversion, here only the positive evidence of the premises will be used as positive evidence for the conclusion, within a unit amount. In the spirit of induction and abduction, the following restrictions are put in the truth-value function F_{exe}:

$$w^+ = and(f_1, c_1, f_2, c_2),$$
$$w^- = 0.$$

It follows that $w = and(f_1, c_1, f_2, c_2)$.

The *exemplification rule* can also be replaced by certain combinations of deduction and conversion, but all of them will lead to a conclusion of the same frequency and a lower (or equal) confidence when $k \geq 1$. Therefore, since direct conclusions should be favored over indirect conclusions, this result suggests that k should be at least 1.

From the above analysis of each syllogistic rule, as well as the relations between amounts of evidence and truth-value given in Table 3.1, the truth-value functions of the syllogistic rules are summarized in Table 4.7.

In the four truth-value functions, the *frequency* of the conclusion only depends on the *frequency* of the premises, but not on their *confidence*, because it is about the *ratio* between positive and negative evidence. On the other hand, the *confidence* of the conclusion depends on all the four values in the premises, and is always lower than the *confidence* of either premise.

Table 4.7. The truth-value functions of the syllogistic rules.

Function name	Boolean version	Truth-value version
F_{ded}	$f = and(f_1, f_2)$	$f = f_1 \times f_2$
(deduction)	$c = and(f_1, c_1, f_2, c_2)$	$c = f_1 \times c_1 \times f_2 \times c_2$
F_{abd}	$w^+ = and(f_1, c_1, f_2, c_2)$	$f = f_2$
(abduction)	$w = and(f_1, c_1, c_2)$	$c = \frac{f_1 \times c_1 \times c_2}{f_1 \times c_1 \times c_2 + k}$
F_{ind}	$w^+ = and(f_2, c_2, f_1, c_1)$	$f = f_1$
(induction)	$w = and(f_2, c_1, c_2)$	$c = \frac{f_2 \times c_1 \times c_2}{f_2 \times c_1 \times c_2 + k}$
F_{exe}	$w^+ = and(f_1, c_1, f_2, c_2)$	$f = 1$
(exemplification)	$w = and(f_1, c_1, f_2, c_2)$	$c = \frac{f_1 \times c_1 \times f_2 \times c_2}{f_1 \times c_1 \times f_2 \times c_2 + k}$

Beside the above common properties, the truth-value functions fall into two groups, according to the maximum *confidence* of the conclusions:

Strong Inference: The upper bound of the confidence is 1. Such an inference rule has a binary version in IL. In NAL-1, only the *deduction rule* belongs to this group.

Weak Inference: The upper bound of the confidence is $1/(1+k) \leq 1/2$. Such an inference rule has no binary version in IL, but corresponds to a "reversed" version of a strong inference. In NAL-1, the *abduction rule*, the *induction rule*, and the *exemplification rule* belong to this group.

This distinction also applies to immediate inference rules. In NAL-1, there is only one immediate inference rule, the *conversion rule*, which is weak. Here we can also explain the role k plays in a more general way: It indicates the relative contributions the weak inference rules make, compared to the strong inference rules — the larger the k is, the less the system depends on them.

This "strong versus weak" distinction is similar to the "deductive versus inductive" and the "explicative versus ampliative" made in the literature of logic [Flach and Kakas (2000)]. Here I use two new words, because to call the weak rules "inductive" would blur the differences among the rules in that group — it is better to define "induction" by its formal features.

On the other hand, to call this group "ampliative" may be misleading. As analyzed previously, when the truth-value of such a conclusion is taken into account, it does not really say more than the premises. What is "ampliative" is the binary version of the rule, without the proper restriction of a truth-value. Actually, it is *the choice rule* that is the ampliative part of NAL, since it uses an imperfect (though the best it can find) belief to answer a request for a perfect relation.

Though "deduction" in NAL can also produce tentative conclusions that are revisable by new evidence (so it is not the "deduction" in the "infallible" sense), it is still different from the other types of forward inference introduced so far, and the difference is in how high its *confidence* can be.

A more comprehensive discussion about induction and abduction in NAL can be found in Wang (1999, 2001a), respectively.

4.3.   Backward Inference Rules

As shown in Table 3.2, NAL-1 can process two types of Narsese sentences: judgments and questions. When the system is given a question Q, the *choice rule* can select the best answer among the candidate answers provided by the system's existing beliefs. At the same time, some other candidate answers can be derived by inference rules, guided by Q.

The second possibility does not exist in IL-1, where a question is answered by simply searching the beliefs of the system. Such a strategy cannot be used in NAL-1, since under AIKR, new sentences (both judgments and questions) may show up at any moment, and the system must make real-time responses to the questions, without assuming that all the implications of the given judgments have been exhaustively listed in the knowledge base K^*. Instead, the system must *selectively* carry out some inference processes among all the possible ones.

In this situation, one important way (though not the only way) for the system to make the selection is by *backward inference*, where a question Q produces a *derived question* Q'. Like forward inference, backward inference may also happen in two forms:

Syllogistic Inference: A question Q and belief J (a judgment) produce question Q', if and only if an answer for Q can be derived from the J and an answer for question Q', by a forward syllogistic inference rule.

Immediate Inference: A question Q produces question Q', if and only if an answer for Q can be derived from an answer for question Q', by a forward immediate inference rule.

For example, if the question is *"robin → animal"*, and the system already has the belief *"robin → bird $\langle 1, 0.9 \rangle$"*, backward inference will produce a question *"bird → animal"*, since from its answer and the existing belief, an answer to the original question can be provided by the *deduction rule*. Similarly, another question *"animal → robin"* is produced via backward inference, since from its answer, an answer to the original question can be provided by the *conversion rule*.

Therefore, the function of backward inference is not to directly answer a question, but to "activate" the relevant beliefs so as to realize certain forward inference to produce the answer. It is called "backward" because it starts at where the system wants to reach (the question), and moves "backward" to the relevant beliefs that will eventually derive the required answer. Therefore, the "forward/backward inference" in NAL is similar to the "forward/backward chaining" in some AI systems [Russell and Norvig (2010)].

As a term logic, the inference rules in NAL are *reversible*, in the following sense:

Syllogistic Inference: If there is a forward inference rule that takes two judgments as premises, and produces a third judgment as a conclusion, then from one premise and the conclusion, the other premise can be derived by a forward inference rule (though its truth-value will be different). We have seen this reversibility in the relation among deduction–abduction–induction. Therefore, if in a forward inference rule one premise and the conclusion drop their

Table 4.8. The backward syllogistic
rules of NAL-1.

$J\backslash Q$	$M \to P$	$P \to M$
$S \to M \ \langle f, c \rangle$	$S \to P$	$S \to P$
	$P \to S$	$P \to S$
$M \to S \ \langle f, c \rangle$	$S \to P$	$S \to P$
	$P \to S$	$P \to S$

truth-values to become questions, the rule becomes a valid one for backward inference.

Immediate Inference: If there is a forward inference rule that takes one judgment as a premise, and produces another judgment as a conclusion, then from the conclusion, the premise can be derived by a forward inference rule (though its truth-value will be different). Therefore, if in a forward inference rule the premise and the conclusion drop their truth-values to become questions, the rule becomes a valid one for backward inference.

Because of this property, the backward syllogistic rules of NAL-1, listed in Table 4.8, can be obtained from Table 4.4, by letting the first premise and the conclusion be questions, and the term P can be either a normal term, or a question mark to be instantiated.

NAL-1 has only one immediate inference rule: conversion. Its backward form is the same as its forward form, except no truth-value involved.

This reversibility of inference is not limited to NAL-1, but also holds in the higher layers of NAL. To simplify the description, in the following chapters, only the forward inference rules are listed, though they can all be used for backward inference, by dropping the truth-values from one premise and the conclusion, so as to turn them from judgments into questions.

CHAPTER 5

NARS: BASIC MEMORY AND CONTROL

As mentioned in Chapter 1, a reasoning system has two parts: a "logic" part specifying what sentences can be expressed and what inference steps can be carried out, and a "control" part specifying how the steps are organized into inference processes, so as to accomplish certain overall functions. Since this book is about NAL, the logic part of NARS, it will not describe the control part of the system in detail. On the other hand, since the two parts are closely related, it is impossible to fully understand NAL without understanding the basics of the control part. For this reason, this chapter describes how NAL-1 is implemented in a computer system to become NARS (in its simplest form). The control parts for the upper layers of NAL are based on similar ideas.

5.1. Inference Tasks

When NARS only implements NAL-1, an input sentence (in Narsese) is either a *judgment* or a *question* (as specified in Table 3.2), and the system's overall function is to answer the given questions according to the beliefs derived from the given judgments. For this purpose, the system treats each input or derived sentence as an *inference task* to be processed.

Each task is processed in two stages: the *initial processing* which happens only once when the task is accepted into the system, and the *continued processing* may happen any number of times. What the system does is:

Judgment - initial: using the local inference rules

- turn it into a belief of the system,
- revise it using existing beliefs on the same statement,
- answer pending questions that match its content.

Judgment - continued: using the forward inference rules to derive new judgments.

Question - initial: using the local inference rules to answer it with the best matching beliefs.

Question - continued: using the backward inference rules to derive new questions.

Here the initial processing part functions like a database, and the continued processing part is what makes a reasoning system more powerful than an information retrieval system, such as a database.

As mentioned in the previous chapter, NARS carries out both forward inference and backward inference, because the system cannot afford the resources to only reason forward exhaustively to reach the answers, nor can it only reason backward, since all the truth-value functions are associated with forward rules. Backward inference is used to activate the relevant beliefs, and forward inference is used to produce answers from the activated beliefs, as well as to spontaneously derive the implications of new knowledge, so as to adapt the system's beliefs to its experience.

Therefore, a Narsese sentence in NARS can be a *task* which is actively processed, a *belief* (if it is a judgment) which is passively used to process tasks, or both. At any moment, the system typically has a large number of tasks, and a even larger number of beliefs. Since NARS is open and works in real time, it cannot process the tasks sequentially, one after another, but has to process them in parallel by dynamically allocating its computational resources among the tasks. In this context, "parallel processing" does not mean multiple processors or threads, but that the processing periods of tasks overlap in time.

Using this terminology, what NARS does is nothing but task processing, and a task is processed by interacting with beliefs. In each inference step, a task and a belief are selected as premises, and their formal properties fully determine the applicable inference rules, then the conclusions will be handled as derived tasks. Consequently, how a task is processed is determined by the beliefs it interacts with, and what the control mechanism does is to select the task and the belief in each inference step.

Due to insufficient resources, the system cannot allow every task to interact with all relevant beliefs exhaustively; due to insufficient knowledge, the system does not know the optimal way to distribute its resources. Again, here the solution is *adaptation*, that is, to allocate the resources among the tasks and the beliefs, so as to achieve the highest overall efficiency in resource usage, under the implicit assumption that the future will be similar to the past.

The above analysis means that tasks in NARS are with different processing "speeds", and beliefs are at different accessing "depths". Their ranks depend on multiple factors, and some of them change constantly. This "controlled concurrency" [Wang (1995, 1996c)] is unique to NARS, though it is inspired by many other ideas, including heuristic search [Newell and Simon (1976)], time sharing [McCarthy (1992)], anytime algorithm [Dean and Boddy (1988)], genetic algorithm [Holland (1986)], spreading activation [Smolensky (1988)], and parallel terraced scan [Rehling and Hostadter (1997)].

5.2.   Bag-Based Storage

The problem of insufficient resources is not a new problem to AI at all. In many situations, a system has to stop a process before reaching its "logical end", due to the shortage of processor time. Various situations have been discussed in other AI projects, where a common solution is to do a "meta-level planning" in advance to decide how far (or deep) each process should go to achieve the highest overall efficiency of resource usage [Boddy and Dean (1994); Russell and Wefald (1991); Horvitz (1989)].

This approach cannot be used in NARS, which works in real time, and is always open to new input. If the system makes a resource allocation plan at one moment, there may be a new task showing up in the next moment that renders the plan useless. Consequently, NARS has to allocate its resources *dynamically*, that is, to adjust the allocation plan while using it to arrange the inference process.

The problem can be abstractly described as this: in the system there are some data "items" to be processed, and the processing can be sliced into smaller steps. An item can be processed for any number of steps, though the more, the better. With insufficient resources, few items can be processed to the end, so here we do not even need to specify what this "to the end" means, but simply continue the processing if there are still resources available for this item. Obviously, the processing time an item got is proportional to the number of times it was selected for processing. However, given the dynamic nature of the situation, the number of times cannot be predetermined, but has to be adjusted from time to time. Therefore, the system does not assign an *absolute* time budget to each item (as the number of times the item gets selected for processing), but a *relative* one, indicating the *chance* for the item to be selected for processing in the next moment.

Since dynamic resource allocation happens in several places in NARS, a data structure called "bag" is specially designed to provide this functionality [Wang (1995, 1996c)]. A bag can contain items up to a constant maximum number. Each item has a unique key, a priority in [0, 1], and some other fields. Three major operations are defined on a bag:

put(item): The given item is put into the bag. If there is already an item with the same key, the two are merged; if the bag already reaches its full maximum capacity, an item with the lowest priority is taken out of the bag to make space for the new item.

get(): A selected item is taken out of the bag, and the probability for an item to be selected is propositional to its priority value.

get(key): The item with the given key, if it exists, is taken out of the bag.

Though the last operation is ordinary, the first two are different from the common "insertion" and "deletion" operations defined on data structures, since they are designed under AIKR — the first operation admits the limited storage space, and the second admits the limited processing time.

Conceptually, a bag is a probabilistic priority-queue. It differs from the ordinary priority-queues in that the items are not removed exactly according to the order of their priority, but probabilistically, with their priority values used to decide their chances in each removal. The reason to use it is to distribute the resources *unevenly* according to the system's experience, while still giving low-priority items some opportunity to be processed. It can be considered as an approach to achieve a tradeoff between exploitation and exploration [Russell and Norvig (2010)].

It is important to realize that "priority" is a relative measurement. To know the priority value of an item alone tells us little about how much resources it will get, because that depends on what priority values the other items in the same bag have. Like evolutionary systems, items in a bag compete for resources, and a priority value indicates the level of competitiveness of the item.

A bag can be implemented with an array of buckets (for the first two operations) combined with a hash table (for the last operation). The "put" operation registers the item in the hash table by its key, and stores it in a bucket by its priority (as in bucket sort). The "get" operation visits each bucket at a frequency that is propositional to the rank of the bucket, and the "get by key" operation directly gets the item via the hash table. Therefore, each operation can be finished in a (small) constant time, independent of the number of items in the bag. Of course, the access frequency is only approximately propositional to the priority values, but accuracy is not important here, since the priority values are rough estimations themselves.

5.3.   Concept as a Unit

As mentioned before, a feature that distinguishes a term logic like NAL from propositional/predicate logic is the use of syllogistic inference rules, which requires the premises to have a shared term in each inference step. An important implication of this requirement is that the beliefs that can be directly used for a task "$S \to P$" must have S or P in it.

In NARS, a "concept" is an object that is uniquely named by a term, and it contains the tasks and beliefs with that term as subject or predicate.[1] In this way, a concept is a data structure, or object (as in object-oriented programming), that is both a unit of storage and a unit of processing. All inference steps happen "locally" within concepts. This feature greatly reduces the range of beliefs to be considered for a given task, and also makes distributed implementation of NARS possible. It is perfectly fine to run different concepts on different hardware devices, and let them cooperate by exchanging tasks.

Since inference happens locally within concepts, so does the resource competition among tasks and beliefs within a concept. Now we can specify a concept C_t as a data structure that is named by term t, and consists of a bag of tasks and a bag of beliefs, where the items in both bags are Narsese sentences that have t as subject or predicate.

For example, the belief "$robin \to bird \langle 1, 0.9 \rangle$" is stored in concepts C_{robin} and C_{bird} only. When question "$robin \to animal$" is processed, it only directly interacts with beliefs in C_{robin} and C_{animal}, but not with beliefs in other concepts, such as C_{water} or C_{bird}, though the latter concept will probably be involved *indirectly*, via a derived question like "$bird \to animal$".

We can talk about "the meaning of a concept" in a way that is parallel to "the meaning of a term" — just like the meaning of term *robin* is determined by its experienced relations with other terms (including *bird*), the meaning of concept C_{robin} is determined by its experienced relations with other concepts (including C_{bird}). The difference is just that a term is an identifier, while a concept is a data structure named by a term.

Under AIKR, resource competition not only happens *within* concepts, but also *among* concepts, that is, the system must dynamically

---

[1]This is true for NAL-1, though not exactly the case for the upper layers of NAL.

allocate time–space resources among concepts. Using the same data structure at a larger scale, the concepts are contained in a bag, and form the system's "memory" or "mental space". This memory is more than a collection of beliefs (like the K^* defined in Chapter 2), because it also contains the tasks under processing, plus the "structural knowledge" about the priority among the concepts, as well as among the tasks and beliefs within each concept.

The concept-level space competition causes some low-priority concepts to lose space, while their correspondent terms may still exist in the tasks and beliefs stored in other concepts. Consequently, while each concept is still named by a term, some terms may no longer name any existing concept.

In NARS, concepts provide an important intermediate unit between the overall memory and the individual tasks and beliefs. In AI research, the need for *structured* knowledge representation has been realized long ago, and various approaches have been used, including frame, semantic network, description logic, etc. [Russell and Norvig (2010)]. The knowledge representation in NARS are similar to them here or there.

5.4.   Inference Cycle

As a reasoning system, the running process of NARS consists of an unlimited number of inference steps, each of which carries out following routine:

(1) get a concept from the memory,
(2) get a task from the concept,
(3) get a belief from the concept,
(4) derive new tasks from the selected task and belief,
(5) put the involved items back into the corresponding bags,
(6) put the new tasks into the corresponding bags.

This routine is referred to as the *inference cycle* of the system. In it, the first two steps are straightforward, carried out by the "probabilistic retrieval" operation "get" on the whole memory and the task-bag of the selected concept, respectively. The third step is similar, but with the additional requirements that the belief cannot have overlapping evidential basis with the task, nor has already interacted with the task recently (the implementation details are omitted here).

Step four is where inference actually happens. In NARS, inference is fully "data driven", in the sense that it is the selected premises that decide which inference rules are applied in each step. If the task is a judgment, then the inference is either forward or revision; if the task is a question, then the inference is either backward or choice. In this way, the system usually does not decide on an inference type (deduction, induction, etc.) and search for premises to do it, but lets the selected premises lead the direction of the inference. It is possible to have multiple applicable rules for a given task/belief pair, and they will be applied in parallel to get multiple conclusions. After the inference rule decides the content and truth-value of a derived task, other functions will be used to decide its other attributes, including its initial priority value, which depends on the priority values of its "parents" (the task/belief pair), the type of inference, etc. For example, in backward inference, if the corresponding forward rule is strong (like deduction), the priority of the derived question will be higher than the cases where the forward rule is weak (like induction).

In the fifth step, each item (belief, task, and concept) is returned to the bag it came from, with an adjusted priority value. The adjustment is made according to several factors:

- All priority values "decay" over time, though at different rates. Each item is given a "durability" factor in $(0, 1)$ to specify the percentage of priority level left after each reevaluation [Wang (1995, 1996c)]. In this way, there is both relative and absolute forgetting in memory: an item has a tendency to become less and less accessible over time, which may eventually lead to its removal from the memory.

- A task or belief is activated if it is relevant to the current context, judged by the current priority of the other term (not the one of its "hosting" concept). Partly because of this, and partly because of the effect of derived tasks, activation spreads through the memory, similar to that in a neural network [Smolensky (1988)].

- The result of the current inference step is used as feedback. For example, if the task is a question, and the belief provides an answer that is better than the current best, then the priority of the belief is increased (as a reward), while the priority of the task is decreased (since the problem has been partially solved). Furthermore, this belief is "activated" to become a task, so as to carry out forward inference.

Since there is no "perfect answer" to a question, and there are always more beliefs to be taken into account, no task is removed because its processing has been completed. Instead, a task is removed only when its priority value has become the lowest in the corresponding bag. On the other hand, a question can get any number of answers, each of which is better than the previous ones, though none of them should be considered as "the final answer" when it is found, since there is always a possibility for the system to find a better one later.

In the last (sixth) step, the "new tasks" include the ones just produced and the ones arrived from the outside in the previous cycle, and they are all accumulated in a task buffer. For most purposes, these two types of tasks will be processed in the same way. Especially, a derived task is not explicitly linked to its parent task, so it can still exist in the system when its parent has been forgot. This treatment produces effects that are similar to the functional autonomy of motives studied in psychology [Allport (1937)]. While the priority of the derived tasks are determined by the system, those of the input tasks can be specified by the users or other systems, or take the default values associated with its type (for example, questions have higher priority than judgments). When a task is added into a concept, the priority of the latter is increased (which is how a concept becomes activated). After a new task is put into a bag, it goes immediately through the initial inference process mentioned at the beginning of this chapter.

Since each of the above steps can be finished in a constant time, so is the inference cycle as a whole.

5.5.   Properties of NARS

As a reasoning system, NARS has the following properties:

- For each input judgment, the system will reveal some of its implications (by letting it interact with some beliefs), but not all of them.
- For each input question, the system will provide the best answer(s) when it is found, then continues to look for better ones.
- Each belief of the system is based on the evidence collected from the system's experience, though there is no guarantee that all evidence has been taken into consideration.
- A task-processing process consists of multiple inference steps, each carried out according to a predetermined rule, though the process as a whole is formed at run time according to many ever-changing factors. The system processes each task in a "case by case" manner, without following a predetermined algorithm [Wang (2009b)].
- When a concept is used in the processing of a task, only part of its meaning (i.e., its relations with other terms) is used. Therefore, the "current meaning" of a concept depends not only on what the system knows about a term, but also on which pieces of that knowledge are recalled at the moment.
- Since the system's knowledge consists of a network of beliefs and tasks, and the system's reasoning activity constantly modifies the network by adding new edges and nodes as well as removing some old ones, "learning" and "reasoning" are carried out by the same process [Wang (2000)].

For different purposes, the running process of NARS can be described with different focuses and time scopes.

For each inference step, if the task and the belief are taken as the input, and the conclusion as output, what the system does is still deterministic, except that the priority values involved may depend on factors elsewhere in the system.

However, if we move to a wider scope to consider the processing of tasks, the situation is very different. In question-answering systems, it is conventional to take the question as the input, and the answer as the output, of a computation that follows an algorithm. It means that the same question always gets the same answer, and the process takes the same path and spends the same amount of resources.

As described previously, NARS does not work in this way. For a given task at a certain moment, the processing path and result depends on many factors, including the existence of relevant beliefs, the order for them to be accessed, as well as the processing time the task gets, which in turn depends on the priority values of other competing tasks. When the system becomes complicated enough, the processing context of a task becomes unrepeatable. Since the system is open to new tasks with arbitrary content and timing, the future context for the processing of a task becomes practically unpredictable. Therefore, the processing of a task in NARS cannot be described as following an algorithm that takes the task as input, and nor does it make sense to talk about the computability and computational complexity at the task-processing level.

Finally, if we move further to the scope of whole life cycle of NARS, starting from the state when its memory is empty, with its life-long input as a "problem", and its life-long output as a "solution", then the system is still a Turing Machine doing computation, and the problem-solving process is both repeatable and predictable in principle.

NARS shows a different nature when "observed from a different distance", because as an adaptive system, it does not repeat its internal states in a life cycle. On the contrary, the traditional theory of computation and algorithm focuses on repeatable processes in a system that returns to its initial states at the end of each problem-solving process. This type of theory is suitable for the design and analysis of systems that has sufficient knowledge and resources with respect to the problems to be solved, but cannot be applied to analyze the processing of a task in NARS.

In principle, the initial state of NARS does not include any empirical knowledge, and the system starts with an empty memory. However, for practical reasons, it is perfectly fine for the system to start from a preloaded memory, which may come as a copy of another system's memory, or the result of some manual editing. Even in such cases, the acquired (object-level) knowledge and innate (meta-level) knowledge of NARS are still clearly separated from each other. While everything in the former can be modified by the system's experience, the latter remains fixed.[2]

---

[2]The topic of self-control and meta-cognition will be addressed in Chapter 13.

CHAPTER 6

NAL-2: DERIVATIVE COPULAS

Though NAL-1 is fully based on AIKR and therefore provides a logical foundation for AI, its expressive and inferential powers are still far below what is expected from a general-purpose AI system. Therefore, higher layers of NAL will be added one by one, each of which expands the grammar and inference rules of the logic in a certain way, and makes related adjustments in the semantics (as well as in the memory structure and control mechanism, though those parts are only mentioned briefly in this book). As in NAL-1, in each layer we start by adding new grammar and inference rules into IL. Then, AIKR is acknowledged and the logic is extended from binary to multi-valued to become NAL, with the NAL-specific inference rules added.

For inference rules, the dependence on *copula* is the key aspect distinguishing term logics from propositional/predicate logics. In NAL-1, *inheritance* is the only copula. In NAL-2, several derivative copulas are introduced, as variants of inheritance.

6.1. Similarity Copula

The essence of the *inheritance* copula is the generalization/specialization relationship between concepts, which allows one concept *to be used as* another. It is natural to add a symmetric variant of *inheritance* into IL.

Definition 6.1. For any terms S and P, *similarity* '$\leftrightarrow$' is a copula defined by $(S \leftrightarrow P) \Longleftrightarrow ((S \rightarrow P) \wedge (P \rightarrow S))$.

Since '$\Longleftrightarrow$' and '$\wedge$' are the *equivalence* and *conjunction* connectives in propositional logic, respectively, the expression in the definition is not a statement in IL, but in its meta-language, though it introduces *similarity* statement '$S \leftrightarrow P$' into IL.

Theorem 6.1. *Similarity is a reflexive, symmetric, and transitive relation between two terms.*

So for any term T, "$T \leftrightarrow T$" is *true*, a tautology.

In all the following definitions and theorems, symbols like S, P, M, and T are used for arbitrary terms, so they will not be explicitly declared as so.

Theorem 6.2. $(S \leftrightarrow P) \Longrightarrow (S \rightarrow P)$.

So in their binary form *inheritance* is a special case of *similarity*. On the other hand, in general *inheritance* does not imply *similarity*.

Theorem 6.3. $(S \leftrightarrow P) \Longleftrightarrow (S \in (P^E \cap P^I)) \Longleftrightarrow (P \in (S^E \cap S^I))$.

If two terms are similar to each other, they are in the extension and intension of each other.

Theorem 6.4. $(S \leftrightarrow P) \Longleftrightarrow (S^E = P^E) \Longleftrightarrow (S^I = P^I)$.

In its binary form, "$S \leftrightarrow P$" means the two terms have the same meaning, or are *identical* to each other.

The above definitions and theorems lead to the new inference rules in IL-2 listed in Table 6.1 (the transitivity-based rule of IL-1 is

Table 6.1. The inference rules of IL-2.

premise$_1$	premise$_2$	conclusion
$S \leftrightarrow P$		$S \rightarrow P$
$S \leftrightarrow P$		$P \leftrightarrow S$
$S \rightarrow P$	$P \rightarrow S$	$S \leftrightarrow P$
$M \rightarrow P$	$S \leftrightarrow M$	$S \rightarrow P$
$M \leftrightarrow P$	$S \leftrightarrow M$	$S \leftrightarrow P$

still valid). To simplify the description, here different types of rules, such as *immediate* and *syllogistic*, are listed together.

Redundancies in IL inference rules are allowed. For example, the last two rules in Table 6.1 can be replaced by certain combinations of the other rules.

To extend the binary *similarity* statement in IL-2 to the multi-valued *similarity* judgment in NAL-2, the evidence of a *similarity* statement is defined, alike the evidence of an *inheritance* statement.

Definition 6.2. For similarity statement "$S \leftrightarrow P$", its positive evidence is in $(S^E \cap P^E)$ and $(P^I \cap S^I)$, and its negative evidence is in $(S^E - P^E)$, $(P^E - S^E)$, $(P^I - S^I)$, and $(S^I - P^I)$.

That is, the common extension and intension of the two terms are positive evidence, and their differences are negative evidence. Formally, the evidence of "$S \leftrightarrow P$" is the union of the evidence of "$S \rightarrow P$" and "$P \rightarrow S$".

In NAL-2 a similarity statement is true to a degree, where the amount of evidence and truth-value are defined in the same way as in NAL-1. In the following, the word "identical" will be reserved for the binary relation "$S \leftrightarrow P$" in IL, which is an extreme case of "similar" in NAL, though we can also use the latter word in IL for the same relation.

Corresponding to the basic syllogistic rules in NAL-1, in NAL-2 there are three possible combinations of *inheritance* and *similarity*, and are referred to as *comparison*, *analogy*, and *resemblance*, respectively, listed in Table 6.2. The three rules are discussed one by one in the following.

Table 6.2. The similarity-related syllogistic rules.

$J_2 \backslash J_1$	$M \rightarrow P \langle f_1, c_1 \rangle$	$P \rightarrow M \langle f_1, c_1 \rangle$	$M \leftrightarrow P \langle f_1, c_1 \rangle$
$S \rightarrow M \langle f_2, c_2 \rangle$		$S \leftrightarrow P \langle F_{\text{com}} \rangle$	$S \rightarrow P \langle F'_{\text{ana}} \rangle$
$M \rightarrow S \langle f_2, c_2 \rangle$	$S \leftrightarrow P \langle F_{\text{com}} \rangle$		$P \rightarrow S \langle F'_{\text{ana}} \rangle$
$S \leftrightarrow M \langle f_2, c_2 \rangle$	$S \rightarrow P \langle F_{\text{ana}} \rangle$	$P \rightarrow S \langle F_{\text{ana}} \rangle$	$S \leftrightarrow P \langle F_{\text{res}} \rangle$

Comparison

The *comparison rule* of NAL-2 has an extensional version and an intensional version, with the same premises as the *induction rule* and the *abduction rule* respectively, and derives a *similarity* statement as conclusion. Here is the extensional version:

$$\{M \to P \,\langle f_1,\, c_1\rangle,\ M \to S \,\langle f_2,\, c_2\rangle\} \vdash S \leftrightarrow P \,\langle F_{\text{com}}\rangle.$$

Just as with induction and abduction, such an inference step provides at most the evidence of a unit amount, except that for a similarity statement, the negative evidence comes from both terms symmetrically. That is, any shared property or instance is positive evidence, and any property or instance of only one term is negative evidence, for the two term to be similar to each other. Consequently, the truth-value function can be derived from the following Boolean equations:

$$w^+ = and(f_1, c_1, f_2, c_2),$$
$$w = and(or(f_1, f_2), c_1, c_2).$$

Unlike induction and abduction, the comparison function is symmetric with respect to the two premises, and the same function is used in the intensional version of the rule.

For example, given a common instance of *animal* and *bird*, a *similarity* statement will be made between the two:

$$\{robin \to animal \,\langle 1,\, 0.9\rangle,\ robin \to bird \,\langle 1,\, 0.9\rangle\} \vdash$$
$$bird \leftrightarrow animal \,\langle 1, 0.45\rangle.$$

Analogy

The *analogy rule* of NAL-2 is similar to the *deduction rule* of NAL-1, except that one premise is a similarity judgment. This rule has four versions, each for a different position of the shared term, as listed in Table 6.2. The following is one of them, where the shared term is the subject of the first premise (which is the inheritance judgment):

$$\{M \to P \,\langle f_1,\, c_1\rangle,\ S \leftrightarrow M \,\langle f_2,\, c_2\rangle\} \vdash S \to P \,\langle F_{\text{ana}}\rangle.$$

Intuitively, this rule is about an inference step, in which a term (M) is replaced by a similar term (S) in its relation with a third term (P).

Unlike the *deduction rule*, which only derives confident positive conclusion, this rule also derives confident negative conclusion — if M and S are very similar to each other, then premise "There is no inheritance relation from M to P" should lead to conclusion "There is no inheritance relation from S to P". On the other hand, if the similarity judgment is negative, i.e., M and S are not similar, no confident conclusion can be reached — whether there is an inheritance relation from M to P does not tell us much about whether there is an inheritance relation from S to P.[1]

This analysis suggest the following Boolean restrictions for the truth-value function F_{ana}:

$$f = and(f_1, f_2),$$
$$c = and(f_2, c_1, c_2),$$

which is just like F_{ded}, except that the *confidence* of the conclusion does not depend on the *frequency* of the *inheritance* premise.

For example, if *robin* and *lark* are known to be quite similar, then a description for one can be transformed into a description of the other, with a relatively high confidence:

$$\{robin \rightarrow bird \langle 1, 0.9 \rangle, \ robin \leftrightarrow lark \langle 0.9, 0.9 \rangle\} \vdash$$

$$lark \rightarrow bird \langle 0.9, 0.73 \rangle.$$

As a limit case, when the similarity is perfect (i.e., $f_2 = c_2 = 1$), the conclusion has the truth-value of the *inheritance* premise (i.e., $f = f_1$, $c = c_1$). This covers the case of perfect substitution between terms.

In the everyday usage of the word, "analogy" is used for several different types of inference. The *analogy rule* of NAL only captures the simplest usage among them, that is, "Similar terms have similar relations with other terms". However, when used together with other

---

[1] Here "M and S are not similar" is not the same as "M and S have nothing in common", which will be handled in a higher layer, using explicit *negation*.

rules, various types of analogy can still be carried out by NAL, though not by the *analogy rule* alone. For more detailed discussions on this topic, see Wang (2009a).

Resemblance

The *resemblance rule* of NAL-2 takes two similarity judgments as premise, and produces a similarity judgment as conclusion:

$$\{M \leftrightarrow P \langle f_1, c_1 \rangle, \ S \leftrightarrow M \langle f_2, c_2 \rangle\} \vdash S \leftrightarrow P \langle F_{\text{res}} \rangle.$$

This rule is the multi-valued form of the transitivity of the *similarity copula*. It is also similar to the *deduction rule*, except it can still get a confident conclusion when one of the two premises is negative (and the other positive). Please note that if M is similar to neither S nor P, it does not provide a reason for S and P to be considered as similar to each other. For anything to be derived by this rule, at least one premise should be positive. Therefore, Boolean restrictions for the truth-value function F_{res}:

$$f = and(f_1, f_2),$$
$$c = and(or(f_1, f_2), c_1, c_2).$$

For example, if *robin* is similar to both *swallow* and *lark*, then *swallow* and *lark* can be judged as similar to each other to a degree:

$$\{robin \leftrightarrow swallow \langle 1, 0.9 \rangle, \ lark \leftrightarrow robin \langle 1, 0.9 \rangle\} \vdash$$

$$lark \leftrightarrow swallow \langle 1, 0.81 \rangle.$$

The three new truth-value functions are summarized in Table 6.3. Using the terminology introduced in NAL-1, we say that *comparison* is *weak* inference (like *induction* and *abduction*), while *analogy* and *resemblance* are *strong* inferences (like *deduction*), and correspond to the last two binary rules in Table 6.1, respectively.[2] Furthermore, *comparison* is reversed *analogy*.

---

[2]How to extend the other IL rules in Table 6.1 to NAL will be discussed in Chapter 9.

Table 6.3. The truth-value functions of the similarity-related rules.

Function name	Boolean version	Truth-value version
F_{com}	$w^+ = and(f_1, f_2, c_1, c_2)$	$f = \frac{f_1 \times f_2}{f_1 + f_2 - f_1 \times f_2}$
(comparison)	$w = and(or(f_1, f_2), c_1, c_2)$	$c = \frac{(f_1 + f_2 - f_1 \times f_2) \times c_1 \times c_2}{(f_1 + f_2 - f_1 \times f_2) \times c_1 \times c_2 + k}$
F_{ana}	$f = and(f_1, f_2)$	$f = f_1 \times f_2$
(analogy)	$c = and(f_2, c_1, c_2)$	$c = f_2 \times c_1 \times c_2$
F_{res}	$f = and(f_1, f_2)$	$f = f_1 \times f_2$
(resemblance)	$c = and(or(f_1, f_2), c_1, c_2)$	$c = (f_1 + f_2 - f_1 \times f_2) \times c_1 \times c_2$

6.2. Instance Copula

Informally speaking, the *inheritance* copula is similar to the *subset* relation, '$\subseteq$', in set theory, which is reflexive and transitive, and can be used to form a generalization hierarchy among sets. In set theory, the subset relation is defined using the *membership* relation, '$\in$', which is neither reflexive nor transitive, but serves as the foundation of the generalization hierarchy among sets, in the sense that all sets correspond to various levels of generalization over individual "elements" or "instances".

In term logic, there is a need for something similar. It has been pointed out long ago, that in Aristotle's Syllogistic the terms correspond to generic nouns in a natural language, such as "robin" and "bird", rather than proper names like "Tweety" and "Aristotle", since the logical relationships in "Robin is a type of bird" and "Tweety is a bird" are different.

In NAL, these two relationships are represented by two different copulas, *inheritance* and *instance*, respectively. Here *inheritance* is defined first, because of its logical simplicity and generality. A term in NAL does not have to represent a set — uncountable nouns (mass nouns and abstract nouns) cannot be naturally seen as sets, but they pose no problem to be handled as terms. For example, "Water is a type of liquid" can be easily represented as "*water* → *liquid*", while the corresponding set-theoretic representation "*water* $\subseteq$ *liquid*" has the trouble of explaining what are the elements of these two "sets".

Therefore, in this set-theory analogy, what happened in NAL is like to take "subset" as fundamental, and to use it to define "membership". Here set theory provides another inspiration: a variant of the relationship can be treated as a variant of the terms involved in the relationship. In set theory, proposition "$i \in S$" is equivalent to proposition "$\{i\} \subseteq S$", therefore, in principle, it is possible to use the latter to replace the former, so as to eliminate the need for the '$\in$' relation, without losing any expressing power. In this treatment, the notation '$\{\}$' can be seen as a marker or operator that changes the nature of the term it is applied upon: the term "$\{i\}$" as a whole is taken to be a term defined by its sole instance, i.

Definition 6.3. If T is a term, the *extensional set* with T as the only component, $\{T\}$, is defined by $(\forall x)((x \to \{T\}) \Longleftrightarrow (x \leftrightarrow \{T\}))$.

That is, a term with such a form is "the most specialized" in the sense that all terms in its extension are identical to it, just like that a set defined by a sole element has no non-empty proper subset. The extension of such a term is minimized to only contain terms identical to it, and all these terms are in its intension, too, by definition. Such a statement is like a *singular statement* in Aristotle's Syllogistic, where "the subject term is the name of an individual that cannot itself be predicated by anything else" [Kneale and Kneale (1962)].

Theorem 6.5. *For any term T, $\{T\}^E \subseteq \{T\}^I$.*

On the other hand, $\{T\}^I$ is not necessarily included in $\{T\}^E$.

For the naturalness of the representation, the specialty of an extensional set can be equivalently represented by a special copula.

Definition 6.4. The *instance* statement "$S \circ\!\!\to P$" is defined by the inheritance statement "$\{S\} \to P$", where '$\circ\!\!\to$' is the "instance" copula.

Therefore, "Tweety is a bird" can be represented in Narsese either as "$\{Tweety\} \to bird$" or as "$Tweety \circ\!\!\to bird$", and there is no semantic difference between the two. In both representations, the subject term corresponds to a "source vertex" in the graphical representation of the beliefs — as defined in graph theory, such a vertex has no incoming edge.

The properties of this new copula can be easily derived from the above definition.

Theorem 6.6. $((S \circ\!\!\rightarrow M) \wedge (M \rightarrow P)) \Longrightarrow (S \circ\!\!\rightarrow P)$.

However, "$S \rightarrow M$" and "$M \circ\!\!\rightarrow P$" does not imply "$S \circ\!\!\rightarrow P$", nor does "$S \circ\!\!\rightarrow M$" and "$M \circ\!\!\rightarrow P$". This *instance* relation is not transitive, so no inference rules can be defined on it by itself, which is a major reason for *inheritance* to be taken as the primary copula in NAL, with *instance* as a variant or derivative.

6.3. Property Copula

According to the duality between extension and intension, another special type of term and the corresponding copula are defined.

Definition 6.5. If T is a term, the *intensional set* with T as the only component, $[T]$, is defined by $(\forall x)(([T] \rightarrow x) \Longleftrightarrow ([T] \leftrightarrow x))$.

That is, a term with such a form is like a set defined by a sole attribute or property. In the notation of set theory, T is taken as a predicate name, which defines a set $\{x|T(x)\}$. In Narsese, on the contrary, both T and $[T]$ are taken as terms, with different, though related, meanings.

Term $[T]$ corresponds to a concept defined by its sole property. In a natural language, examples of these concepts include adjectives and adverbs. For example, "Apples are red" can be represented in Narsese as "*apple* $\rightarrow$ [*red*]", where the predicate term represents "red things", which is not the same as the concept "red" but closely related to it.

The duality between extension and intension leads to the following conclusions, which have correspondence in the description of *extensional set*.

The *intensional set* has a special property: all terms in the intension of $[T]$ must be identical to it, and no term can be more *general* than it (though it is possible for some terms to be more general than T).

Theorem 6.7. *For any term T, $[T]^I \subseteq [T]^E$.*

On the other hand, $[T]^E$ is not necessarily included in $[T]^I$.

Definition 6.6. The *property* statement "$S \rightarrow\circ P$" is defined by the inheritance statement "$S \rightarrow [P]$", where '$\rightarrow\circ$' is the "property" copula.

So "Apples are red" can also be represented as "*apple*$\rightarrow\circ$ *red*". In graphical representations, terms with the form of $[T]$ correspond to "sink vertices" that have no outgoing edge.

Theorem 6.8. $(S \rightarrow M) \wedge (M \rightarrow\circ P) \Longrightarrow (S \rightarrow\circ P)$.

However, "$S \rightarrow\circ M$" and "$M \rightarrow P$" do not imply "$S \rightarrow\circ P$", and nor do "$S \rightarrow\circ M$" and "$M \rightarrow\circ P$".

We can easily get another variant of *inheritance* by combining an *instance* copula and a *property* copula.

Definition 6.7. The *instance-property* statement "$S \circ\!\rightarrow\!\circ P$" is defined by the *inheritance* statement "$\{S\} \rightarrow [P]$", where '$\circ\!\rightarrow\!\circ$' is the "instance-property" copula.

The above statement states that an instance S has a property P, so "Tweety is yellow" can be represented in Narsese either as "*Tweety* $\circ\!\rightarrow\!\circ$ *yellow*" or as "$\{Tweety\} \rightarrow [yellow]$".

Theorem 6.9. *For any term S and P*

$$(S \circ\!\rightarrow\!\circ P) \Longleftrightarrow (\{S\} \rightarrow\circ P) \Longleftrightarrow (S \circ\!\rightarrow [P]).$$

In summary, while all the grammar rules of NAL-1 are still valid in NAL-2, there are additional grammar rules as listed in Table 6.4.[3] These grammar rules do not *replace* the rules defining *term* and *copula* in NAL-1 (Table 3.2), but *add* alternative substitutions.

---

[3]In Table 6.4, symbols '{', '}', '[', and ']' are written within quotation marks, to indicate that here they are used literally, not as special symbols used in the grammar rules.

Table 6.4. The new grammar rules of
NAL-2.

$\langle copula \rangle ::= \leftrightarrow \mid \circ\!\!\rightarrow \mid \rightarrow\!\!\circ \mid \circ\!\!\rightarrow\!\!\circ$
$\langle term \rangle ::= \text{'\{'} \langle term \rangle \text{'\}'} \mid \text{'['} \langle term \rangle \text{']'}$

Table 6.5. The copula mapping rules.

external statement	$\Longleftrightarrow$	*internal statement*
$S \circ\!\!\rightarrow P$		$\{S\} \rightarrow P$
$S \rightarrow\!\!\circ P$		$S \rightarrow [P]$
$S \circ\!\!\rightarrow\!\!\circ P$		$\{S\} \rightarrow [P]$

As far as IL-2 and NAL-2 are concerned, the function of extensional and intensional sets is equivalent to the function of the derived copulas *instance, property*, and *instance-property*, in the sense that the implemented system can either only use the sets without the copulas, or only use the copulas without the sets. A system can support both groups at the interface, and only use one of the two within the system. However, since all the inference rules on NAL-1 are defined on the *inheritance* copula, it is simpler to use the sets, not the new copulas.[4] As a result, no new inference rule is introduced for the derived copulas *instance, property*, and *instance-property*.

The same thing cannot be said to the copula *similarity*, since the same *similarity* judgment summarizes many different pairs of *inheritance* judgments, and therefore cannot be uniquely reduced into the latter. Consequently, *similarity* has its own inference rules, as listed in Tables 6.1 and 6.2. Therefore, NAL-2 actually uses two copulas in internal inferences, though can use three additional copulas for external communication, as listed in Table 6.5.

The semantics of NAL-2 remains the same as that of NAL-1, except that terms in experience can be sets. The idealized experience still only uses the inheritance copula, not the derivative copulas.

---

[4]We will see more reasons for this decision in the next layer, NAL-3, where the sets become necessary.

Table 6.6. The equivalence
rules on sets.

$statement_1$	$\Longleftrightarrow$	$statement_2$
$S \rightarrow \{P\}$		$S \leftrightarrow \{P\}$
$[S] \rightarrow P$		$[S] \leftrightarrow P$

The extensional/intensional sets can be used as normal terms by the inference rules of IL and NAL. The only special inference rules that directly recognize their structure are the two "equivalence rules" in Table 6.6. These rules derive one statement from the other, in either direction, without changing the truth-value of the statement, in both IL and NAL, since the two statements are defined as having the same meaning. Obviously, the second rule in Table 6.1 (coming from the symmetry of *similarity*) belongs to this type, too.

CHAPTER 7

NAL-3: SET-THEORETIC TERMS

Even with five copulas, the expressive and inferential powers of NAL-2 is still quite limited. To express more complicated content, *compound terms* are introduced in NAL-3. Especially, compound terms can be composed by combining or restricting the extension or intension of existing terms.

7.1. Compound Term

An obvious shortage of NAL-2 (as well as many term logics) is that a statement consists of a subject term and a predicate term, and each of the two is either an atomic identifier or a single-component set. A natural way to overcome this limitation is to use "compound" or "structured" terms. It is similar to natural languages, where a sentence often takes the "subject–predicate" format, with the "subject" and "predicate" being phrases.[1]

Definition 7.1. A *compound term* (*con* $C_1 \ldots C_n$) is a term formed by a *term connector*, *con*, that connects one or more terms $C_1, \ldots, C_n$ ($n \geq 1$), called the *component(s)* of the compound.

By default, the order of the components matters, and the components are not necessarily different from each other. Otherwise it will be explicitly mentioned when a type of compound term is defined.

---

[1] The "subject/predicate phrase" distinction in natural languages is not the same as the "subject/predicate term" distinction in term logics, though the two are closely related.

A term connector is a logical constant without internal structure. All the connectors are predefined as part of NAL, rather than learned from the system's experience. Consequently, the "meaning" of a connector is given by its definition, and realized in the related inference rules.

Now we can treat the *extensional set* and *intensional set* defined in NAL-2 as compound terms, each with a single component, even though they are not written in the above default format of compound terms, but represent their connectors using special delimiters ('{}' and '[]').

Since a component of a compound term can be a compound term itself, a syntactic hierarchy of terms can be formed.

Definition 7.2. Each term in NAL has a *syntactic complexity*. The syntactic complexity of an atomic term (i.e., word) is 1. The syntactic complexity of a compound term is 1 plus the sum of the syntactic complexity of its components.

Usually, the syntactic complexity of a compound is just the number of symbols (words and connectors) in its structure (including the substructures). Using this measurement, in the following discussions we can meaningfully say that one term is "syntactically simpler" than another term.

In some types of compound term, the "infix" format is more natural than the "prefix" format, so $(con\ C_1 \ldots C_n)$ can be rewritten as $(C_1\ con \ldots con\ C_n)$, and the syntactic complexity of the two forms are defined to be the same (so the repeated connectors are counted as one).

For term connectors with two or more components, they are usually only defined with two components, and the general case (for both the prefix format and the infix format) is translated into the two-component case by the following definition.

Definition 7.3. If $C_1 \ldots C_n$ $(n > 2)$ are terms, and *con* is a term connector defined as taking two or more arguments, then both $(con\ C_1 \ldots C_n)$ and $(C_1\ con \ldots con\ C_n)$ are defined recursively as (*con* (*con* $C_1 \ldots C_{n-1}$) C_n), though the latter form has a higher syntactic complexity.

Please note that among terms this *syntactic* hierarchy (where terms are related by a relationship between a component and a compound) and the *semantic* hierarchy (where terms are related by a copula) are not the same.

In ideal situation, the meaning of a compound term and the meaning of its components are related by the following definition.

Definition 7.4. In IL, two compound terms are *identical* if they have the same term connector and pairwise identical components, that is, for arbitrary term connector *con* and terms $C_1 \ldots C_n$ and $D_1 \ldots D_n$,

$$((C_1 \leftrightarrow D_1) \wedge \ldots \wedge (C_n \leftrightarrow D_n)) \implies$$
$$((con\ C_1 \ldots C_n) \leftrightarrow (con\ D_1 \ldots D_n)).$$

The ' $\implies$ ' in the above theorem cannot be replaced by ' $\iff$ ', since the interrelations among components influence the meaning of a compound, so identical compound terms do not necessarily have identical pairwise components. Exceptions are the compounds with a sole component.

Definition 7.5. In IL, two compound terms with sole component are *identical* if and only if they have the same term connector and identical components, that is, $(C \leftrightarrow D) \iff ((con\ C) \leftrightarrow (con\ D))$.

Since the extensional/intensional sets defined in NAL-2 are compound terms with sole component, the meaning of the compound and that of the component mutually determine each other.

Theorem 7.1. $(S \leftrightarrow P) \iff (\{S\} \leftrightarrow \{P\}) \iff ([S] \leftrightarrow [P])$.

Based on the above results and the definitions of derived copulas, we can get the following results.

Theorem 7.2. $(S \leftrightarrow P) \iff (S \circ\!\!\rightarrow \{P\}) \iff ([S] \rightarrow\!\!\circ P)$.

"$T \circ\!\!\rightarrow \{T\}$" and "$[T] \rightarrow\!\!\circ T$" follow as a special cases. On the other hand, neither "$T \circ\!\!\rightarrow T$" nor "$T \rightarrow\!\!\circ T$" is an analytical truth in IL, though either of the two can be an empirical truth for a given term T. Therefore, some form of self-reference is allowed in IL and NAL.

After compound terms are introduced into NAL, the meaning of a term is no longer completely determined by its empirical (i.e., experienced) relations with other terms (as defined in NAL-1), but also by the *literal meaning* of the compound terms that are in the vocabulary of the system at the moment.

The existence of a compound term ($con\ C_1\ C_2$) in the system's memory will contribute to the meaning of C_1, C_2, and the compound term itself. In the graphical representation of the system's memory, we can use a special type of edge between C_1 and ($con\ C_1\ C_2$) to indicate that the former is a syntactic part of the latter (and the same for C_2), though this edge is not stored explicitly as a belief — instead, it is part of the innate knowledge of the system that is implicitly embedded in the inference rules. In this way, the meaning of a term is still represented by all the edges coming into and going out of the corresponding vertex, except that now an edge can be either syntactic (literal knowledge) or semantic (empirical knowledge).

Consequently, in NAL the meaning of a compound term is not *completely reducible* to the meanings of its components plus the meaning of the term connector — the compound terms are "semi-compositional". When initially created, the meaning of a compound term is fully determined by its connector and components, as specified in its definition. However, as the system gets experience involving a compound term as a whole, this experience is not necessarily derivable from the components. For example, the meaning of "blackboard" cannot be fully derived from the meaning of "black" and "board", though is still related to them, especially at the beginning.

7.2. Intersections

According to the experience-grounded semantics of NAL, the system's beliefs are summaries of its experience, and, its concepts, named by terms, are constituents and their patterns in the experience. Under AIKR, a major function of concepts is to efficiently organize the experience. Consequently, compound terms are widely used to summarize the meaning of other terms in a more compact way, without losing too much information.

Since the empirical meaning of a term consists of its extension and intension, which are (classical) sets in IL, it is natural to introduce compound terms into IL-3 by set operations, such as to "merge" or "split" existing concepts to get new ones.

Definition 7.6. Given terms T_1 and T_2, their *extensional intersection* is a compound term $(T_1 \cap T_2)$ defined by

$$(\forall x)((x \to (T_1 \cap T_2)) \iff ((x \to T_1) \wedge (x \to T_2))).$$

From right to left, the equivalence expression defines the extension of the compound, since "$(x \to T_1) \wedge (x \to T_2)$" implies "$x \to (T_1 \cap T_2)$"; from left to right, it defines the intension of the compound, since the tautology "$(T_1 \cap T_2) \to (T_1 \cap T_2)$" implies "$(T_1 \cap T_2) \to T_1$" and "$(T_1 \cap T_2) \to T_2$", and there is nothing else in this intension, so any M satisfying "$(T_1 \cap T_2) \to M$" must satisfy either "$T_1 \to M$" or "$T_2 \to M$", except the trivial case when M is the compound itself.[2]

Graphically, the above definition means that if a vertex has an (*inheritance*) edge going into $(T_1 \cap T_2)$, then it must have edges into T_1 and T_2; if a vertex has an (*inheritance*) edge coming from $(T_1 \cap T_2)$, then it must have an edge from T_1 or T_2. Therefore, $(T_1 \cap T_2)$ is more specific than T_1 and T_2. This result is given by the following theorem, which can also be taken as an equivalent definition of the compound term $(T_1 \cap T_2)$.

Theorem 7.3. $(T_1 \cap T_2)^E = T_1^E \cap T_2^E$, $(T_1 \cap T_2)^I = T_1^I \cup T_2^I \cup \{(T_1 \cap T_2)\}$.

In the above expressions, the '$\cap$' sign is used in two different senses. On the right-side of the first expression, it indicates the intersection

---

[2]The intension part of the definition should not be interpreted in set theory by treating "inheritance" as "subset", because if T_1 and T_2 are sets, "$(T_1 \cap T_2) \subseteq x$" does not imply "$(T_1 \subseteq x) \vee (T_2 \subseteq x)$".

of sets, but on the left-side of the two expressions, it is the term connector of *extensional intersection*.

For example, $([yellow] \cap bird)$ represents "yellow bird", whose instances belong to both "yellow thing" and "bird", and whose properties include those of "yellow thing" plus those of "bird". If the system's experience contains many occurrences of yellow birds, the compound term can be used to represent them, which is more efficient, both in processing time and in storage space, than using two terms for "yellow" and "bird", separately.

Like an atomic term, the meaning of a compound term is also determined by both its extension and intension, rather than by its extension alone, as in most traditional models of categorization. Some long-standing issues can be resolved in this way. As argued in Wang (2011), the well-known Conjunction Fallacy [Tversky and Kahneman (1983)], also known as the "Linda Problem", can be explained as application of intensional evidence.

Similarly, a compound term can be formed to generalize two given terms.

Definition 7.7. Given terms T_1 and T_2, their *intensional intersection* is a compound term $(T_1 \cup T_2)$ defined by

$$(\forall x)(((T_1 \cup T_2) \to x) \iff ((T_1 \to x) \wedge (T_2 \to x))).$$

From right to left, the equivalence expression defines the intension of the compound, since "$(T_1 \to x) \wedge (T_2 \to x)$" implies "$(T_1 \cup T_2) \to x$"; from left to right, it defines the extension of the compound, since the tautology "$(T_1 \cup T_2) \to (T_1 \cup T_2)$" implies "$T_1 \to (T_1 \cup T_2)$" and "$T_2 \to (T_1 \cup T_2)$", and there is nothing else in this extension, so any M satisfying "$M \to (T_1 \cup T_2)$" must satisfy either "$M \to T_1$" or "$M \to T_2$", except the case when M is the compound itself.

Theorem 7.4. $(T_1 \cup T_2)^I = T_1^I \cap T_2^I$, $(T_1 \cup T_2)^E = T_1^E \cup T_2^E \cup \{(T_1 \cup T_2)\}$.

For example, $(dog \cup cat)$ is a term that covers all kinds of dogs and cats as its instances, while the properties of the term consist of the common properties of dogs and cats.

The above definition and theorem show that the duality of *extension* and *intension* in NAL corresponds to the duality of *intersection* and *union* in set theory — *intensional intersection* corresponds to *extensional union*, and *extensional intersection* corresponds to *intensional union*. Since set theory is purely extensional, the '∪' operator is associated to *union* only. To stress the symmetry between extension and intension in NAL, here it is called "intensional intersection", rather than "extensional union", though the latter is also correct, and sounds more natural to people familiar with set theory.

Both term connectors '∩' and '∪' can be extended to take more than two components. Since they are both associative and symmetric, the order of their components does not matter. Consequently, they are isomorphic to the corresponding set operators, and all the following NAL theorems map into theorems in set theory, if the terms are interpreted as sets, *inheritance copula* as subset relation, *similarity copula* as equal-set relation, and the term connectors as the corresponding set operators.

Theorem 7.5.

$$(T_1 \cap T_2) \leftrightarrow (T_2 \cap T_1),$$
$$(T_1 \cup T_2) \leftrightarrow (T_2 \cup T_1).$$

Theorem 7.6.

$$(T_1 \cap T_2) \to T_1,$$
$$T_1 \to (T_1 \cup T_2).$$

As mentioned previously, even though the above statements are true in IL, in NAL they are not remembered as beliefs, which are purely *empirical*.[3]

The following theorem can be used to reduce a term into a syntactically simpler but semantically equivalent term.

---

[3]Instead, this *analytical* knowledge is embedded in the relevant inference rules, to be introduced in NAL-5.

Theorem 7.7.

$$(T \cap T) \leftrightarrow T,$$
$$(T \cup T) \leftrightarrow T.$$

The definitions of the intersections can also be used to decompose a compound term. According to propositional logic, for any propositions P, Q, and R, "$(P \wedge Q) \Longrightarrow R$" is equivalent to "$(P \wedge \neg R) \Longrightarrow \neg Q$", and "$P \Longrightarrow (Q \vee R)$" is equivalent to "$(\neg R \wedge P) \Longrightarrow Q$", so the following theorems are true.

Theorem 7.8.

$$M \to T_1 \wedge \neg(M \to (T_1 \cap T_2)) \implies \neg(M \to T_2),$$
$$\neg(T_1 \to M) \wedge (T_1 \cap T_2) \to M \implies T_2 \to M,$$
$$T_1 \to M \wedge \neg((T_1 \cup T_2) \to M) \implies \neg(T_2 \to M),$$
$$\neg(M \to T_1) \wedge M \to (T_1 \cup T_2) \implies M \to T_2.$$

Finally, an arbitrary term M in the system's vocabulary V_K can be added to both sides of a copula by a term connector, if needed.

Theorem 7.9.

$$S \to P \implies (S \cap M) \to (P \cap M),$$
$$S \to P \implies (S \cup M) \to (P \cup M),$$
$$S \leftrightarrow P \implies (S \cap M) \leftrightarrow (P \cap M),$$
$$S \leftrightarrow P \implies (S \cup M) \leftrightarrow (P \cup M).$$

The '$\Longrightarrow$' in the above theorems cannot be replaced by '$\Longleftrightarrow$'.

7.3. Differences

To specialize a given term means to reduce its extension. In *extensional intersection*, this is achieved by selecting the elements that are *also* in the extension of another term. Clearly, a similar effect can be achieved by selecting the elements that are *not* in the extension of another term.

Definition 7.8. If T_1 and T_2 are different terms, their *extensional difference* is a compound term $(T_1 - T_2)$ defined by

$$(\forall x)((x \to (T_1 - T_2)) \iff ((x \to T_1) \wedge \neg(x \to T_2))).$$

From right to left, the equivalence expression defines the extension of the compound, since "$(x \to T_1) \wedge \neg(x \to T_2)$" implies "$x \to (T_1 - T_2)$"; from left to right, it defines the intension of the compound, since the tautology "$(T_1 - T_2) \to (T_1 - T_2)$" implies "$(T_1 - T_2) \to T_1$", and there is nothing else in this intension, so any M satisfying "$(T_1 - T_2) \to M$" must satisfy "$T_1 \to M$", except being the compound itself.

Obviously, $(T_2 - T_1)$ can also be defined, but it will be different from $(T_1 - T_2)$. For example, $([yellow] - bird)$ means "yellow thing that is not bird", while $(bird - [yellow])$ means "bird that is not yellow". Here T_1 and T_2 are required to be different, otherwise their difference will have an empty extension, and therefore cannot be a meaningful term. This case is different from $(T \cap T)$, which is meaningful, though it can be reduced to a simpler term.

Since the extension of $(T_1 - T_2)$ is obtained from that of T_1, using negative restriction provided by T_2, its intension cannot be increased from that of T_1 by adding something from T_2 (as in $(T_1 \cap T_2)$). For example, the properties of "bird that is not yellow" are merely the properties of "bird", since "not yellow" does not provide any (positively defined) property.

Theorem 7.10. $(T_1 - T_2)^E = T_1^E - T_2^E$, $(T_1 - T_2)^I = T_1^I \cup \{(T_1 - T_2)\}$.

Similarly, according to the duality between extension and intension, a term can be generalized by selecting part of its intension (properties). To do it with *positive* criteria has produced *intensional intersection*, and now we will do that with *negative* criteria.

Definition 7.9. If T_1 and T_2 are different terms, their *intensional difference* is a compound term $(T_1 \ominus T_2)$ defined by

$$(\forall x)(((T_1 \ominus T_2) \to x) \iff ((T_1 \to x) \wedge \neg(T_2 \to x))).$$

From right to left, the equivalence expression defines the intension of the compound, since "$(T_1 \rightarrow x) \land \neg(T_2 \rightarrow x)$" implies "$(T_1 \ominus T_2) \rightarrow x$"; from left to right, it defines the extension of the compound, since the tautology "$(T_1 \ominus T_2) \rightarrow (T_1 \ominus T_2)$" implies "$T_1 \rightarrow (T_1 \ominus T_2)$", and there is nothing else in this extension, so any M satisfying "$M \rightarrow (T_1 \ominus T_2)$" must satisfy "$M \rightarrow T_1$", except being the compound itself.

Theorem 7.11. $(T_1 \ominus T_2)^I = T_1^I - T_2^I$, $(T_1 \ominus T_2)^E = T_1^E \cup \{(T_1 \ominus T_2)\}$.

For example, $(bird \ominus animal)$ is a term defined by those properties of *bird* that are not shared by other types of *animal*, or "Whatever that differ bird from other animal" (a form of "bird-ness"). This term is more general than *bird*, since it requires less properties than the latter, though from the definition alone its instances are still the same as *bird*. This *intensional difference* is obviously different from the *extensional difference* of the same terms, $(bird - animal)$, which means "birds that are not animals".

These *difference* connectors have many properties that are in parallel to those of the *intersection*, though the *difference* connectors cannot take more than two components. Also, neither $(T - T)$ nor $(T \ominus T)$ is a meaningful term.

Theorem 7.12.

$$(T_1 - T_2) \rightarrow T_1,$$
$$T_1 \rightarrow (T_1 \ominus T_2).$$

Theorem 7.13.

$$M \rightarrow (T_1 - T_2) \implies \neg(M \rightarrow T_2),$$
$$(T_1 \ominus T_2) \rightarrow M \implies \neg(T_2 \rightarrow M).$$

Theorem 7.14.

$$M \rightarrow T_1 \land \neg(M \rightarrow (T_1 - T_2)) \implies M \rightarrow T_2,$$
$$\neg(M \rightarrow T_1) \land \neg(M \rightarrow (T_2 - T_1)) \implies \neg(M \rightarrow T_2),$$
$$T_1 \rightarrow M \land \neg((T_1 \ominus T_2) \rightarrow M) \implies T_2 \rightarrow M,$$
$$\neg(T_1 \rightarrow M) \land \neg((T_2 \ominus T_1) \rightarrow M) \implies \neg(T_2 \rightarrow M).$$

Theorem 7.15.

$$S \to P \implies (S - M) \to (P - M),$$
$$S \to P \implies (M - P) \to (M - S),$$
$$S \to P \implies (S \ominus M) \to (P \ominus M),$$
$$S \to P \implies (M \ominus P) \to (M \ominus S),$$
$$S \leftrightarrow P \implies (S - M) \leftrightarrow (P - M),$$
$$S \leftrightarrow P \implies (M - P) \leftrightarrow (M - S),$$
$$S \leftrightarrow P \implies (S \ominus M) \leftrightarrow (P \ominus M),$$
$$S \leftrightarrow P \implies (M \ominus P) \leftrightarrow (M \ominus S).$$

As in set theory, the intersections and differences connectors can cancel out each other in certain ways:

Theorem 7.16.

$$T \leftrightarrow ((T \cap M) \cup (T - M)),$$
$$T \leftrightarrow ((T \cup M) \cap (T \ominus M)).$$

Theorem 7.17.

$$((T \cup M) - M) \to T,$$
$$((T \ominus M) \cap M) \to T,$$
$$T \to ((T - M) \cup M),$$
$$T \to ((T \cap M) \ominus M).$$

7.4. Multi-Component Sets

Now we can extend the definitions of *extensional set* and *intensional set* from containing one component (as defined in NAL-2) to containing any number of components.

Definition 7.10. Given different terms $T_1, \ldots, T_n$ $(n \geq 2)$, an *extensional set* $\{T_1, \ldots, T_n\}$ is defined as $(\cup\{T_1\} \ldots \{T_n\})$; an *intensional set* $[T_1, \ldots, T_n]$ is defined as $(\cap[T_1] \ldots [T_n])$. The new format has a lower syntactic complexity, so should be used whenever possible.

In this way, an *extensional set* is defined by enumerating its *instances*, and an *intensional set* is defined by enumerating its *properties*. The order of the components does not matter, and duplicate components are not allowed.

It is important to remember that in IL the extension of an *extensional set* not only include the singleton sets of its instances, but also its subsets. For example, the extension of term $\{a,\ b,\ c\}$ includes $\{a\}$, $\{b\}$, $\{c\}$, $\{a,\ b\}$, $\{a,\ c\}$, $\{b,\ c\}$, and $\{a,\ b,\ c\}$. The same is true for intensional sets.

These multi-component sets no longer have certain properties of single-component sets such as the minimum extension or intension. On the other hand, they have properties that are not there in single-component sets.

Theorem 7.18.

$$((M \circ\!\!\rightarrow \{T_1, \ldots, T_n\}) \iff ((M \leftrightarrow T_1) \vee \ldots \vee (M \leftrightarrow T_n))),$$
$$(([T_1, \ldots, T_n] \rightarrow\!\!\circ M) \iff ((T_1 \leftrightarrow M) \vee \ldots \vee (T_n \leftrightarrow M))).$$

Theorem 7.19.

$$(\{T_1, \ldots, T_n\} - \{T_n\}) \leftrightarrow \{T_1, \ldots, T_{n-1}\},$$
$$([T_1, \ldots, T_n] \ominus [T_n]) \leftrightarrow [T_1, \ldots, T_{n-1}].$$

Now we see that IL can represent and process a set, which is defined either by instances or by properties, similar to the "set" defined in set theory. The *intersection* and *difference* connectors can be applied to them just like how the corresponding operators are applied to sets. For example, if the given term T_1 is $\{Mars, Pluto, Venus\}$ and T_2 is $\{Pluto, Saturn\}$, then the compound term $(T_1 \cup T_2)$ is $\{Mars, Pluto, Saturn, Venus\}$, $(T_1 \cap T_2)$ is $\{Pluto\}$, $(T_1 - T_2)$ is $\{Mars, Venus\}$, and $(T_2 - T_1)$ is $\{Saturn\}$. Intensional sets are handled in the same way.

A set is a special type of term, but a term in general is not necessarily identical to any set. Even though the extension and intension of a term are defined as sets in the meta-level, in the object-level it is usually impossible to decide their *cardinality* in a meaningful way. On the contrary, the cardinality of an extensional or intensional set is a syntactic feature, so can be decided effectively. Therefore, as in mathematics, in NAL sets provide the foundation for counting and other mathematical operations and notions.

Table 7.1. The new grammar rules of NAL-3.

$$\langle term \rangle ::= '\{'\langle term \rangle^+ '\}' \mid '['\langle term \rangle^+ ']'$$
$$\mid (\cap \langle term \rangle \langle term \rangle^+)$$
$$\mid (\cup \langle term \rangle \langle term \rangle^+)$$
$$\mid (- \langle term \rangle \langle term \rangle)$$
$$\mid (\ominus \langle term \rangle \langle term \rangle)$$

Given the necessity of sets in NAL, its functional equivalence with the derivative copulas *instance*, *property*, and *instance-property* no longer exists in NAL-3 and the higher layers. Consequently, NAL should be implemented to use sets for internal representation and external communication, while only to use the three derivative copulas for communication, so as to reduce the redundancy in the internal representation and processing.

In summary, the above definitions introduce the new forms for *term* in Table 7.1.

The grammar rule in Table 6.4 for *extensional* and *intensional* *sets* becomes a special case of the new rule in Table 7.1. Following the common convention, comma (',') can be used to separate the components in a compound term (especially, a set), though its usage is optional. Narsese does not allow a compound term without component, so an "empty set" cannot be represented as '{ }' or '[]', but as an atomic term, like "*empty-set*" or "*nothing*". This is another difference between IL/NAL and set theory in the representation and processing of sets.

7.5. Inference on Compound Terms

In the previous sections, the syntax and semantics of compound terms in general, and intersections and differences in particular, are described. The description applies to both IL-3 and NAL-3, and the latter also needs to handle numerical truth-value. In the following the inference rules of NAL-3 are introduced.

Almost all of the inference rules introduced in the lower layers can be directly applied to compound terms, by treating them as atomic (i.e., non-compound) terms. In that situation, a compound term is used as a whole, and its internal structure and literal meaning are all ignored.

Choice

To handle compound terms in NAL-3, the only change in the existing rules happens in the *choice rule*, when used to compare competing answers T_1 and T_2 for a *selective question* "$S \rightarrow$?" (or "? $\rightarrow P$"). In NAL-1, the system compares the truth-values of "$S \rightarrow T_1$" and "$S \rightarrow T_2$", and chooses the one with a higher *expectation* value. In NAL-3, however, the *syntactic complexity*, or its opposite, the *syntactic simplicity*, of the answer is also taken into account.

Definition 7.11. If the *syntactic complexity* of a term is n, then its *syntactic simplicity* is $s = 1/n^r$, where $r > 0$ is a system parameter.

Since $n \geq 1$, s is in $(0, 1]$. Atomic terms have the highest simplicity, 1.0.

For a selective question, when the candidate answers have the same *expectation* value, NAL prefers the simplest answer, because it usually costs less resources than the others to process. It is a form of "Occam's Razor" that favors simplicity when the other factors are the same. When the candidates have different *expectation* values, however, *expectation* e and (syntactic) *simplicity* s must be combined together, so as to make the candidates comparable in general. Since a good answer should have high values on both dimensions, the *and* operator is used, and as a result, the preferred answer is the one that has a large $e \times s$, that is, a larger e/n^r. By adjusting the value of the "razor parameter" r, we can control the relative weights of the two factors in the *choice rule*. To simplify the discussion, in the following we assume $r = 1$. Clearly, the *choice rule* defined in NAL-1 becomes a special case of the above rule, with $s = n = 1$ for atomic terms.

After expended to handle compound terms, the *choice rule* can serve additional functions, such as *pattern recognition* or (high-level) *perception*: when S is a compound term, question "$S \rightarrow$?" asks the system to find a simple term T that covers S as a special case. Again, here the simplicity of T and its "fitness" with the "pattern" (measured by the expectation of "$S \to T$") are balanced against each other when multiple candidates exist.[4]

Various forms of "Occam's Razor" have been widely used in AGI systems [Baum (2004); Hutter (2005)]. The major differences between the above treatment in NAL and the other approaches are:

- "Occam's Razor" is not accepted as a postulate for its own sake, but as an implication of AIKR. For this reason, it is only accepted in NAL, but not in IL.

- Though high simplicity and high expectation are both preferred, they are not taken to be correlated, as assumed by Solomonoff (1964). Instead, they are treated as measurements that are defined independently, though can be combined to make choices.

Composition

New compound terms can be either *introduced* in the (idealized or actual) experience of the system, or *composed* by inference rules from the existing terms.

To compose *intersections* and *differences* in NAL-3, the inference rules in Table 7.2 use the same premises as the rules in Table 4.4 (though the terms are named differently). However, this time the conclusions are not between the two terms unshared in the premises, but between the shared term and a compound term composed by the other two. Therefore they are not *syllogistic*, but *compositional*, though the truth-values of conclusions are still calculated from those of the premises, as before. Such a rule is applicable only when T_1 and T_2 are different, and do not have each other as component. Also, the two premises cannot have overlapping evidential bases.

Each of the three truth-value functions appearing in Table 7.2 is used at least in two compositional rules, one extensional and

---

[4]More factors can be taken into account when answering this question, such as the *relevance* of T to the current context, or the *usefulness* of T in the history of the system. However, these factors are not contributed by the *logic* part of NARS, but the *control* part, as mentioned in Chapter 5 — candidates with those properties have higher accessibility. This issue will not be discussed in detail in the book.

Table 7.2. The compositional rules of NAL-3.

$J_2 \backslash J_1$	$M \to T_1 \langle f_1, c_1 \rangle$	$T_1 \to M \langle f_1, c_1 \rangle$
$T_2 \to M \langle f_2, c_2 \rangle$		$(T_1 \cup T_2) \to M \langle F_{\text{int}} \rangle$
		$(T_1 \cap T_2) \to M \langle F_{\text{uni}} \rangle$
		$(T_1 \ominus T_2) \to M \langle F_{\text{dif}} \rangle$
		$(T_2 \ominus T_1) \to M \langle F'_{\text{dif}} \rangle$
$M \to T_2 \langle f_2, c_2 \rangle$	$M \to (T_1 \cap T_2) \langle F_{\text{int}} \rangle$	
	$M \to (T_1 \cup T_2) \langle F_{\text{uni}} \rangle$	
	$M \to (T_1 - T_2) \langle F_{\text{dif}} \rangle$	
	$M \to (T_2 - T_1) \langle F'_{\text{dif}} \rangle$	

Table 7.3. The truth-value functions of the composition rules.

Name	Inference	Frequency	Confidence
F_{int}	intersection	$f = and(f_1, f_2)$	$c = and(c_1, c_2)$
F_{uni}	union	$f = or(f_1, f_2)$	$c = and(c_1, c_2)$
F_{dif}	difference	$f = and(f_1, not(f_2))$	$c = and(c_1, c_2)$

another intensional, and the *difference* rule is also used for both orders between the two terms. The three truth-value functions are listed in Table 7.3.

In these functions, the *frequency* of the conclusion is determined by the *frequency* of the premises with the same Boolean operator that defines the extension or intension of the compound, while the *confidence* of the conclusion is determined conjunctively by the *confidence* of the premises. All these three functions are strong, so have binary versions in IL.[5]

As in binary logic, here a conclusion may be derived from a single premise. Since $T_1 \to (T_1 \cup T_2)$ is an analytical truth, if $M \to T_1$ has a high *frequency* and a high *confidence*, the system should be able

---

[5]How to represent *negative* statements in IL will be introduced in Chapter 9.

to assign a similar truth-value to $M \rightarrow (T_1 \cup T_2)$, without evidence about $M \rightarrow T_2$.[6]

Equipped with these compositional rules, NAL-3 not only can derive new tasks and beliefs among the existing terms (as in the lower layers), but can also derive new compound terms, using the existing terms as components. In other words, a system using NAL can not only learn new knowledge about existing concept, but also "learn new concepts", in several senses:

- The system is open to input sentences containing novel (atomic or compound) terms that are not in the system's current vocabulary.
- The compositional rules may create compound terms that are not in the system's current vocabulary.
- Even when a conclusion only contains existing terms, it may more or less change the meaning of the terms by adding new relations into them.
- Since each time a concept is used with its "current meaning", which is influenced by the priority distribution among the beliefs in the concept (as explained in Chapter 5), concept learning also happens when this priority distribution is adjusted.

Clearly, in NAL-3 the system's vocabulary does not only contain terms obtained from the system's experience (as in the lower layers), but also the compound terms that have been composed from them.

Some people may think that since the "new concepts" in NAL are all composed from existing concepts, they are not really "new". This opinion is incorrect, because as soon as a compound term is formed, its meaning will no longer be fully determined by its "literal meaning" (which links it to the meaning of its components), but also depends on the conceptual relation between the concept *as a whole* and the other concepts, and this part of meaning usually cannot be

---

[6]This type of immediate inference will be introduced in NAL-5. In the previous versions of NARS [Wang (2006b)], this type of inference is also carried out by the composition rules. Now they are covered separately to simplify the design. The overall results are similar, since when the composition rules and the single-premise rules produce conflicting conclusions, the choice rule will pick the high confident one to use.

reduced into that of its components. This aspect of concept learning is discussed in Wang and Hofstadter (2006).

One important nature of NARS is that it is not a reasoning system in the traditional sense, but an attempt to build an "Artificial General Intelligence" (AGI) [Wang and Goertzel (2007)] in the framework of a reasoning system. It follows that the notion of "reasoning" is greatly expended to include other cognitive processes. Here we have seen that "reasoning" and "learning" are two aspects of the same underlying process, rather than two separate (though related) processes, as assumed by many other AGI projects, especially various "Cognitive Architectures" [Newell (1990); Chong *et al.* (2007)].

When learning new concepts, NARS does not exhaustively search a "vision space", and evaluate every possible concept according to a fixed criterion, like some traditional AI systems. For example, though it is syntactically legitimate to pick two arbitrary terms in the system's vocabulary, then to evaluate their intersections and differences, NARS does not try that. Instead, an intersection (or difference) is composed only when it can be used to summarize some experience obtained in the system. This is why no new term is composed from "$M \rightarrow T_1\langle f_1, c_1 \rangle$" and "$T_2 \rightarrow M\langle f_2, c_2 \rangle$" in Table 7.2.

Furthermore, whether a concept is valuable or fruitful is not a decision made *when* the concept is created, but *after* it is created, in the process in which all existing concepts compete for resources.

All these properties make the concept learning process in NARS different from that in traditional machine learning algorithms [Mitchell (1997); Russell and Norvig (2010)].

CHAPTER 8

NAL-4: RELATIONAL TERMS

An often claimed advantage of predicate logic over term logic is that the former can represent any conceptual relation (as *function* over *arguments*), while the latter can only represent a small number of relations (as *copulas* between *terms*) [Frege (1999)]. Though this criticism is valid toward traditional term logics, like that of Aristotle (1882), it is an issue that can be resolved within term logic, using *compound terms*.

NAL-4 has the capability of representing and processing arbitrary relations among terms.

8.1. Product and Acquired Relation

The approach taken in IL/NAL to represent relation is similar to the approach used in set theory, where a "relation" is defined as a set of ordered pairs or tuples.

Definition 8.1. The *product* connector '$\times$' takes two or more terms as components, and forms a compound term that satisfies

$$((\times S_1 \cdots S_n) \rightarrow (\times P_1 \cdots P_n))$$
$$\iff ((S_1 \rightarrow P_1) \wedge \cdots \wedge (S_n \rightarrow P_n)).$$

Therefore, this compound term is simply a way to put two or more terms into a sequence, and to extend the *inheritance* relation from the components to the compounds. Intuitively, a product represents an anonymous relation among the components, and the role played by each of them is indicated only by their relative order. As usual, the connector can be used both in the prefix format and the infix format. To simplify the description, in the following products of two terms are used, though the results can be easily extended to products of more than two terms.

Theorem 8.1. $((S_1 \times S_2) \leftrightarrow (P_1 \times P_2)) \iff ((S_1 \leftrightarrow P_1) \wedge (S_2 \leftrightarrow P_2))$.

Theorem 8.2.

$$(S \to P) \iff ((M \times S) \to (M \times P)) \iff ((S \times M) \to (P \times M)),$$
$$(S \leftrightarrow P) \iff ((M \times S) \leftrightarrow (M \times P)) \iff ((S \times M) \leftrightarrow (P \times M)).$$

The above result intuitively says that a term can be "multiplied" to both sides of a copula.

The definition of *product* in NAL is like how *Cartesian product* is defined in set theory, except that here all the involved items are *terms*, not *sets* or their elements. Furthermore, the definition in set theory is purely extensional (defining a product by enumerating its elements), while the NAL definition is both extensional and and intensional — the above definition specifies the extension of $(P_1 \times P_2)$ and the intension of $(S_1 \times S_2)$ at the same time.

When S_1 and S_2 are singleton sets, this definition can be rewritten as

$$(((\{T_1\} \times \{T_2\}) \to (P_1 \times P_2)) \iff ((T_1 \circ\!\!\to P_1) \wedge (T_2 \circ\!\!\to P_2)).$$

With the following definition, the above result can be mapped into the set theory definition perfectly.

Definition 8.2. A product of singleton extensional sets ($\{T_1\} \times \{T_2\}$) is identical to a singleton extensional set of a product $\{(T_1 \times T_2)\}$, and the latter format has a lower syntactic complexity. The same is true for intensional sets, that is, $([T_1] \times [T_2]) \leftrightarrow [(T_1 \times T_2)]$. The two can be further simplified into $\{T_1 \times T_2\}$ and $[T_1 \times T_2]$, respectively, without changing their syntactic complexity.

Now we can see the *product* of NAL as an extension of the Cartesian product in set theory. Once again, while the membership relation is fundamental in set theory, in NAL it is the inheritance relation that is used to define the other constituents of the logic.

The '×' operator is used, because in set theory a Cartesian product between a set of cardinality m and a set of cardinality n has a cardinality $m \times n$. This result only holds in special cases in NAL, though the intuition remains, as shown by the following meta-level result.

Theorem 8.3.

$$\{(x \times y)|x \in T_1^E, y \in T_2^E\} \subseteq (T_1 \times T_2)^E,$$

$$\{(x \times y)|x \in T_1^I, y \in T_2^I\} \subseteq (T_1 \times T_2)^I.$$

In the above theorem, the '$\subseteq$' relation cannot be replaced by '$=$', because $(T_1 \times T_2)^E$ and $(T_1 \times T_2)^I$ may contain other terms that are not *products*.

Unlike a *set*, a *product* may have duplicate components, and the order of components matters. As a special case of the definition of *product*, when the terms involved are products with common components, the system can "concatenate" them into longer products:

Theorem 8.4.

$$(((\times\ S_1\ S_2)\ \rightarrow\ (\times\ P_1\ P_2)) \wedge ((\times\ S_1\ S_3) \rightarrow (\times\ P_1\ P_3)))$$

$$\Longleftrightarrow ((\times\ S_1\ S_2\ S_3) \rightarrow (\times\ P_1\ P_2\ P_3)).$$

Now "relation" can be formally defined in IL-4 as a term that has a *product* in its extension or intension. Once again, this definition covers the "relation" in set theory as a special case.

Definition 8.3. A *relational term*, or a *relation*, is a term R such that in K^* there is a *product* $(T_1 \times\ T_2)$ satisfying "$(T_1 \times T_2) \rightarrow R$" or "$R \rightarrow (T_1 \times T_2)$".

Since "$(T_1 \times T_2) \rightarrow (T_1 \times T_2)$" is true by definition, a *product* is a *relation*, though a *relation* is not necessarily a *product* — a *relation* can be an atomic term. Therefore, a *relation* may not be a compound term, nor is it marked syntactically. A term is referred to as a "relation" when it is related to a *product* by a copula.

For example, "Water dissolves salt" can be represented as "$(water \times salt) \rightarrow dissolve$", so *dissolve* is a *relation* in NAL. Similarly, "Dissolving is between a liquid and a solid" can be represented as "$dissolve \rightarrow (liquid \times solid)$", which also shows that *dissolve* is a relation. Clearly, the last statement is different from "$(liquid \times solid) \rightarrow dissolve$", which means "Liquid dissolves solid". Like other terms, the extension of a relational term includes more *specific* relational terms, while its intension includes more *general* relational terms. In this way, relations also form a conceptual hierarchy.

8.2.   Types of Conceptual Relation

In summary, a "conceptual relation" is a relation between terms, therefore it is also a relation between the concepts named by the terms. Conceptual relations in NAL are divided into three types:

Syntactic relation: A syntactic relation is between a compound term and its components, like the relation between *raven* and $(raven - [black])$. These relations are indicated by the term connector of the compound ('$-$' here), and, optionally, by the location of the component in the compound ('*raven*' is the first component in the compound).

Semantic relation: A semantic relation is between the subject term and the predicate term of a statement, like the relation between *raven* and *bird* in "$raven \rightarrow bird$". These relations are indicated by the copula of the statement ('$\rightarrow$' here).

Acquired relation: An acquired relation is among components of a *product*, like the relation between *raven* and *worm* in "$(raven \times worm) \rightarrow food$". These relations are indicated by terms.

In NAL, the first type of relation is binary and literal, while the latter two are multi-valued and empirical. Furthermore, the meanings of "relations" of the first two types above are defined at the meta-level (as in this book) and embedded in the grammar and inference rules. That is, the meaning of such a relation to the system is fixed, though it may be only gradually revealed to an observer by how it is treated by the system. On the contrary, the meaning of a "relation" of the last type is completely determined by what the system has experienced about it, and therefore changes over time. Even if the system has acquired concepts like "part of", "component of", "inheritance", and "is a", which have similar meanings with certain innate relations, they will not become identical to the innate ones.[1]

In a predicate logic, the above three types of relations are represented uniformly by predicate names, which have no innate meaning recognized by the inference rules. On the contrary, a key feature of term logic is to give the relations represented by copulas a special status. All inference rules in term logic are justified according to the defining properties of copulas, as exemplified by Aristotle's Syllogistic. Though such a treatment seems unnecessary in theorem-proving (which is binary deduction), limitations of predicate logic have been well known when commonsense reasoning is under consideration.

In study on knowledge representation and reasoning, AI researchers have recognized the special function of the "is-a" relation (which is similar to the *inheritance* in NAL), and treated it differently (both in representation and inference) from other relations in techniques including frame, semantic network, and description logic [Woods (1975); Brachman (1983); Donini *et al.* (1996); Russell and Norvig (2010)]. Compared to them, what makes NAL special is that the whole logic (rather than parts of it) is built on a few copulas, which are used to represent the other (acquired) relations, with the help of compound terms.

Copulas are special in that each of them is defined on all terms with the same meaning (substitutability), while an acquired relation is meaningful only on certain terms, and its meaning changes according to experience and context [Wang (2006b)]. As to be discussed in the following chapters, many major issues in predicate logics disappear in term logics, due to the use of copulas.

---

[1]This issue is related to the topic of "self-knowledge", to be addressed in NAL-9.

8.3.   Image and Structural Transformation

Though any conceptual relation can be represented as one of the three types listed previously, it does not mean that such a representation is good enough for the system's inference need. For example, we expect knowledge "Water dissolves salt" and "Rain is water" can be used as premises to derive "Rain dissolves salt" by deduction, but "$(water \times salt) \to dissolve$" and "$rain \to water$" do not fit into the pattern of the *deduction rule* defined in NAL-1 (or any NAL inference rule defined so far), because the common term *water* is neither the subject nor the predicate of the first premise, but a component of its subject.

In principle, this issue can be resolved by defining another version of deduction rule, where the premises have such a pattern. However, that would lead to too many versions of each rule. The solution used in NAL is to use inference rules for "structural transformation", by which the same statement is equivalently rewritten into other formats, so as to allow a component of the subject term or predicate term of the original statement to be treated as the subject term or predicate term of the new statement, which has the same truth-value as the original. This is similar to the case in natural language, where a statement can be expressed in either "active voice" or "passive voice", which have different grammatical structures (and different subject phrases), but similar (if not equivalent) semantic content.[2]

Definition 8.4. For a relation R and a product $(\times T_1 \ T_2)$, the *extensional image* connector, '$/$', and *intensional image* connector, '$\backslash$', are defined as the following, respectively:

$$((\times T_1 \ T_2) \to R) \Longleftrightarrow (T_1 \to (/R \diamond T_2)) \Longleftrightarrow (T_2 \to (/R \ T_1 \diamond)),$$
$$(R \to (\times T_1 \ T_2)) \Longleftrightarrow ((\backslash R \diamond T_2) \to T_1) \Longleftrightarrow ((\backslash R \ T_1 \diamond) \to T_2),$$

where '$\diamond$' is a special symbol indicating the location of T_1 or T_2 in the product, and in the component list it can appear in any place,

---

[2]Different structures also influence inference control, which will not be discussed here.

except the first (which is reserved for the relational term). When it appears at the second place, the image can also be written in infix format as (R / T_2) or $(R \backslash T_2)$.

The above definition can be extended to include products with more than two components, where the image can only be written in the prefix format.

The notion of "image" also comes from set theory, though in NAL it is not restricted to sets, nor is it defined only on the extension of relations.

For the previous example, now the conceptual relationship among *water*, *salt*, and *dissolve* can be equivalently expressed in three statements:

- $(water \times salt) \to dissolve$
- $water \to (/ \ dissolve \diamond salt)$
- $salt \to (/ \ dissolve \ water \ \diamond)$

Roughly speaking, $(/dissolve \diamond salt)$ is "whatever dissolves salt", and $(/ \ dissolve \ water\diamond)$ is "whatever dissolved by water". Now the *deduction rule* can be applied in the following form:

$$\{water \to (/ \ dissolve \diamond salt), rain \to water\} \vdash$$
$$rain \to (/ \ dissolve \diamond salt)$$

and the conclusion can be transformed into "$(rain \times salt) \to dissolve$", which is the expected result. To simplify the description, truth-value calculation is omitted in this example, as well as in similar examples in the following.

In general, (R / T) and $(R \backslash T)$ are different, since the former is defined *extensionally*, while the latter *intensionally*. Even so, there are special cases where they get the same result.

Theorem 8.5.

$$((T_1 \times T_2) / T_2) \leftrightarrow T_1,$$
$$((T_1 \times T_2) \backslash T_2) \leftrightarrow T_1.$$

Here (extensional or intensional) *image* serves as the reverse operation of *product*, by canceling its effect.[3]

However, when an *image* connector is followed by a *product* connector, with the same component, the two cancel each other only in one direction of *inheritance*.

Theorem 8.6.

$$((R \; / \; T) \times T) \to R,$$
$$R \to ((R \setminus T) \times T).$$

The *inheritance* copula in the above result cannot be replaced by the *similarity* copula, because the extension and intension of the relational term R may contain terms that are not in the form of $(M \times T)$, and information about those terms will not be kept in the *image*, so cannot be recovered by the *product*.

It follows from the above results that in IL the *image* connectors can be applied to both sides of an *inheritance* copula, and in certain cases the order of the terms in the conclusion is switched.

Theorem 8.7.

$$S \to P \Longrightarrow (S \; / \; M) \to (P \; / \; M),$$
$$S \to P \Longrightarrow (M \; / \; P) \to (M \; / \; S),$$
$$S \to P \Longrightarrow (S \setminus M) \to (P \setminus M),$$
$$S \to P \Longrightarrow (M \setminus P) \to (M \setminus S).$$

In summary, NAL-4 introduces the new grammar rules in Table 8.1.

There are additional restrictions in the grammar rules for the *images* that cannot be easily expressed in the grammar notations: the two "$\langle term \rangle^*$" expressions on both sides of '$\diamond$' cannot both be empty, that is, an *image* must contain at least two terms as components,

---

[3]Intuitively, with respect to the size of the involved extensions or intensions, *intersection* and *difference* correspond to "addition" and "subtraction", *product* to "multiplication", and *image* to "division". This is the reason for *image* to be named *quotient* in Wang (1995). The current name is used to be consistent with set theory.

Table 8.1. The new grammar rules of NAL-4.

$$\langle term \rangle ::= (\times \langle term \rangle \langle term \rangle^{+})$$
$$|(/\langle term \rangle \langle term \rangle^{*} \diamond \langle term \rangle^{*})$$
$$|(\backslash \langle term \rangle \langle term \rangle^{*} \diamond \langle term \rangle^{*})$$

and the first one is taken to be a *relation*. As mentioned previously, a *"relational term"* is not defined by Narsese grammar rules as a type of compound term, but refers to any term that is semantically related with a *product* in the system's experience.

As for semantics, the situation in NAL-4 is the same as that in NAL-3. The meaning of a compound term, such as a *product* or an *image*, is partially determined by its syntactic relations with its components, and partially determined by its semantic and acquired relations with other terms. For example, literally speaking, (/ *dissolve* ⋄ *salt*) is "whatever dissolves salt", but at the same time, the system's knowledge on whether various liquids have this property also forms an important part of the meaning of this compound term, and this kind of meaning cannot be fully derived from the meaning of *dissolve* and *salt*. Now it is more clear why it has been said several times that "The meaning of a term (either atomic or compound) depends on all the relations between the term and other terms".

There is no new inference rule directly defined in NAL-4. Obviously, the equivalence and implication propositions in the definitions and theorems of IL-4 can be used in inference, which is a topic to be addressed in the next chapter.

CHAPTER 9

NAL-5: STATEMENTS AS TERMS

In a natural language, there are compound and complex sentences that contain other sentences as parts. Similarly, in Narsese a statement can be used as a (compound) term to form "statements on statements", or "higher-order statements", and the inference on such statements is "higher-order inference". This chapter introduces the basic grammar rules of higher-order statement and inference rules of higher-order inference in NAL. Compared to them, the statements in the previous layers of NAL, as well as the inference on them, are "first-order", where a statement only relates terms that are not statements themselves.

9.1. Higher-Order Statement

Syntactically, it is easy to extend Narsese to cover *higher-order statements* — it is enough to allow a *statement*, as defined previously, to be used as a *term*. To avoid ambiguity, such a statement is enclosed by a pair of parentheses, and it can be used in inference like other (first-order) terms.

Many conceptual relations between a human and a statement, including the "propositional attitudes" [McKay and Nelson (2010)], can be represented in Narsese as higher-order relations. For example, "John knows that the Earth is round" can be represented as

$$\{John \times (\{Earth\} \to [round])\} \to know,$$

where *know* is a relation between a cognitive system (*John*) and a statement ($\{Earth\} \to [round]$), and its meaning is determined like the other acquired relations in the system. All the previously defined inference rules can be used on this type of higher-order statements, by simply treating statements as terms. Except their syntactic forms, there is nothing special about this type of higher-order statements.

Obviously, this structure can be used recursively, such as "Mary believes that John knows that the Earth is round", and there is no logical reason to restrict the number of recursions. Though it is possible to further classify higher-order statements into "second-order", "third-order", etc., such distinctions are not made in NAL, since they make no difference in the grammar and inference rules. Therefore in NAL they are called "higher-order" all together.

From the above description, it becomes very clear that the "first-order versus higher-order" distinction in NAL, which is a *term logic*, is completely different from the distinction under the same name in a *predicate logic* — in the former, "higher-order" means "statements on statements", while in the latter it means "predicates on predicates" [Enderton (2009)].

In other approaches, propositional attitudes like "know" and "believe" are usually formalized in a special type of modal logic, known as "epistemic logic", where the meaning of the propositional attitudes are captured by special logical constants [Hendricks and Symons (2009)]. On the contrary, in NAL these propositional attitudes are represented as *acquired* relations with experience-grounded meaning.[1]

Not only can a *statement* be treated as a *term*, a *term* can also be treated as a *statement*, even though it is not in the "subject–copula–predicate" format. For example, if to the system "Columbus' belief" means "the Earth is round", then the former can be used as the latter in many beliefs, and is effectively a statement. Furthermore,

---

[1]In NAL, propositional attitudes are still different from other acquired relational terms, because they are associated with the system's internal operations, which will be introduced in NAL-9. Even so, their meaning nevertheless depends on the system's experience with these relations, which is not the case in an epistemic logic.

a statement in NAL can be identified by an atomic term, such as "*round-Earth* ↔ ({*Earth*} → [*round*])".

Therefore, in NAL the real difference between a "term" and a "statement" is not *syntactic* (even though they are listed as separate items in the grammar rules) but *semantic*, since a statement has both a truth-value and a meaning, while the other (non-statement) terms only have meanings, but no truth-value — "Columbus' belief" can be true to an extent, but "Columbus' ship" cannot. Therefore, in NAL *a statement is a term with truth-value*, while a non-statement term is a term that has not got any truth-value yet.[2]

9.2. Implication and Inheritance

In IL-1, the *inheritance* copula is defined to express that one *term* is related to another in *meaning* in such a way that one can be used as the other; similarly, in IL-5 another copula is defined to express that one *statement* is related to another in *truth-value* in such a way that one can be used as the other.

Definition 9.1. If S_1 and S_2 are statements, "$S_1 \Rightarrow S_2$" is true if and only if in IL S_2 can be derived from S_1 in a finite number of inference steps. Formally, it means $(S_1 \Rightarrow S_2) \Longleftrightarrow \{S_1\} \vdash S_2$. Here '$\Rightarrow$' is the *implication* copula.

Though at the meta-level we can say that "$S_1 \Rightarrow S_2$" if and only if "$\{S_1\} \vdash S_2$", the two are not the same at the object-level: the former is a *statement*, while the latter is a *process*.[3]

Since *implication* is defined between statements, it is a "higher-order copula" involved in higher-order inference, in the sense clarified previously. Intuitively speaking, "$S_1 \Rightarrow S_2$" means "If S_1, then S_2", or "S_1 implies S_2". It is different from the "material implication" in propositional logic (written as '$\Longrightarrow$' in this book), which is defined as "$\neg S_1 \vee S_2$", and does not requires S_1 to be related to S_2 in content.

---

[2]It is put in this way because a term may initially enter the system's experience without a truth-value, but then get it at a later time.

[3]To confuse the two will cause conceptual confusions, as revealed by Carroll's "What the Tortoise Said to Achilles" [Carroll (1895)].

Since IL is a term logic, it is impossible for S_2 to be derived from S_1 if the two are not related in content.

Theorem 9.1. *The* implication *copula is a reflexive and transitive relation from one statement to another statement.*

Since the above theorem on *implication* is parallel to the definition of *inheritance* in IL-1, higher-order inference in IL-5 can be defined as *partially isomorphic* to first-order inference, as shown in the following definitions.

Definition 9.2. An *implication statement* consists of two statements related by the implication copula. In implication statement "$A \Rightarrow C$", A is the *antecedent* statement, and C is the *consequent* statement.

Definition 9.3. Given idealized experience K expressed in the formal language of IL-5, the *sufficient conditions* of a statement T is the set of statements $T^S = \{x | x \in V_K \land x \Rightarrow T\}$; the *necessary conditions* of T is the set of statements $T^N = \{x, | x \in V_K \land T \Rightarrow x\}$.

Theorem 9.2. *If both A and C are statements in V_K, then*

$$(A \Rightarrow C) \Longleftrightarrow (A^S \subseteq C^S) \Longleftrightarrow (C^N \subseteq A^N).$$

To extend the usage of *implication* from IL to NAL, its evidence can be defined in a similar way as that of *inheritance*.

Definition 9.4. For an implication statement "$A \Rightarrow C$", its *evidence* are statements in A^S and C^N. Among them, statements in $(A^S \cap C^S)$ and $(C^N \cap A^N)$ are *positive evidence*, while statements in $(A^S - C^S)$ and $(C^N - A^N)$ are *negative evidence*.

The amounts of evidence and the truth-value for a higher-order statement are defined in the same way from evidence as for a first-order statement. Therefore, the semantics of NAL-5 is similar to that of NAL-1.

In IL-2, *similarity* is defined as symmetric *inheritance*, while in IL-5, *equivalence* is defined as symmetric *implication*.

Definition 9.5. The *equivalence* copula, '$\Leftrightarrow$', is defined by

$$(A \Leftrightarrow C) \Longleftrightarrow ((A \Rightarrow C) \wedge (C \Rightarrow A)).$$

As a special type of compound terms, *compound statements* can be used to summarize existing statements.

Definition 9.6. When S_1 and S_2 are different statements, their *conjunction*, $(S_1 \wedge S_2)$, is a compound statement defined by

$$(\forall x)((x \Rightarrow (S_1 \wedge S_2)) \Longleftrightarrow ((x \Rightarrow S_1) \wedge (x \Rightarrow S_2))).$$

Their *disjunction*, $(S_1 \vee S_2)$, is a compound statement defined by

$$(\forall x)(((S_1 \vee S_2) \Rightarrow x) \Longleftrightarrow ((S_1 \Rightarrow x) \wedge (S_2 \Rightarrow x))).$$

These two statement connectors are symmetric, and can be extended to take more than two arguments. In the definition, the symbol '$\wedge$' is used in two different meanings: in $(S_1 \wedge S_2)$, it is the new statement connector to be defined; in the right-hand side of the definitions, it is the *conjunction* operator of propositional logic, used as a meta-language in IL and NAL. The *disjunction* connector is defined by the *conjunction* of *necessary conditions* of its two components, though it can be equivalently defined by the *disjunction* of *sufficient conditions* of its two components, that is, as:

$$(\forall x)((x \Rightarrow (S_1 \vee S_2)) \Longleftrightarrow ((x \Rightarrow S_1) \vee (x \Rightarrow S_2)))$$

which may look more natural to some readers. Even so, the previous definition is preferred, since it gives sufficient and necessary conditions a symmetric treatment.

Theorem 9.3.

$$(S_1 \wedge S_2) \Rightarrow S_1,$$
$$S_1 \Rightarrow (S_1 \vee S_2).$$

The isomorphism between first-order IL and higher-order IL is summarized in Table 9.1.

The isomorphism given in Table 9.1 is not completely unnoticed in the previous works, even though it is not presented explicitly in this way. In FOPL, categorical sentences (which are represented as

Table 9.1. Isomorphism between first-order and higher-order IL.

First-order IL	Higher-order IL
term	statement
inheritance	implication
similarity	equivalence
subject	antecedent
predicate	consequent
extension	sufficient condition
intension	necessary condition
extensional intersection	conjunction
intensional intersection	disjunction

Table 9.2. The copulas of NAL.

	First-order	Higher-order
asymmetric	*inheritance* ($\rightarrow$)	*implication* ($\Rightarrow$)
symmetric	*similarity* ($\leftrightarrow$)	*equivalence* ($\Leftrightarrow$)

first-order statements in Narsese) are all expressed as conditional sentences (which are represented as higher-order statements in Narsese). For example, the English sentence "Robin is a type of bird" is not directly represented as a relation between concepts "robin" and "bird", but between sentences "x is a robin" and "x is a bird", where x is a universally quantified variable. Later we will see that these two representations do not have the same meaning exactly.

Though *implication* and *equivalence* are isomorphic to *inheritance* and *similarity*, respectively, they are not the same. The higher-order copulas indicate the substitutability between statements in *truth-value*, while the first-order copulas indicate the substitutability between terms in *meaning*. They both specify the extent to which one item *can be used as* another, though in different ways.

For this reason, in NAL both first-order copulas and higher-order copulas are recognized and processed by the inference rules. Overall, there are only four copulas to be implemented in NARS, as listed in Table 9.2.

Table 9.3. The new grammar rules of NAL-5.

$\langle term \rangle ::= (\langle statement \rangle)$
$\langle statement \rangle ::= \langle term \rangle$
$\quad \mid (\neg \langle statement \rangle)$
$\quad \mid (\wedge \langle statement \rangle \langle statement \rangle^{+})$
$\quad \mid (\vee \langle statement \rangle \langle statement \rangle^{+})$
$\langle copula \rangle ::= \Rightarrow \mid \Leftrightarrow$

There are three derivative copulas that are used in the system interface only: *instance* ($\circ\!\!\rightarrow$), *property* ($\rightarrow\!\!\circ$), and *instance-property* ($\circ\!\!\rightarrow\!\!\circ$). They do not have higher-order correspondence.

The new grammar rules of IL-5 and NAL-5 are listed in Table 9.3, where the new copulas and term connectors have been defined previously, except the *negation* connector '¬', which will be discussed separately in a following section.

Because of the isomorphism in definitions, there are isomorphic inference rules in NAL-5 (with the same truth-value function) for the following rules defined previously[4]:

- The NAL-1 rules for deduction, abduction, induction, exemplification, and conversion.
- The NAL-2 rules for comparison, analogy, and resemblance.
- The NAL-3 rules for the composition and decomposition of intersections.
- The backward inference rules corresponding to the above forward inference rules.

The term connectors for (extensional/intensional) sets, product, and (extensional/intensional) images are not involved in the isomorphism between first-order and higher-order terms. They are still defined using the *inheritance* copula, and treat higher-order terms just like first-order terms, so there is no special rule added. Similarly, the revision rule and the choice rule work the same way on first-order and higher-order statements.

---

[4]Some of the inference rules in the list have been studied in the existing literature under different names. For example, the higher-order deduction rule of IL is traditionally called "hypothetical syllogism".

9.3.   Implication as Conditional

Higher-order inference includes more than the above isomorphism with first-order inference. Beside being reflexive and transitive, the *implication* copula is also defined to correspond to an inference process, that is, the *implication* statement "$S_1 \Rightarrow S_2$" is true if and only if the inference process $\{S_1\} \vdash S_2$ can happen in IL. This result is similar to the Deduction Theorem in propositional logic [Kleene (2002)].

According to the experience-grounded semantics of IL, this relation between implication and derivation can be extended to any true statement S. By definition, S is true if and only if it can be derived from the experience of the system, K, that is, $K \vdash S$. We can use E to represent the conjunction of all statements in K, so the above derivation is represented as $\{E\} \vdash S$, which is equivalent to implication statement "$E \Rightarrow S$".

When this equivalence is extended into NAL, both the truth-value of the *implication* statement and the validity of the inference process becomes a matter of degree, though the two should still be measured as the same. By definition, in NAL a judgment "$S\langle f, c\rangle$" states that "The degree of belief the system has on statement S, according to available evidence, is measured by $\langle f, c\rangle$". Assume that the available evidence currently used on the evaluation of S can be written as a compound statement E, then the same meaning can be represented as "$\{E\} \vdash S\langle f, c\rangle$", that is, "$E \Rightarrow S\langle f, c\rangle$", which states that "The degree of belief the system has on statement 'If E is true, then S is true' is measured by $\langle f, c\rangle$". In this way, a statement "S" is equivalently translated into a *conditional* statement "$E \Rightarrow S$", by explicitly mentioning its *evidence* as its *condition*.

This translation is a conceptual one, not an actual one, since there is no need to actually spell out E in Narsese. Nevertheless, the translation provides an important insight that every judgment is *conditional*, or based on implicitly represented evidence. Furthermore, the truth-value of the judgment is also the truth-value of the corresponding conditional judgment, if the condition is explicitly

Table 9.4. The conditional syllogistic rules.

(1) Premises	(2) Condition added	(3) Conclusion	(4) Condition dropped
$M \Rightarrow P$, M	$M \Rightarrow P$, $E \Rightarrow M$	$E \Rightarrow P \langle F_{\text{ded}} \rangle$	$P \langle F_{\text{ded}} \rangle$
$P \Rightarrow M$, M	$P \Rightarrow M$, $E \Rightarrow M$	$E \Rightarrow P \langle F_{\text{abd}} \rangle$	$P \langle F_{\text{abd}} \rangle$
$M \Leftrightarrow P$, M	$M \Leftrightarrow P$, $E \Rightarrow M$	$E \Rightarrow P \langle F'_{\text{ana}} \rangle$	$P \langle F'_{\text{ana}} \rangle$

spelled out. This insight, as well as the conceptual translation, can be used to establish a group of inference rules. In such a rule, the implicit condition E is made explicit in the premises, so as to change the premise combination into one for which NAL already has inference rules. Finally, the condition is turned implicit in the conclusion. Table 9.4 contains three rules obtained in this way, where the truth-values of the premises are omitted.

The inference rules in Table 9.4 are called "Conditional Syllogistic Rules", because they are variants of the higher-order syllogistic rules, obtained by treating one of the premises as a conditional statement. When used in inference, the two middle-columns in the table are omitted, and the rules are taken as directly from the first column (as premises) to the last column (as conclusions).

Let us discuss the first case as an example. This inference rule is the NAL version of *modus ponens*, a well-known form of deduction [Kleene (2002)]:

$$\{M \Rightarrow P \langle f_1, c_1 \rangle, \; M \langle f_2, c_2 \rangle\} \vdash P \langle F_{\text{ded}} \rangle.$$

This rule is a variant of the higher-order deduction rule (its binary form is traditionally called "hypothetical syllogism"):

$$\{M \Rightarrow P \langle f_1, c_1 \rangle, \; S \Rightarrow M \langle f_2, c_2 \rangle\} \vdash S \Rightarrow P \langle F_{\text{ded}} \rangle,$$

where the statement S is replaced by the implicit condition E, which is added into the second premise before the inference, then dropped from the conclusion.

Similarly, when two judgments can be seen as based on the same implicit condition, conclusions can be derived according to the existing rules, as in Table 9.5.

Table 9.5. The conditional compositional rules.

(1) Premises	(2) Condition added	(3) Conclusion	(4) Condition dropped
P, S	$E \Rightarrow P,\ E \Rightarrow S$	$S \Rightarrow P \langle F_{\text{ind}} \rangle$	$S \Rightarrow P \langle F_{\text{ind}} \rangle$
P, S	$E \Rightarrow P,\ E \Rightarrow S$	$S \Leftrightarrow P \langle F_{\text{com}} \rangle$	$S \Leftrightarrow P \langle F_{\text{com}} \rangle$
P, S	$E \Rightarrow P,\ E \Rightarrow S$	$E \Rightarrow (P \wedge S) \langle F_{\text{int}} \rangle$	$(P \wedge S) \langle F_{\text{int}} \rangle$
P, S	$E \Rightarrow P,\ E \Rightarrow S$	$E \Rightarrow (P \vee S) \langle F_{\text{uni}} \rangle$	$(P \vee S) \langle F_{\text{uni}} \rangle$

The rules in Table 9.5 are not *syllogistic*, but *compositional*, since the statements in the conclusions are compound terms composed by the terms in the premises. Because they are applicable only when the premises "can be seen as based on the same implicit condition", NAL does not take two arbitrary judgments as premises and apply these rules on them.[5]

As limit cases of F_{int} and F_{uni}, respectively, in IL *conjunction* and *disjunction* correspond to the same truth tables as in propositional logic, even though the two are not *defined* by their truth tables in IL, and such a compound statement is formed only when its components are related in content. Also different from propositional/predicate logic, in IL the truth-values of "$S \Rightarrow P$" and "$S \Leftrightarrow P$" cannot be decided according to the truth-values of S and P. In NAL, in certain situations these truth-values can be derived from those of their component statements by a "weak" rule (*induction* or *comparison*), so the conclusions are inconclusive (i.e., with relatively low confidence values).

Now we see that the notion of "syllogistic rules" has been extended from its traditional sense into multi-valued and multi-copula in NAL. However, these rules still follow the basic request that each takes two premises that share a common term, and produces a conclusion between the other two terms, though one of the terms may be implicitly represented.

So far, NAL has included three different (though related) forms of the deduction–abduction–induction trio, as summarized in Table 9.6. They share the same group of truth-value functions.

---

[5]The applicable situations of these rules are introduced in the following chapters.

Table 9.6. Deduction–abduction–induction in NAL (2).

First-order	Higher-order	Conditional
$\{M \to P, S \to M\} \vdash S \to P$	$\{M \Rightarrow P, S \Rightarrow M\} \vdash S \Rightarrow P$	$\{S \Rightarrow P, S\} \vdash P$
$\{P \to M, S \to M\} \vdash S \to P$	$\{P \Rightarrow M, S \Rightarrow M\} \vdash S \Rightarrow P$	$\{P \Rightarrow S, S\} \vdash P$
$\{M \to P, M \to S\} \vdash S \to P$	$\{M \Rightarrow P, M \Rightarrow S\} \vdash S \Rightarrow P$	$\{P, S\} \vdash S \Rightarrow P$

Table 9.7. Deduction–abduction–induction in NAL (3).

$\{(S \wedge M) \Rightarrow P, M\} \vdash S \Rightarrow P$	$\{(C \wedge M) \Rightarrow P, S \Rightarrow M\} \vdash (C \wedge S) \Rightarrow P$
$\{(S \wedge P) \Rightarrow M, S \Rightarrow M\} \vdash P$	$\{(C \wedge P) \Rightarrow M, (C \wedge S) \Rightarrow M\} \vdash S \Rightarrow P$
$\{M \Rightarrow P, S\} \vdash (S \wedge M) \Rightarrow P$	$\{(C \wedge M) \Rightarrow P, M \Rightarrow S\} \vdash (C \wedge S) \Rightarrow P$

A conditional statement can have conditions itself, and such a statement can be equivalently transformed into a statement with a conjunctive condition.[6]

Theorem 9.4. *For any statements S_1, S_2, and S_3,*

$$(S_1 \Rightarrow (S_2 \Rightarrow S_3)) \Longleftrightarrow ((S_1 \wedge S_2) \Rightarrow S_3).$$

Based on this relation, two more variant forms of the deduction–abduction–induction rules can be established, as listed in Table 9.7.

In each of the five forms of syllogisms listed in Tables 9.6 and 9.7, the *deduction rule* corresponds to a valid inference rule in IL, from which the *abduction rule* is obtained by exchanging the second premise and the conclusion (plus proper renaming of the terms), and the *induction rule* is obtained by exchanging the first premise and the conclusion (plus proper renaming of the terms). This "reversing" relationship among the three types of inference is exactly what Peirce proposed, though the syntax and semantics of the rules are not the same as his rules [Peirce (1931)].

---

[6]Implication statements with conjunctive conditions play an important role in inference, as to be shown in the later layers of NAL. This structure also corresponds to *Horn clauses*, a form of proposition widely used in logic programming [Kowalski (1979)].

We can image the two premises and one conclusion in each first-order or higher-order syllogistic rule as forming a triangle, with the three terms involved as vertices, and the three statements as edges. In this triangle, from any two sides the third one can be derived.

When all three edges of the above triangle are asymmetric statements (i.e., *inheritance* or *implication*), the *deduction rule* is an extended version (from binary to multi-valued) of the transitivity of the asymmetric copula, while in the other two rules one copula in the premises is used in the reverse direction, which is why the rule is "weak" and produces only low-confidence conclusions. This reversion is possible, because the evidence supporting the original statement also provides some information for the reversed statement, though not as strongly.

When the triangle is formed by two asymmetric statements (*inheritance* or *implication*) and a symmetric statement (*similarity* or *equivalence*), in the three possible premise–conclusion combinations, two of them are strong inference (with the symmetric statement as a premise, using the *analogy rule*), and the other is weak (with the symmetric statement as the conclusion, using the *comparison rule*). Here the symmetric statement can be used in either directions to get a confident conclusion.

Finally, if all the three statements are symmetric statements (*similarity* or *equivalence*), the inference uses the *resemblance rule*, and is strong in all cases.

The above discussion provides a more clear picture about the relationship among different types of syllogistic inference, which are unified in NAL, in syntax, semantics, and pragmatics. Furthermore, it suggests a procedure to extend NAL into a higher layer:

(1) Add new grammar rules into Narsese to increase the expressing power of the language,
(2) Add new inference rules into IL, so as to process and generate the new sentences,
(3) Extend the new IL rules into strong rules of NAL,
(4) Get weak rules of NAL by reversing the strong rules.

In the following chapters, we will see the applications of this "NAL expansion procedure".

9.4. Negation

Since the *negation* connector in NAL-5 takes exactly one argument, it is not isomorphic to the (extensional/intensional) *difference* connectors defined in NAL-3, though still related to them.

Definition 9.7. Compound statement $(\neg S)$ is the *negation* of statement S. In IL the truth-value of $(\neg S)$ is the opposite that of S. In NAL the truth-value of $(\neg S)$ is obtained by switching the positive and negative evidence of S.

As explained before, if a statement has truth-value *true* in IL, then it has truth value $\langle 1, 1 \rangle$ in NAL (though not explicitly represented there as a belief). However, its negation in IL (which has a truth-value *false*) and in NAL (which has a truth-value $\langle 0, 1 \rangle$) do not exactly map into each other — any statement in NAL not supported by "full positive evidence" will be considered as *false* in IL. It is not really a problem (since a binary logic and a multi-valued logic cannot have one-to-one mappings between their truth-values), though we need to be careful when moving between these two systems. For example, after *negation* is introduced into IL, we cannot simply say that *true* in IL is always mapped into $\langle 1, 1 \rangle$ in NAL anymore, since if "$S \rightarrow P$" has truth-value *false* in IL, "$(\neg(S \rightarrow P))$" will be *true* there, but the latter statement should not be given the truth-value $\langle 1, 1 \rangle$ in NAL, because it may have both positive and negative evidence. Therefore, the mapping from *true* to $\langle 1, 1 \rangle$ will be restricted to statements that have the "$\langle term \rangle \langle copula \rangle \langle term \rangle$" format, and not applied to compound statements.

As far as the truth-values of statements are concerned, in IL the three statement-connectors (*conjunction, disjunction,* and *negation*) are handled as in propositional logic, that is, the two logics have the same truth tables for them, as well as the same theorems like double negations and De Morgan's laws.

Theorem 9.5. $(\neg(\neg S)) \Longleftrightarrow S$.

Theorem 9.6.

$$\neg(S_1 \wedge S_2) \Longleftrightarrow (\neg S_1) \vee (\neg S_2),$$
$$\neg(S_1 \vee S_2) \Longleftrightarrow (\neg S_1) \wedge (\neg S_2).$$

Theorem 9.7.

$$(S_1 \wedge (\neg(S_1 \wedge S_2))) \Longrightarrow (\neg S_2),$$
$$((\neg S_1) \wedge (S_1 \vee S_2)) \Longrightarrow S_2.$$

As mentioned previously, the *implication* and *equivalence* in IL are defined differently from propositional logic. Even so, the two logics still have some common results here, though they are not proved in the same way.

Theorem 9.8. $(S_1 \Leftrightarrow S_2) \Longleftrightarrow ((\neg S_1) \Leftrightarrow (\neg S_2))$.

When the discussion moves into NAL where a statement is multi-valued, the definition of negation connector directly leads to the *negation rule* of NAL-5, as specified in Table 9.8.

The *negation rule* is a type of immediate inference, since it derives a conclusion from a single premise. Another such rule in Table 9.8, the *conversion rule*, has been introduced by its isomorphism with the *conversion rule* in NAL-1. In the following we can get the same result in another way.

In NAL, the truth-values of "$S \Rightarrow P$" and "$P \Rightarrow S$" can be obtained in many different ways. To analyze their relationship, we focus on a "normal case" in higher-order inference where all implication statements get their truth-values from the truth-values

Table 9.8. The immediate inference rules in NAL-5.

Type	Premise	Conclusion	Truth-function
negation	S	$(\neg S)$	$F_{neg} : f = 1 - f_1,\ c = c_1$
conversion	$S \Rightarrow P$	$P \Rightarrow S$	$F_{cvn} : w = w^+ = f_1 \times c_1$
contraposition	$S \Rightarrow P$	$(\neg P) \Rightarrow (\neg S)$	$F_{cnt} : w = w^- = (1 - f_1) \times c_1$

of their components. Here the only applicable inference rule in NAL is the *induction rule* in Table 9.5, which has the following form:

$$\{P \langle f_1, c_1 \rangle, \ S \langle f_2, c_2 \rangle\} \vdash S \Rightarrow P \langle F_{\text{ind}} \rangle.$$

Therefore, in the extreme (binary) situations, the conclusion gets positive evidence when $(P \wedge S)$ is true, negative evidence when $((\neg P) \wedge S)$ is true, and no evidence when $(\neg S)$ is true.

Comparing "$S \Rightarrow P$" and "$P \Rightarrow S$", we see that they have the same *positive* evidence $(P \wedge S)$, but distinct *negative* evidence $(((\neg P) \wedge S)$ and $((\neg S) \wedge P)$, respectively). Since it has been established in NAL-1 that when a conclusion is derived from a single premise with a different evidence scope, the amount of evidence for the conclusion is at most 1, for the *conversion rule* in NAL-5 we get the truth-function in Table 9.8, which gives the truth-value $f = 1$ and $c = f_1 \times c_1 / (f_1 \times c_1 + k) \leq 1/(1 + k)$, exactly the same as the *conversion rule* in NAL-1.

Now we can establish the *contraposition rule* in Table 9.8 in the same way. According to the previous analysis, "$S \Rightarrow P$" and "$(\neg P) \Rightarrow (\neg S)$" have the same *negative* evidence, $((\neg P) \wedge S)$, but distinct *positive* evidence $((P \wedge S)$ and $((\neg S) \wedge (\neg P))$, respectively). Consequently, the truth-function is the one defined in Table 9.8, which gives the truth-value $f = 0$ and $c = (1 - f_1) \times c_1 / ((1 - f_1) \times c_1 + k) \leq 1/(1 + k)$ — Like the *conversion rule*, the *contraposition rule* is also weak inference.

This result is very different from the corresponding one in propositional logic, where propositions "$S \Longrightarrow P$" and "$(\neg P) \Longrightarrow (\neg S)$" are equivalent to each other, meaning that they have the same truth-value. This difference between propositional logic and NAL is caused by the fact that in propositional logic the (binary) truth-value of a proposition depends only on whether there is negative evidence, while in NAL the (non-binary) truth-value of a statement depends on the amount of both positive and negative evidence. Consequently, in NAL "$S \Rightarrow P$" and "$(\neg P) \Rightarrow (\neg S)$" usually have different truth-values, though the negative evidence for one is also counted as negative evidence for the other.

The above discussion is directly related to the well-known "Confirmation Paradox" [Hempel (1965)], and the solution provided by NAL is explained in detail in Wang (2009d).

9.5.   Analytic Truth in Inference

So far, three logic systems have been involved in this discussion:

Non-Axiomatic Logic (NAL). As the subject matter of this book, this logic is based on AIKR.

Inheritance Logic (IL). This logic is introduced as an idealized version of NAL. It is not based on AIKR, though share many other properties with NAL.

Propositional Logic (PL). Together with predicate logic, PL is used as a meta-logic of IL to express definitions and theorems involving IL statements. It does not obey AIKR, neither.

The relationship between NAL and IL can be summarized as the following:

- The two logic systems are defined on the same categorical language, Narsese, except that IL uses binary truth-values, while NAL uses (two-dimensional) numerical truth-values.
- Both IL and NAL use an experience-grounded semantics, in which truth-value and meaning in Narsese are defined using *ideal experience* expressed as IL statements. However, NAL depends on *actual experience* (consisting of NAL judgments) in inference.
- Both IL and NAL use syllogistic inference rules. The strong rules of NAL (*deduction, analogy, resemblance, intersection, union, difference,* and *negation*) have corresponding rules in IL, while the weak rules of NAL (*abduction, induction, exemplification, comparison, conversion,* and *contraposition*) do not, but correspond to certain reversed versions of IL rules.

On the other hand, IL and PL have some important similarity and difference, too:

- The operators *conjunction* ('∧'), *disjunction* ('∨'), and *negation* ('¬') are basically used in the same way in IL and PL, except that in IL a compound statement is formed only when its components are semantically related.

- Both the IL *implication* statement "$S \Rightarrow P$" and the PL *implication* proposition "$S \Longrightarrow P$" correspond to the derivation relation "$\{S\} \vdash P$" in the logic, and the *equivalence* ('$\Leftrightarrow$' and '$\Longleftrightarrow$', respectively) relation is defined as symmetric *implication*.
- The most important difference between IL and PL is that in the former the truth-value of "$S \Rightarrow P$" and "$S \Leftrightarrow P$" cannot be determined by the truth-values of S and P alone. Especially, "$S \Rightarrow P$" is not equivalent to "$(\neg S) \vee P$".

Therefore, the *implication* in IL is not the "material implication" in PL, but more like the "strict implication" in some non-classical logic [Mares (2011)].

Because of the above relations, every definition and theorem in IL corresponds to a true proposition in PL, but not the other way around when *implication* and *equivalence* are involved. Consequently, the definitions and theorems introduced in the meta-level usually can be used in the inference of NAL in the following way:

(1) Re-interpret a definition or theorem (originally expressed as a PL proposition) as an analytic truth in IL whenever possible.[7]

(2) If the analytic truth has the "$\langle term \rangle \langle copula \rangle \langle term \rangle$" format, use it in a strong rule of NAL as a judgment with a truth-value $\langle 1, 1 \rangle$.

As a result, each strong rule in NAL has several variants, each of them takes an explicit premise (a belief in NAL) and an implicit premise (an analytic truth in IL), and derives a conclusion that is a derived belief. For example, since "$P_1 \rightarrow (P_1 \cup P_2)$" is true in IL, "$P_1 \rightarrow (P_1 \cup P_2) \langle 1, 1 \rangle$" and "$S \rightarrow P_1 \langle f_1, c_1 \rangle$" can be used as premises by the *deduction rule* defined in NAL-1 to derive "$S \rightarrow (P_1 \cup P_2) \langle f_1, f_1 c_1 \rangle$". Since analytical truths in IL are not actually stored as beliefs in NAL, in this step the inference is carried out by

---

[7] As analyzed before, not all true propositions in PL can be used in NAL, but when introducing the definitions and theorems, the related issues have been taken into consideration, so the improper ones have been avoided.

the following single-premise rule:

$$\{S \to P_1 \langle f_1, c_1 \rangle\} \vdash S \to (P_1 \cup P_2) \langle f_1, f_1 c_1 \rangle.$$

This rule is used only when the compound term $(P_1 \cup P_2)$ already exists in the system, rather than to create such a compound term with an arbitrary P_2 from the single premise alone.

Similarly, the definition "$((\times T_1 T_2) \to R) \Longleftrightarrow (T_1 \to (/R \diamond T_2))$" provides an inference rule

$$\{(\times T_1 T_2) \to R \langle f_1, c_1 \rangle\} \vdash T_1 \to (/ R \diamond T_2) \langle f_1, c_1 \rangle.$$

Therefore, every meta-level *equivalence* statement corresponds to a NAL rule where the conclusion and the single premise have the same truth-value.

The inference rules derived in this way are called "structural rules" in NAL, because they all come from definitions of the *syntactic structures* (as compound terms) in Narsese. *Structural inference* is a special case of *immediate inference*, where only one premise is needed. Conceptually, there is a second premise, which is an analytical truth, so does not need to be mentioned. Such a rule can be seen as an extension of a rule in IL, where the conclusion is true to a degree, because a premise is true to a degree itself.

However, the weak rules (induction, abduction, etc.) of NAL cannot use IL truths in this way, because these rules are invalid in IL. Otherwise, for every $(T_1 \cap T_2)$ in the system, "$T_1 \to T_2 \langle 1, 1/(1+k) \rangle$" would be derived from the analytical truths "$(T_1 \cap T_2) \to T_1$" and "$(T_1 \cap T_2) \to T_2$" by the *induction rule*, without any empirical evidence. Similarly, after deriving a belief on "$S \to (P_1 \cup P_2)$" from truth "$P_1 \to (P_1 \cup P_2)$" and a belief on "$S \to P_1$" by deduction, the conclusion would be used by the abduction rule with "$P_2 \to (P_1 \cup P_2)$" to derive a belief on "$S \to P_2$". To avoid these consequences, analytical truths are not allowed to be used by the weak inference rules.

Consequently, the reversibility among inference rules is not maintained among structural rules. An asymmetric analytical truth cannot be used in the "reverse direction", while an empirical belief can, though the different directions may have different "strengths", in terms of the confidence of the conclusions derived along that path. A strong inference rule follows all the copulas in the indicated direction, while a weak inference rule uses some copula in the reverse direction, which is allowed only when the judgment has empirical evidence.

In this way, many (though not all) analytical truths in Narsese, that is, the definitions and theorems of IL, are *embedded* in the structural inference rules of NAL, and are implicitly used in the inference process of NARS. However, the system does not explicitly store them among its beliefs, nor accept them as absolute truth in experience, which only contains empirical truths with confidence lower than 1. As its name suggests, NARS does not accept any axiom at the object-level, nor is the system built as a theorem prover in IL. The system is equipped with a logic for which it has no explicit knowledge, though can use it to process tasks.[8]

---

[8]It is possible for the system to learn about its own native logic via self-monitoring, a function to be introduced in NAL-9. Even after that, it does not necessarily become a perfect theorem prover in IL, nor an "expert" on NAL.

CHAPTER 10

NAL-6: VARIABLE TERMS

NAL-6 adds variable terms into the system, so as to support several advanced types of inference.

10.1. Variable Terms Defined

The terms introduced so far are all *constant* terms, in the sense that each of them names a specific concept. Therefore, when such a term appears in multiple sentences, all the occurrences refer to the same concept. On the contrary, a *variable term*, or simply a *variable*, is used as a *symbol* that represents another term, and the same variable may refer to different concepts in different sentences.[1]

Variable terms are similar to pronouns in natural languages. In NAL, they serve several functions, some of which have been touched before.

At the meta-level, all the definitions and theorems of IL and NAL, as well as the grammar and inference rules, contain symbols (such as the T, S, P, and M) that can be replaced by arbitrary terms, though they are not part of Narsese, but its meta-language.

In NAL-1 (Table 3.2), the question mark '?' in questions is effectively a variable term, though it is not defined in that way in NAL-1, but treated as a special sign in the language. To express

---

[1] Here the "constant versus variable" distinction is not about whether the meaning of a term changes over time. With an experience-grounded semantics, the meaning of a constant term may change over time, though such changes are usually gradual and continuous. On the contrary, when a variable changes its reference, the change in meaning is sudden and discontinuous.

more complicated questions, a special symbol is not enough, since it cannot represent multiple variable terms in a sentence, nor variable terms that do not appear as a subject or predicate term in a sentence, but as a component of a compound term. The following definition provides a more general form for this type of variable term.

Definition 10.1. A *query variable* is a variable term in a question that represents a constant term to be found to answer the question, and it is named by '?', optionally followed by a word or a number.

Therefore, in Narsese, query variables may take the form of "?x", "?y", "?1", or simply "?", and in general they play the same role as words like "what" in English.

The expressive power of Narsese can be extended by using variable terms, not only in questions, but also in judgments. As defined in IL-1, the *inheritance* statement "$S \to P$" states that the extension of S is included in the extension of P, and the intension of P is included in the intension of S. When its truth-value is defined in NAL-1, the extensional evidence and intensional evidence are mixed together. Such a uniform treatment of extension and intension is necessary for NAL [Wang (2006b)], though in some situations it is also desired to separate the extensional relation and the intensional relation between two terms.

In IL, the extension and intension of terms are classical sets. Between any two sets, there are two basic binary relations: whether the two include each other, and whether the two have common elements. These two relations between the extensions of S and P can be expressed as "If a term is in the extension of S, then it is also in the extension of P" and "There is a term that is both in the extension of S and the extension of P." Obviously, they correspond to compound statements formed by *implication* and *conjunction*, respectively, with an unspecified term that links S and P.[2]

---

[2]Though it is not hard to introduce new copulas, as in Wang (1994b), or to treat them as different types of sentences, as in Aristotle (1882), NAL uses variable terms to express them, which is an approach that fits better with the other aspects of the logic.

Though both statements above contain variable terms, they are different: in the former, the variable represents an *arbitrary* term in the extension of S, while in the latter, it only represents a certain *anonymous* term. Therefore, two types of variables are defined.

Definition 10.2. An *independent variable* represents any unspecified term under a given restriction, and it is named by a word preceded by '#'. A *dependent variable* represents a certain unspecified term under a given restriction, and it is named as an independent variable with a *dependency list* consisting of independent variables it depends on, which can be empty.

Using variable terms, the previously mentioned extensional and intensional statements can be naturally represented as the following in IL:

	independent variable	**dependent variable**
extensional	$(\#x \to S) \Rightarrow (\#x \to P)$	$((\#x() \to S) \wedge$ $(\#x() \to P))$
intensional	$(P \to \#x) \Rightarrow (S \to \#x)$	$((P \to \#x()) \wedge$ $(S \to \#x()))$

According to the definitions of the related copulas and term connectors introduced previously, there are variants of the above statements in Narsese:

	independent variable	**dependent variable**
extensional	$(\#x \to S) \Leftrightarrow (\#x \to P)$	$\#x() \to (S \cap P)$
intensional	$(P \to \#x) \Leftrightarrow (S \to \#x)$	$(P \cup S) \to \#x()$

On the other hand, if we focus on extensional statements, and also include negative statements on the P part, we get four Narsese statements that correspond to the four types of sentences (that are traditionally marked as A, E, I, and O) in Aristotle's logic, respectively [Smith (2012)]:

	independent variable	dependent variable
affirmation	$(\#x \to S) \Rightarrow (\#x \to P)$	$((\#x() \to S) \wedge$
		$(\#x() \to P))$
denial	$(\#x \to S) \Rightarrow (\neg(\#x \to P))$	$((\#x() \to S) \wedge$
		$(\neg(\#x() \to P)))$

Obviously, the two types of variable terms in IL roughly correspond to the *universally quantified variable* and *existentially quantified variable* in FOPL, especially under the "substitution interpretation" [Haack (1996)]. The two extensional statements in the first table roughly corresponds to propositions "$(\forall x)(S(x) \implies P(x))$" and "$(\exists x)(S(x) \wedge P(x))$", respectively. However, the two treatments of variables are still different in the following aspects:

- In IL, a variable can represent either an instance (in the extension) or a property (in the intension) of a given term, while in FOPL a variable can only represent an instance. To talk about "every property" or "an existing property", a higher-order predicate logic is needed.
- In IL, a variable represents a term under a given restriction (i.e., in the *extension or intension* of a given term), while in FOPL a variable represents an object in the whole *domain*. For this reason, statement "$(\#x \to S) \Rightarrow (\#x \to P)$" and proposition "$(\forall x)(S(x) \implies P(x))$" do not have exactly the same meaning.[3]
- In IL, variables are used to relate two (or more) terms, so each variable appears more than once in the statement, either at both sides of an implication or equivalence statement (for an independent variable), or within two or more components of a

---

[3]This subtle difference is important for the definition of evidence. To decide the truth-values of the two samples, in FOPL every object in the domain needs to be taken into account. On the contrary, in NAL only the terms in the extension of S are relevant.

Table 10.1. The new grammar rules of NAL-6.

$$\begin{aligned}
\langle term \rangle &::= \langle variable \rangle \\
\langle variable \rangle &::= \langle independent\text{-}variable \rangle \\
&\quad | \ \langle dependent\text{-}variable \rangle \\
&\quad | \ \langle query\text{-}variable \rangle \\
\langle independent\text{-}variable \rangle &::= \#\langle word \rangle \\
\langle dependent\text{-}variable \rangle &::= \#[\langle word \rangle(\langle independent\text{-}variable \rangle^*)] \\
\langle query\text{-}variable \rangle &::= ?[\langle word \rangle]
\end{aligned}$$

conjunction or intersection term (for a dependent variable). There is no sentence in Narsese that directly corresponds to "$(\forall x)P(x)$" or "$(\exists x)P(x)$".

A dependent variable can refer to a term without naming it (so as to use it only as a place holder). Such an *anonymous* term is simply marked as '#'. Please note that when multiple '#'s appear in a sentence, they do not necessarily refer to the same constant term. A similar treatment is given to query variables, so the '?' used in the previous layers are now considered an anonymous variable term. An independent variable must appear more than once in a statement, so cannot be anonymous.

The variable-related grammar rules introduced in NAL-6 are summarized in Table 10.1.

Clearly, the grammar rules only specify the *necessary* condition for a sentence to be meaningful in NAL, rather than the *sufficient* condition, since it does not include the additional requirements mentioned previously, which exclude "$\#x \to P$" and "$(\#x \to S) \Rightarrow (P \to \#x())$" from acceptable statements, even though they satisfy the grammar. The same thing happens in other places of NAL, too.

Definition 10.3. In a sentence, the *scope* of a variable is the smallest statement that contains all occurrences of the variable.[4]

---

[4]According to this definition, in IL statement "$(\neg((\#x \to S) \Rightarrow (\#x \to P)))$" the negation is beyond the scope of the variable, so its corresponding proposition in FOPL is "$\neg((\forall x)(S(x) \Longrightarrow P(x)))$", not "$(\forall x)\neg(S(x) \Longrightarrow P(x))$". The latter corresponds to "$(\#x \to S) \Rightarrow (\neg(\#x \to P))$" in IL.

In a sentence with multiple variables, as far as each of them uses a different name, their scopes do not need to be explicitly specified. The scope of a variable can be embedded in that of another variable. Especially, if the scope of a dependent variable is included in the scope of an independent variable, the latter appears in the dependency list of the former.

For two variables, there are four meaningful combinations (though the grammar allows more). For example, in Narsese the following beliefs can be represented:

- $((\{\#x\} \to key) \land (\{\#y\} \to lock)) \Rightarrow (\{\#x \times \#y\} \to open)$ ["Every key opens every lock."]
- $((\{\#x()\} \to key) \land ((\{\#y\} \to lock) \Rightarrow (\{\#x() \times \#y\} \to open)))$ ["There is a key that opens every lock."]
- $(\{\#x\} \to key) \Rightarrow ((\{\#y(\#x)\} \to lock) \land (\{\#x \times \#y(\#x)\} \to open))$ ["Every key opens some lock (that depends on the key)."]
- $((\{\#x()\} \to key) \land (\{\#y()\} \to lock) \land (\{\#x() \times \#y()\} \to open))$ ["There is a key that opens a lock."]

Definition 10.4. A variable is *open* in a compound term if its scope goes beyond the compound, otherwise it is *closed* in the compound term. If a compound term contains open variables, it is also a variable.

For example, in statement "$(\#x \to S) \Rightarrow (\#x \to P)$", the statement as a whole is closed, though its two components "$\#x \to S$" and "$\#x \to P$" are both open. Only a closed compound term names a concept, while an open compound term does not. Similarly, only closed statements have truth-values.

Definition 10.5. The meaning of a variable term is determined locally by its relations with the other terms within its scope.

As defined previously, the meaning of a constant term is *global*, in the sense that at any given moment, its occurrences in the whole system have the same meaning, determined by its (empirical and analytical) relations with the other term *in the whole system*. Therefore, the name of a variable term is unique in a *sentence*, while the name of a constant term is unique in a *system*. For example, in two statements "$(\#x \to dog) \Rightarrow (\#x \to mammal)$" and "$(\#x \to mammal) \Rightarrow (\#x \to animal)$", the two occurrences of "*mammal*" refer to the same concept named by that term. On the contrary, the four occurrences of "$\#x$" refer to no concept at all. Among them, the first two occurrences belong to one variable, whose meaning is determined by its relation with "*dog*" and "*mammal*" in the first statement, while the last two occurrences belong to another variable, whose meaning is determined by its relation with "*mammal*" and "*animal*" in the second statement.

When extended from IL to NAL, the truth-value of a statement can be determined by instantiating its closed variables by constant terms. As will be explained in detail in the following, the truth-value of "$(\#x \to S) \Rightarrow (\#x \to P)$" is determined just like that of "$(S \to P)$", except that only the extensional evidence of the latter is considered.

In this way, the truth-value of "$(\#x \to S) \Rightarrow (\#x \to P)$" in NAL is more similar to (though not identical with) the probability value $\Pr(P(x)|S(x))$, rather than to $\Pr((\forall x)(S(x) \Longrightarrow P(x)))$ — If some instances of S are in P but some are not, the latter value will be 0, while the former will not be. As in the case of "$S \to P$", negative evidence will decrease the *frequency*, but not completely "falsify" it. This is another fundamental difference between FOPL and NAL: a piece of "general knowledge" is represented in the former as a proposition with universally quantified variables, and corresponds to a conjunction of the same proposition on every object in the domain; on the latter, however, the "general knowledge" is statistical by nature, and a statement with an independent variable does not correspond to a conjunction anymore. Formally, in FOPL, if the domain consists of individuals $a_1, \ldots, a_n$, then "$(\forall x)P(x) \Longleftrightarrow P(a_1) \wedge \ldots \wedge P(a_n)$" and "$(\exists x)P(x) \Longleftrightarrow P(a_1) \vee \ldots \vee P(a_n)$". In NAL, the variable terms do not satisfy such an equivalence.

10.2.   Variable Elimination and Introduction

Since a variable represents another term, one common operation in variable-related inference is "substitution", as defined in symbolic logic [Kleene (2002)] and its computer implementation [Russell and Norvig (2010)], except that a substitution in NAL can go in both directions: not only substituting a variable by a constant (variable elimination), but also substituting a constant by a variable (variable introduction).

Definition 10.6. For given terms R, S, T, a *substitution* $R\{S/T\}$ produces a new term by replacing all occurrences of S by T in R, under the condition that S does not occur in T.

A *valid* substitution in a statement does not change the truth-value of the statement. When reasoning on judgments, it is valid to substitute an independent variable by an arbitrary term, or to substitute an arbitrary term by a dependent variable. When a question is matched to a judgment, it is valid to substitute a query variable by a constant term. This result directly comes from the definitions of the variable terms: an "independent variable" represents an arbitrary term, a "dependent variable" represents a specific (though unnamed) term in a judgment, and a "query variable" represents a specific term that needs to be found.

The procedure of finding a possible substitution is called "unification", which has been specified in the study of reasoning systems [Russell and Norvig (2010)]. Two terms R and S can be *unified* if and only if there is a substitution θ such that $R\theta$ and $S\theta$ are identical.

Most of the inference rules defined in NAL can be extended to take statements with variables as premises or conclusions, by applying a proper substitution on the premises (before the inference) or on the conclusion (after the inference). Consequently, most of the new inference rules introduced in IL-6 and NAL-6 are obtained by adding unification and substitution to the existing rules.

For example, some *independent-variable elimination rules* are given in Table 10.2, and each of them can be seen as carrying a substitution $\{\#x/M\}$, followed by an inference defined in NAL-5. Almost all the syllogistic and compositional rules defined previously can be used in this way, where the previous request on a "common term" in the two premises is replaced by "two terms that can be unified".

Table 10.2. Sample independent-variable elimination rules.

$$\{(\#x \to M) \Rightarrow (\#x \to P),\ S \to M\} \vdash S \to P\ \langle F_{\mathrm{ded}} \rangle$$
$$\{(\#x \to P) \Rightarrow (\#x \to M),\ S \to M\} \vdash S \to P\ \langle F_{\mathrm{abd}} \rangle$$
$$\{(\#x \to M) \Leftrightarrow (\#x \to P),\ S \to M\} \vdash S \to P\ \langle F'_{\mathrm{ana}} \rangle$$

Table 10.3. Sample independent-variable introduction rules.

$$\{M \to P, M \to S\} \vdash (\#x \to S) \Rightarrow (\#x \to P)\langle F_{\mathrm{ind}} \rangle$$
$$\{M \to P, M \to S\} \vdash (\#x \to S) \Leftrightarrow (\#x \to P)\langle F_{\mathrm{com}} \rangle$$

Table 10.4. Sample dependent-variable introduction rule.

$$\{M \to T_1,\ M \to T_2\} \vdash (\#x() \to T_1) \wedge (\#x() \to T_2)\ \langle F_{\mathrm{int}} \rangle$$

These rules are referred to as "independent-variable elimination", because, conceptually speaking, an independent variable in a premise is substituted by a constant first, then a previously defined rule is applied to the premises.

The reversibility among inference rules is maintained in NAL-6, that is, whenever there is a rule *eliminating* a variable from a premise, there is another rule *introducing* a variable into its conclusion. The reverse of *independent-variable elimination* is *independent-variable introduction*, as given in Table 10.3.

The rules in Table 10.3 can be seen as concrete cases of the first two rules in Table 9.5, followed by a substitution $\{M/\#x\}$. When these rules are introduced in NAL-5, it is mentioned that they can be applied only when the premises "can be seen as based on the same implicit condition". In Table 10.3 the condition is satisfied, since the premises contain a common term M. On the other hand, these rules can be justified in the same way as the corresponding rules in NAL-1 and NAL-2, except that here the "extensional inheritance" and "intensional inheritance" between S and P are separated, due to the using of independent variables.

The rule in Table 10.4 introduces a dependent variable into conjunction, which can be seen as the intersection-composition

Table 10.5. Sample dependent-variable elimination rule.

$$\{M \to T_1, (\#x() \to T_1) \wedge (\#x() \to T_2)\} \vdash M \to T_2 \langle F_{\text{ana}-\text{cvn}} \rangle$$

rule defined in Table 7.2 (with the statement in the conclusion equivalently rewritten as a conjunction), followed by a substitution $\{M/\#x()\}$.

The reverse of the rule in Table 10.4 is given in Table 10.5.

Conceptually, the inference rule in Table 10.5 is an implicit *comparison* followed by an *analogy*. First, in "$(\#x() \to T_1) \wedge (\#x() \to T_2) \langle f_2, c_2 \rangle$" the anonymous term provides positive evidence for a similarity statement "$T_1 \leftrightarrow T_2$". However, the truth-value function is not F_{com} (which expects two premises) but F_{cvn} (which expects one premise and only provides positive evidence, up to one unit amount, as required here):

$$f_2' = 1, \quad c_2' = f_2 \times c_2/(f_2 \times c_2 + k).$$

Then, "$M \to T_1 \ \langle f_1, c_1 \rangle$" and "$T_1 \leftrightarrow T_2 \ \langle f_2', c_2' \rangle$" are used by the *analogy rule* to derive "$M \to T_2 \ \langle F_{\text{ana}} \rangle$". Therefore, the truth-value function $F_{\text{ana}-\text{cvn}}$ is just the analogy function F_{ana}, except that the second premise's truth-value is processed by function F_{cvn} first. This inference is a weak one, since the confidence of the conclusion is lower than $1/(1 + k)$.

The rules in Tables 10.2 to 10.5 are only about the *extensions* of S, P, T_1 and T_2, and that is why the previous four tables are named as "sample rules" — they are incomplete. Similarly, there are rules that only process the *intensions* of the terms involved. In all these rules a dependent variable is only introduced into a *conjunction* or *intersection*, and an independent variable into (both sides of) an *implication* or *equivalence*.

Now we see that NAL can derive "$(\#x \to bird) \Rightarrow (\#x \to animal)$", "$(animal \to \#x) \Rightarrow (bird \to \#x)$", and "$bird \to animal$". The first statement is purely extensional, the second is purely intensional, and the last a mixture of the two. The system needs all of them. Usually, the "pure" ones provide more specialized information,

Table 10.6. Sample multi-variable introduction rules.

$$\{(\#x \to P) \Rightarrow (M \to (/\ R\ \#x\ \diamond)),\ M \to S\}$$
$$\vdash ((\#y \to S) \land (\#x \to P)) \Rightarrow (\#y \to (/\ R\ \#x\ \diamond))\ \langle F_{\text{ind}} \rangle$$
$$\{(\#x \to P) \Rightarrow (M \to (/\ R\ \#x\ \diamond)),\ M \to S\}$$
$$\vdash (\#y() \to S) \land ((\#x \to P) \Rightarrow (\#y() \to (/\ R\ \#x\ \diamond)))\ \langle F_{\text{int}} \rangle$$
$$\{(\#x() \to P) \land (M \to (/R\ \#x()\diamond)),\ M \to S\}$$
$$\vdash ((\#y \to S) \Rightarrow ((\#x(\#y) \to P) \land (\#y \to (/\ R\ \#x(\#y)\ \diamond)))\ \langle F_{\text{ind}} \rangle$$
$$\{(\#x() \to P) \land (M \to (/\ R\ \#x()\ \diamond)),\ M \to S\}$$
$$\vdash ((\#y() \to S) \land (\#x() \to P) \land (\#y() \to (/\ R\ \#x()\ \diamond))\ \langle F_{\text{int}} \rangle$$

while the "mixed" one is more general, and helps to keep the coherence between the extension and intension of a term.

All the above variable introduction/elimination rules can be extended to the situations where a variable appears more than twice in a statement, as well as to situations where more than one variable appears in a statement. Most of such extensions are straightforward.

For example, variables can be introduced into statements where other variables exist. When an independent variable is introduced, the existing dependent variables in its scope become its functions. The four rules for variable introduction in Table 10.6 are extended version of the rules in Tables 10.3 and 10.4, and they are responsible for producing the four sentences in the "key–lock" example in the previous section, respectively.

There are variable-related rules that neither eliminate nor introduce variables, but merely unify them. for example, a version of deduction derives "$(\#x \to S) \Rightarrow (\#x \to P)$" from "$(\#x \to M) \Rightarrow (\#x \to P)$" and "$(\#x \to S) \Rightarrow (\#x \to M)$" by unifying the two variables in the premises — which are indeed different terms, by definition, despite of the shared name.

The revision rule is also extended to unify independent variables. For example, statements "$(\#x \to S) \Rightarrow (\#x \to P)$" and "$(\#y \to S) \Rightarrow (\#y \to P)$" can be merged together, since an independent variable can be substituted by another one. On the contrary, the revision rule cannot be applied to two judgments containing dependent variables, such as two copies of "$((\#x() \to S) \land (\#x() \to P))$" even if they have different evidential bases, since the dependent variables in them do not necessarily correspond to the same (constant) term, even though they share the same variable name. Consequently, there may be more than one such judgments that have the same statement, but different evidential bases. When a question is raised on this statement, the *choice* rule will pick the answer with the highest *expectation* value.

In logic programming languages like Prolog, "existential variables in queries" and "query variables" are the same thing, which is not the case in NAL. For example, the question "$?x \rightarrow (S \cap P)$" asks for a constant term T that gives "$T \rightarrow (S \cap P)$" the highest *expectation* value; on the other hand, the question "$\#x() \rightarrow (S \cap P)$" only asks for a truth-value to be assigned to the statement (with the highest *expectation* value among all candidates), without knowing the constant term.

10.3.   Symbolic Reasoning

Beside separating extension and intension, variable terms also allow the system to infer on symbols and abstract concepts.

Semantically, variable terms in Narsese (such as $\#x$ and $\#y$) and variables in the meta-language of Narsese (such as S and P) are like the "symbols" in traditional "symbolic systems" [Newell and Simon (1976)], in the sense that they represent other (constant) terms, which provide concrete interpretation or "grounding" for the symbols. On the contrary, the constant terms in NARS (such as *robin* and *bird*) are not "symbols" in that sense, since their meaning is already grounded, or determined, by the system's experience, so cannot be freely interpreted anymore.

Consequently, statement "$(\{\#x\} \rightarrow P) \Rightarrow (\{\#x\} \rightarrow Q)$" can represent the knowledge "If an object is an instance of P, then it is also an instance of Q", without demanding any direct experience on P and Q. In this way, the system can have *hypothetical* concepts that are not directly grounded in the system's empirical experience, but can be *applied* to very different contexts to derive valid conclusions.

Moving further in this direction, we get *abstract* terms. Syntactically, these terms look just like ordinary constant terms, and they name concepts in the system. They are however semantically similar to variable terms, since they are not *generalized* from the system's sensorimotor experience, but *abstracted* from them via idealization and simplification, to such an extent that they are applicable to very different situations in experience.

Abstract terms are often introduced using *definitions*, so as to get a fixed or stable meaning to regulate its future usage. For example, in Narsese a term *natural-number* can be defined by another term $(integer - [negative])$, and a *subset* relation between P and Q can be defined by statement "$(\{\#x\} \to P) \Rightarrow (\{\#x\} \to Q)$". To represent this conceptual relation in Narsese, a term *define* can be used, so the above examples can be represented as "$\{(integer - [negative]) \times natural\text{-}number\} \to define$" and "$\{((\{\#x\} \to \#p) \Rightarrow (\{\#x\} \to \#q)) \times (\{\#p \times \#q\} \to subset)\} \to define$", respectively.

The meaning of *define* in this two examples is like the *similarity* copula and the *equivalence* copula, respectively, except that it is an acquired relation, with experience-grounded meaning, which indicates that the system should follow the convention established by a definition. While "$S \leftrightarrow P$" means the two terms are *observed* to be exchangeable, "$\{S \times P\} \to define$" means the two terms are *required* to be exchangeable.

In NAL a definition itself is *true* as a binary statement, though the judgment "$\{(integer - [negative]) \times natural\text{-}number\} \to define$" still has a numerical truth-value like the others, indicating the system's degree of belief that this statement is indeed a definition. In this way, NAL can embed an axiomatic subsystem, call it a "theory", with its definitions, axioms, and theorems. They are not represented in Narsese as judgments with truth-value $\langle 1, 1 \rangle$, but using terms like *define*, *axiom*, *theorem*, and *prove*. It is often necessary to indicate the theory they belong to by using longer words or compound terms.

For example, the system can have a belief "$\{((\#x(\#y) \to axiom) \land (\{\#x(\#y) \times \#y\} \to prove)) \times (\#y \to theorem)\} \to define$", which defines a theorem as something that can be proved from an axiom. In this way, NARS can carry out binary deduction *within* this theory, only using special inference rules represented as *implication* or *equivalence* statements in Narsese. At the same time, NARS can still carry out various types of inference *outside* the theory, using NAL inference rules, to form hypothetical or heuristic knowledge about the system. The ability of reasoning both inside and outside a theory plays important roles in thinking, as pointed out in Hofstadter (1979).

The above description shows that NAL can handle two types of "truth": beside the native truth-value (which is experience-grounded, multi-valued, and system-wide), it also allows "theory-specific" truth to be used, like "true in number theory" or "true in Euclidean geometry", which is binary, axiom-based, and restricted within a theory. These two types of truth are related, but cannot replace each other. For example, if a mathematical hypothesis has passed many testing cases, its truth-value will be $\langle 1, c \rangle$ with a c near 1, but it will still not be considered as a theorem until a proof is found.

By allowing terms to be numbers, NAL can carry out various types of numerical calculations. For example, it can compute probability values according to probability theory and statistics, without confusing it with the truth-value calculations performed by the truth-value functions, which do not follow probability theory.

When an abstract theory is applied to a concrete situation, an object is proximately treated as an instance of an abstract concept, so as to get concrete implications in the domain. That is, if the system believes that P is a subset of Q and "$\{Tweety\} \to P$", then from them and the theory-specific truth "$(\{\#x\} \to P) \Rightarrow (\{\#x\} \to Q)$", by deduction the system can get "$\{Tweety\} \to Q$", which is no longer in the theory, so has an empirical truth-value.

When the theory to be embedded is not represented in Narsese, but a different language L, a translation process will be needed between the two, which maps the terms in Narsese into and from words, phases, and sentences in L, mainly using a relation *represent*, which is similar to the above *define* relation, though is between a term in Narsese and whatever represents it in another language.

For example, to represent set theory in Narsese, we can have:

- "$\{`\subset` \times subset\} \to represent$", which means "Symbol '$\subset$' (in set theory) represents term *subset* (in Narsese)";

- "$(\{\times \#x \ ` \subset ` \#y\} \times \{(\#x \times \#y) \rightarrow subset\}) \rightarrow represent$", which means "Sequence '$\#x \subset \#y$' (in set theory) represents term '$(\#x \times \#y) \rightarrow subset$' (in Narsese)".

In the two examples, the *represent* relation is similar to the *similarity* copula and the *equivalence* copula, respectively, except that it is an acquired relation, and it uses words, phrases, or sentences in other language to represent terms.

Using this approach, to understand a given sentence S in L means to answer the question "$\{S \times ?\} \rightarrow represent$", and to generate sentences in L to express statement T means to answer the question "$\{? \times T\} \rightarrow represent$", both under some additional requirements.

The same approach can also be applied to the situation where the external language L is a natural language, like English or Chinese. This book does not discuss natural language processing, but only makes the following position statements about the process in NARS:

- Natural language is processed in the same way as other types of symbols, that is, as external representations, or "symbols", of the internal concepts of the system. The processing is carried out by the same logic and control mechanism. The specialty of this process mainly comes from the special nature of linguistic knowledge.

- In both understanding and generating, syntactic, semantic, and pragmatic processing happen in parallel: the overall process is driven by pragmatic goals, the *represent* relation is built using semantic knowledge, and syntactic knowledge helps to map a long sequence of words (in L) into the structure of compound terms (in Narsese).

- Like other types of knowledge, linguistic knowledge is learned by the system from its experience, in an incremental and interactive process. Given linguistic notions and grammar rules will improve the system's performance, though they are not absolutely necessary for language learning and usage.

In general, the natural language processing in NARS will be more similar to the "cognitive linguistics" school [Lakoff (1988); Langacker (1999)] than to the other competing approaches in linguistics.

Narsese is the "native language" of NARS, while all the other languages used by the system are "foreign languages" acquired with Narsese as the meta-language. Consequently, the semantics of the other languages is similar to model-theoretic semantics, since "truth" and "meaning" in them are defined with respect to the "model" specified in Narsese, while the semantics of Narsese cannot be established in this way, since it does not have a meta-language *within the system* to refer to. On the other hand, the experience-grounded semantics of NARS can be uniformly applied to both types of language.

The major issue that makes natural languages harder than artificial languages to learn and use, as well as for model-theoretic semantics to be less proper, is that the *represent* relation (similar to the *interpretation* in model-theoretic semantics) is no longer a static one-to-one mapping with a binary truth-value, but a dynamic many-to-many mapping with a graded truth-value. However, since NAL is already a logic that can handle this type of mappings, there is little to add at the meta-level, though there is still a lot to be learned at the object-level for each new language. Even so, it is unnecessary to train the systems one by one. After one system is properly trained, its memory can be copied, and used as the starting point of other systems, which will have "inherited" (though still modifiable) knowledge about the language.

Given its ability to learn another language, NAL can be used to emulate an arbitrary logic. For example, though NAL is fundamentally different from FOPL, it can serve as the meta-logic of FOPL and emulate the inference process in the latter. All the notions of FOPL can be introduced in Narsese as terms, including "proposition", "true", "false", "valid inference rule", "axiom", "theorem", "conjunction", "implication", and so on. A proposition in FOPL is represented as a term in Narsese, and its (binary) truth-value is represented as a property. The grammar rules and inference rules in FOPL are normally represented as *implication* or *equivalence* statements with variable terms in Narsese. As a result, NAL can carry out inference in FOPL.

Even so, in NARS inference in NAL and inference in FOPL are carried out at deferent levels: the former at the *meta-level*, and the latter at the *object-level*. The NAL rules are *innate* to the system, and they are represented procedurally in the programming language (such as Java or Prolog) and (normally) cannot be modified or violated by the system. On the contrary, the FOPL rules are learned by the system from its experience, and they are represented declaratively in Narsese and can be modified or violated by the system.

Therefore, the relation between NAL and the traditional models of reasoning (such as binary logic, probability theory, set theory, etc.) can be summarized as the following:

- Conceptually and semantically, the traditional models correspond to extreme and idealized situations, where the insufficiency of knowledge and resources can be ignored.
- The grammar and inference rules of NAL are not derived from the traditional models, though are similar to them in certain situations, under certain interpretations.
- NARS can learn and emulate the traditional models (among other things), though does not have them implanted as part of the system's innate knowledge.

Since NAL can emulate an arbitrary logic at object-level, it can do so for its meta-logic, IL, or even NAL itself. This means that the inference rules of IL and NAL can be expressed as Narsese statements, to be used by the related rules (such as deduction) to emulate its own inference steps.[5]

The ability of emulating other logics or theories is not a property possessed only by NAL. Since NAL can be implemented in Prolog, which is based on FOPL, in a sense NAL can be emulated by FOPL. Here it is important to understand that if a logic can be *emulated* (or *implemented*) by another in this way, it does not mean that the

---

[5]This type of self-reference directly leads to the system's self-monitor and self-control ability, to be introduced in Chapter 13.

former is *reduced* into the latter as part of it, nor that the two have identical properties.

For example, though NAL is non-axiomatic and based on AIKR, it can emulate an axiomatic logic assuming sufficient knowledge and resources, that is, it can be "locally axiomatized". Here the situation is just like the notion of "virtual machine" in computer science — when described at different levels of abstraction, the same system can show different, even opposite, properties. For example, decimal calculations are implemented by binary calculations, and declarative programming languages are implemented by procedural programming languages. There is nothing magical or contradictory for an axiomatic system to implement a non-axiomatic system, or the other way around.

In the history of AI, there have been many debates between the supporters of *general-purpose* approaches (in representation, algorithm, architecture, etc.) and those of *special-purpose* approaches. Usually, special-purpose solutions are simpler and more efficient, while a general-purpose solution covers a wider range of problems [Wang and Goertzel (2007)]. The approach taken in NARS is to *design* the system as general-purpose and uniform at the meta-level, but to allow it to *learn* various special-purpose representations and solutions from experience at the object-level. The capability of symbolic reasoning plays a central role in this approach, since it allows the system to move among different representations, rather than to be restricted by the built-in representation or the direct experience of the system.

CHAPTER 11

NAL-7: EVENTS AS STATEMENTS

NAL-7 introduces *time* into the logic. In the lower layers of NAL, time influences the inference process in an implicit way, mainly in the control part of the system. In NAL-7, however, temporal information is explicitly represented in the grammar rules and the inference rules. Furthermore, the reasoning process happens in real time, and takes the changes in the environment into account.

11.1. Time and Events

As mentioned previously, NAL is the logic implemented in a reasoning system NARS. As all other physical systems, NARS exists in *time*, which primarily appears as an order among the events inside and outside the system.

Definition 11.1. An *event* is a statement with a time-dependent truth-value, that is, the evidential support summarized in its truth-value is valid only in its *duration*, which is a certain period of time between the moment the event *starts* and the moment it *ends*.

To be exact, almost all empirical statements are time dependent, and few statements are about eternal relations [Vila (1994)]. However, for practical purposes, it is not always necessary for the temporal attributes of a statement to be taken into consideration. Therefore, whether a *statement* should be treated as an *event* may change from context to context, and events are just the statements whose temporal attributes are specified. On the contrary, the time interval of a "non-event" statement is unspecified, except that it includes all the moments as far as the system is concerned.

For example, "The Earth revolves around the Sun" is usually taken as a statement rather than an event, even though its truth-value (which is *true* to most people living in the present age) does not hold before the Earth was formed. On the other hand, whether "Beijing is the capital of China" should be treated as an event or a statement depends on the context of the description — it may be treated as an event in a history textbook, but a statement in travel guides. For this reason, "event" is not defined as a Narsese grammatical category, but refers to certain statements that have temporal information associated.

Therefore, an event is a statement whose truth-value may change, and this type of belief change is different from the changes caused by the accumulation of evidence. Instead, when an event begins or ends, the evidence collected about the statement during the previous period becomes *outdated*, and should not be taken into account when the current situation is under consideration.

An event often can be considered as a point in the time dimension when its duration is irrelevant to the current reasoning task, and this point is referred to as when the corresponding event "happens". In this way, the temporal relation between two atomic events E_1 and E_2 has the following three basic cases:

- E_1 happens *before* E_2 happens,
- E_1 happens *after* E_2 happens,
- E_1 happens *when* E_2 happens.

Obviously, "*before*" and "*after*" are the opposite directions of the same temporal relation.

Definition 11.2. In IL, there are two basic temporal relations between two events: "*before*" (which is irreflexive, antisymmetric, and transitive) and "*when*" (which is reflexive, symmetric, and transitive).

This selection of the basic temporal relations is supported by the related results in linguistics and psychology [Wierzbicka (1996); Lu and Graesser (2004)].

If the temporal relation between two events is more complicated than these cases, like the ones listed in Allen (1984), it is always possible to divide an event into sub-events (by talking about "the end of E_1" and "the beginning E_2"), then to describe their temporal relations.

If event E_1 is represented as "before" event E_2, the time interval between "E_1 ends" and "E_2 starts" is omitted as negligible, even if the duration of this interval is not zero. When the interval is not negligible, it can be represented as an event E_3, which happens after E_1 and before E_2. Similarly, when two events are described as happening at the same time, it does not mean that their time intervals perfectly coincide, but that their difference in timing is negligible.

While most AI systems represent time *absolutely*, either as a point or an interval on a time dimension [Vila (1994)], NAL takes a *relational* approach and allows different granularity and accuracy, so can be applied to fields where phrases like "at the same time" and "immediately after" are used with very different scales, scopes, and accuracies (such as descriptions in astronomy and electronics).

In NARS, though we can intuitively talk about the time interval of an event (as above), it is not assumed that such an accurately specified interval is known as in Allen (1984), or even well defined, for every event — just like many concepts in NARS do not have a sharp boundary around its instances, many events, such as "the Renaissance" and "the wind last evening", do not have a sharp boundary for their duration. Very often, the system does not need a high accuracy here, otherwise it can use a more accurate concept.

This treatment of time is consistent with the general principle of NARS in perception and categorization, that is, instead of attempting *to describe the world as it is*, what the system does is *to summarize the experience as it needs*.

Since events have time-dependent truth-values, the related terms and concepts will have time-dependent meaning. For example, the term expressing "the President of the USA" may change its extension after each presidential election, though part of its intension remains stable. This is basically what Goodman's "New Riddle" [Goodman (1955)] is really about — after a concept changes parts of its meaning, old judgments about it need to be reevaluated to decide whether the previous evidence is still valid. In NARS, one solution to this type of problem is to explicitly use time-dependent concepts, such as "the President of the USA during WWII" and "the President of the USA after Barack Obama".

As a real-time system, NARS not only needs to reason "about time", but also to reason "in time", which demands a "personal sense of time" [Ismail and Shapiro (2000)], measured in NARS by the system's "internal clock" defined by its own working cycle.

Definition 11.3. Some temporal properties of an event within NARS can be specified with respect to the events defined by an *internal clock*, with the system's inference cycle as unit.

For this definition to make sense, it is necessary for the internal activity to roughly take a constant time (measured in the conventional way), which can be achieved by the current NARS design, as briefly described in Chapter 5 and explained with more details in Wang (1996c, 2009b). Such a time measurement is relative to the system's internal activity, so different copies of NARS implemented in different hardware/software platforms may associate different "subjective time" to an event in their common environment. Therefore, in the following, "NARS" refers to such a concrete system, with its own internal clock, which is neither "universal" nor "absolutely accurate". For this reason, this "personal time" is not explicitly referred to in Narsese, though it can be used to describe the system's interaction with its environment.

Definition 11.4. The *real-time experience* of a NARS is a sequence of Narsese sentences, separated by non-negative numbers indicating the interval between the arriving time of subsequent sentences, measured by the system's internal clock.

That is, for i from 1 to n, let S_i be a Narsese sentence and N_i a non-negative integer, a section of real-time experience of NARS can be expressed as:

$$S_1, N_1, S_2, N_2, S_3, N_3, \ldots.$$

It means that sentence S_1 is received at a certain initial moment, then, after N_1 moments (each has the length of a working cycle), sentence S_2 is received, and then after N_2 moments, S_3 comes, and so on. When N_i is 0, S_i and S_{i+1} are considered as accepted at the same moment.

The interval represented by N_i is between the *arrival times* of sentences S_i and S_{i+1}, which is not necessarily the same as the interval between their *occurring times*, if both S_i and S_{i+1} describe events. For example, it is possible for S_i to be perceived *before* S_{i+1} by the system, though it knows that S_i happened *after* S_{i+1} in the environment.

So far, there have been three notions of *experience* used in NAL:

- In IL-1, *ideal* experience is defined as a (constant) *set* of (*true*) statements. The order of statements in this type of experience does not matter.
- In NAL-1, *actual* experience is defined as a *stream* of sentences. The timing in the stream is omitted in the language, and ignored by the inference rules, though it matters for the inference control mechanism.
- In IL-7, *real-time* experience explicitly indicates time in the input stream, using the internal clock. It covers the previous notions of experience as special cases: actual experience corresponds to the situation where there is one input per moment, and idealized experience is where all inputs arrive at the very beginning.

11.2.   Temporal Connectors and Copulas

In NAL, since temporal attributes are optional in statements, the two temporal relations are never used by themselves, without mentioning any logical relations between the events. Instead, they are used in combination with certain copulas and connectors between statements that have been introduced in NAL-5.

First, "E_1 happens before E_2 happens" and "E_1 happens when E_2 happens" both assume "E_1 and E_2 happen (at some time)", which is "$E_1 \wedge E_2$" plus temporal information.

Definition 11.5. The conjunction connector ('$\wedge$') has two temporal variants: "sequential conjunction" (',') and "parallel conjunction" (';'). "(E_1, E_2)" represents the compound event consisting of E_1 followed by E_2, and "$(E_1; E_2)$" represents the compound event consisting of E_1 accompanied by E_2.

Like ordinary conjunctions, both temporal conjunction connectors can take more than two components, and are associative. The order of the components matters in a sequential conjunction, but not in a parallel conjunction.

Similarly, there are temporal variants of copulas *implication* and *equivalence*.

Definition 11.6. For an implication statement "$S \Rightarrow T$" between events S and T, three different temporal relations can be specified:

(1) If S happens *before* T happens, the statement is called "predictive implication", and is rewritten as "$S /\!\!\Rightarrow T$", where S is called a *sufficient precondition* of T, and T a *necessary postcondition* of S.

(2) If S happens *after* T happens, the statement is called "retrospective implication", and is rewritten as "$S \backslash\!\!\Rightarrow T$", where S is called a *sufficient postcondition* of T, and T a *necessary precondition* of S.

(3) If S happens *when* T happens, the statement is called "concurrent implication", and is rewritten as "$S |\!\!\Rightarrow T$", where S is called a *sufficient co-condition* of T, and T a *necessary co-condition* of S.

Definition 11.7. Three "temporal equivalence" (predictive, retrospective, and concurrent) relations are defined as the following:

(1) "$S /\!\!\Leftrightarrow T$" (or equivalently, "$T \backslash\!\!\Leftrightarrow S$") means that S is an *equivalent precondition* of T, and T an *equivalent postcondition* of S.

(2) "$S \Leftrightarrow T$" means that S and T are *equivalent co-conditions* of each other.

(3) To simplify the language, "$T \setminus\Leftrightarrow S$" is always represented as "$S \not\Leftrightarrow T$", so the copula "$\setminus\Leftrightarrow$" is not actually included in the grammar of Narsese.

As explained in NAL-5, judgment "$S\langle f, c\rangle$" can be equivalently rewritten as "$E \Rightarrow S \langle f, c\rangle$", where E is a virtual compound statement summarizing the currently available evidence. Now if statement S is an event, its temporal attribute can be specified relative to E, taken as an event that is currently occurring. Since in Narsese E is implicitly assumed, the temporal *implication* copulas serve here as "tenses", which indicate the temporal nature of truth-values. In this way, adjectives like "past", "present", and "future" can be represented in Narsese.

Definition 11.8. The *tense* of a sentence indicates the occurring time of an event with respect to "the event happening now", a special event that is implicitly represented. The temporal implication symbols '$\setminus\Rightarrow$', '$\Rightarrow$', and '$/\Rightarrow$' are also used in a sentence to indicate "past tense", "present tense", and "future tense", respectively.

For example, sentences "It rained", "It is raining", and "It will rain" can be represented in Narsese as "$\setminus\Rightarrow rain\text{-}1$", "$\Rightarrow rain\text{-}1$", and "$/\Rightarrow rain\text{-}1$", respectively, where the event $rain\text{-}1$ is further specified by the statement "$\{rain\text{-}1\} \to rain$" with a proper truth-value.

What makes the situation complicated in real-time reasoning systems is that "now" changes constantly [Elgot-Drapkin and Perlis (1990); Ismail and Shapiro (2000)], so "future" gradually becomes "present", then "past". Furthermore, while "now" is unique, the moments referred to as "past" and "future" are not. Multiple judgments may associate different truth-values to the same event that has a "past" or "future" tense, and each of them is actually about a different moment. For example, "It will rain" and "It will not rain" may not form a contradiction if they are talking about different future times. Here the situation is similar to that of statements containing dependent variables (discussed in the previous chapter), where the "same content" expressed in Narsese may have different meanings.

To allow the "now" to be a moving reference, each sentence in NARS is given a *time stamp* to record the moment (according to the internal clock) when the sentence is formed, either from outside (experience) or inside (inference). If the content of the sentence is an event, the time stamp also contains a tense defined above, to indicate the happening time of the event with respect to the moment recorded in the time stamp. If the content of a sentence is not treated as an event, then its time stamp only contains its creation time, while its happening time is taken to be eternal.

Since time stamps are defined with respect to the internal clock of the system, they are not included in Narsese. When a sentence is expressed (in Narsese) for communication, the temporal information in its time stamp may be translated into (and from) a tense with respect to the current time when the communication happens, which can be different from the recorded tense in the time stamp.

The grammar rules introduced in IL-7 are listed in Table 11.1.

In summary, NARS has three alternative ways to represent temporal information:

Relative representation. Some compound terms (*implication, equivalence,* and *conjunction*) may have temporal order specified among its components.

Numerical representation. A sentence has a time stamp to indicate its "creation time", plus an optional "tense" for its truth-value, with respect to this time.

Table 11.1. The new grammar rules of NAL-7.

$$\langle judgment \rangle ::= [\langle tense \rangle]\langle statement \rangle\langle truth\text{-}value \rangle$$
$$\langle question \rangle ::= [\langle tense \rangle]\langle statement \rangle$$
$$\langle statement \rangle ::= (\, , \langle statement \rangle\langle statement \rangle^{+})$$
$$| \ (\, ; \langle statement \rangle\langle statement \rangle^{+})$$
$$\langle copula \rangle ::= \not\Rightarrow \ | \ \backslash\!\!\Rightarrow \ | \ |\!\!\Rightarrow \ | \ \not\Leftrightarrow \ | \ |\!\!\Leftrightarrow$$
$$\langle tense \rangle ::= \not\Rightarrow \ | \ \backslash\!\!\Rightarrow \ | \ |\!\!\Rightarrow$$

Explicit representation. When the above representations cannot satisfy the accuracy requirement when temporal information is needed, it is always possible to introduce terms to explicitly represent an event or a temporal relation.

Each of the three has its intended uses. The first is generally applicable to all events; the second is useful in dealing with short-term events in perception and action; the last approach can meet the requirement of arbitrary temporal concepts (such as using an external clock or calendar) and temporal relations (such as the ones discussed by Allen (1991)). On the other hand, the last one is the least efficient, since it does not get any special treatment from the temporal inference rules (to be introduced in the following), but depends on the atemporal rules that treat a temporal concept just as other concepts.

In other AI systems, the time-dependency of knowledge is usually represented by adding an explicit argument to indicate the "situation" or "moment" for a statement to be true [McCarthy and Hayes (1969); Elgot-Drapkin and Perlis (1990); Ismail and Shapiro (2000)]. In NAL, such indicators can be used (as a form of *explicit representation*), though they are optional, not required, for the representation of temporal information.

11.3. Temporal Inference

The temporal inference rules in NAL-7 are variants of the rules introduced in the previous layers. Here the basic idea is to process the logical information and the temporal information in the premises in parallel, then combine them in the conclusion, if possible.

Let us see a concrete example. The following is a deduction rule introduced in IL-5,

$$\{(C \wedge M) \Rightarrow P, \ S \Rightarrow M\} \vdash (C \wedge S) \Rightarrow P.$$

This rule can be extended into several valid inferences rules in IL-7, including the following one:

$$\{(M, \ C) \not\Rightarrow P, \ S \not\Rightarrow M\} \vdash (S, \ C) \not\Rightarrow P.$$

Table 11.2. Sample temporal inference rules.

$$\{(M,\ C) \not\Rightarrow P,\ S \not\Rightarrow M\} \vdash (S,\ C) \not\Rightarrow P\ \langle F_{\text{ded}} \rangle$$
$$\{(P,\ C) \not\Rightarrow M,\ (S,\ C) \not\Rightarrow M\} \vdash S \not\Rightarrow P\ \langle F_{\text{abd}} \rangle$$
$$\{(M,\ C) \not\Rightarrow P,\ M \not\Rightarrow S\} \vdash (S,\ C) \not\Rightarrow P\ \langle F_{\text{ind}} \rangle$$

This rule is valid, because its logical aspect is the same as the IL-5 rule, and for the temporal aspect, the conclusion keeps the same temporal order among the events as the premises, that is, S, M, C, P.

This rule is the temporal variant of a *deduction* rule listed in Table 9.7.Using the relations among deduction, abduction, and induction displayed in that table, the temporal variants of the other two rules can be obtained by switching the conclusion of deduction with the premise, respectively, and the corresponding NAL-7 rules are listed in Table 11.2.

Please note that the temporal order of events in the conclusion of a weak rule is not necessarily implied by their order in the premises, given the hypothetical nature of such a rule.

Of course, not all combination of premises can derive valid conclusions in this way. For example, no conclusion can be derived from "$M \not\Rightarrow P$" and "$S \backslash\!\!\Rightarrow M$" by deduction, because the temporal order between S and P cannot be deduced from the premises.

Now we can generalize the previous examples into a procedure, by which the inference rules of NAL-7 are established. This procedure is a special case of the "NAL expansion procedure" proposed in Sec. 9.3:

(1) Each inference rule of IL-6 is extended by using the temporal copulas and connectors to replace the atemporal ones in the premises, then identifying the conclusions where both the logical and the temporal relations can be derived, so as to get valid inference rules for IL-7.

(2) Each inference rule of IL-7 is extended into a strong inference rule in NAL-7, using the same truth-value function as the corresponding rule in NAL-6.

(3) Each strong inference rule of NAL-7 suggests one or more weak inference rules according to the reversibility relationship among the types of inference.

Since the logical aspect and the temporal aspect are processed in parallel, the temporal copulas do not really need to be implemented. Instead, the temporal order among the events in a compound term can be stored separately. Then, beside the ordinary inference as in NAL-6, the temporal orders of the premises are checked, and if the temporal order of events in the conclusion can be decided, a temporal conclusion is formed from the atemporal one. In this way, temporal inference is not carried out by the individual inference rules, but by a "meta-rule" that derives conclusions from the premises and other inference rules. This approach is conceptually equivalent to the above approach, though implemented differently.

In the above discussion, it is assumed that the involved truth-values are eternal themselves. Otherwise, if the premises have tenses, the situation becomes more complicated, though the processing principle remains the same, that is, a valid conclusion should be valid both in the logical aspect and the temporal aspect. For example, if all the tenses are expressed with respect to the current time, then from "$\models (M \:/\!\!\Rightarrow P)$" and "$\models (S \:/\!\!\Rightarrow M)$" the system can derive "$\models (S \:/\!\!\Rightarrow P)$" by deduction, but cannot do so if the premises are "$/\!\!\Rightarrow (M \Rightarrow P)$" and "$\backslash\!\!\Rightarrow (S \:/\!\!\Rightarrow M)$", because the two have different tenses.

When a question comes with a tense, the choice rule will look for a belief with a matching tense as the answer. When the question is about the "current situation" and the system does not have a matching answer, the most recent past situation will be provided.

Explaining the past and predicting the future are among the major features of temporal inference [Vila (1994)]. In NARS, the simplest forms of them are invoked by questions "$(?x \:/\!\!\Rightarrow E)$" and "$(E \:/\!\!\Rightarrow ?x)$", respectively, where E is an event whose cause or effect needs to be found. As in other layers of NAL, multiple paths can be followed when answering such a question, with the candidate answers merged by the *revision* rule and selected by the *choice* rule.

Prediction and retrospective explanation are concrete forms of *causal inference*. In AI, it is widely assumed that there is a domain-independent "causal relation" that can be captured using logic or probability theory [Halpern and Pearl (2005); Goodman *et al.*

(2009)]. In NAL, "causal relation" is not defined as a copula, but treated as an acquired relation, with different definitions and interpretations in different domains and contexts. In NARS, "causation" can be represented by a (relational) concept, with an experience-grounded meaning. Together with the built-in mechanism for temporal inference, various forms of causal inference can be carried out. However, there is no inference rule that is specially designed for such a causation relation.

Closely related to prediction, another group of NAL-7 rules are variants of the following inference rules defined in NAL-5:

$$\{P,\ S\} \vdash S \Rightarrow P \langle F_{\mathrm{ind}} \rangle,$$
$$\{P,\ S\} \vdash S \Leftrightarrow P \langle F_{\mathrm{com}} \rangle.$$

Though these rules do not apply to arbitrary P and S, they are applicable when the two are temporally related events. When P and S are events happening at the same time, the conclusions are "$S \Mapsto P \langle F_{\mathrm{ind}} \rangle$" and "$S \Map&left; P \langle F_{\mathrm{com}} \rangle$"; when S happens right before P, the conclusions are "$S \ /\!\Rightarrow P \langle F_{\mathrm{ind}} \rangle$" and "$S \ /\!\Leftrightarrow P \langle F_{\mathrm{com}} \rangle$". Here the situation is different from the previous temporal meta-rule in that without a temporal relation, these rules will not be applied.

The above *temporal induction rule* behaves like classical (Pavlovian) conditioning. Each time event S is followed by event P, the observation will provide positive evidence for the conclusion "$S \Mapsto P$", which will in turn be used by the system to predict the happening of P when S occurs again. Similarly, an observation of P will be explained by a hypothesized occurrence of S. Traditionally, classical conditioning is modeled in the dynamical system framework, and as a stand-alone process [Sutton and Barto (1990)], which in NARS it is captured as a type of inference, carried out together with the other types of inference.

From the observed succession of events, the system also automatically composes compound events to simplify its description of the experience, just like how it produces other compound terms. Among the competing candidates, only the repeated patterns will grow into stable concepts in the system. Such a process is responsible for the self-organization of perceptual concepts.

Due to the difficulty of deciding the valid time period for a judgment with a temporal truth-value, such a judgment can produce a variant with an eternal truth-value, since the latter can be seen as a summary of truth-values of the judgment in each moment of interest. Each tensed truth-value $\langle f_1, c_1 \rangle$ provides a piece of evidence for the eternal truth-value $\langle f, c \rangle$, in an "induction on moments" — "If it is the case in this moment, it may be always the case". The frequency of the conclusion, f, is the same as that of the premise, f_1, and the confidence of the conclusion, c, is determined by using the confidence of the premise as the amount of evidence, so $c = c_1/(c_1 + k)$. In this way, if the same truth-value is obtained at many moments for a given statement, it gradually becomes eternal, which is how stable beliefs come from temporary observations.

CHAPTER 12

NAL-8: OPERATIONS AND GOALS AS EVENTS

In lower layers, sentences in Narsese are judgments and questions, so the system can only interact with its environment by communicating in Narsese. NAL-8 extends the logic by allowing other forms of interactions, as operations executed by the system to achieve goals.

12.1. Operations as Executable Events

Certain interactions between NARS and its environment can be abstractly represented as a sequence of operations executed by the system.

Definition 12.1. An *operation* of NARS is an event that the system can actualize by executing a corresponding procedure.

While statements are *declarative* knowledge and events are *episodic* knowledge, operations are *procedural* knowledge, in the sense that the meaning of an operation is not only revealed by how it is related to the other terms in Narsese, but also by what it *does* to the system and to the environment.

The notion of "procedural interpretation" is used here as in logic programming [Kowalski (1979)], except that in NARS the meaning of an operator is not fully defined by its procedural implementation. As other terms in the system, the meaning of an operation still depends on its experienced relations with other terms, though part of its meaning is *innate* and bound to the associated procedure, which may not be specified in Narsese, but implemented in the responsible software/hardware.

Definition 12.2. An *atomic operation* is represented as an *operator* (an identifier with the prefix '⇑') followed by an *argument list* (a sequence of terms, though can be empty), like "(⇑op $a_1 \ldots a_n$)". It is treated as statement "(× $self$ $a_1 \ldots a_n$) → ⇑op", where ⇑op belongs to a special type of term that has a *procedural interpretation*, and *self* is a special term referring to the system itself.

For a system implementing NAL-8, its list of atomic operators usually remains constant.

For example, NARS may have a built-in procedure to multiply numbers, which is named by the operator "⇑$multiply$". Equipped with such an operator, the system does not need to learn how to do multiplication via addition, but can simply invoke the procedure using the operator, though it may not be able to fully explain the process in Narsese, nor to know when the operator should be applied — that part of the meaning of the operator is normally acquired from experience.

Therefore operation is system-dependent: an *operation* of a system will be observed as an *event* by other systems, and different systems may have different operations. For example, when John walks, to himself it is just an execution of the operator "⇑$walk$" with certain arguments (such as speed, direction, etc.), while to an observer Mary, it is an event "John walks" with certain properties. The operation and the event have many common properties, though the former has a procedure interpretation and the latter does not, and the latter has one more argument to indicate the actor of the event, which does not need to be mentioned in the former, since it is always the system itself who executes the operations. Like the other statements, both the operation and the event can be further specialized (e.g., to "hike") or generalized (e.g., to "move") using the *inheritance* statements. They can also be related to other operations and events by *similarity* statements.

An operation usually distinguishes *input* and *output* among its arguments. When an operation is described abstractly, its input arguments are typically independent variables, and its output are dependent variables (with the inputs in their dependency lists).

Such an operation corresponds to a function that maps certain input values into output values. When an operation is executed, its input arguments are instantiated by some given values, and its output arguments will be instantiated at the end of the execution by the results. Optionally, an operation may bring the system some Narsese sentences as feedback.

Since the main purpose of operations is for the system to achieve various consequences, their *meaning*, or the system's beliefs about them, usually include some *implication* or *equivalence* statements (temporal or not), which indicate the conditions, causes, and effects of an operation. Typically, such a "procedural belief" takes the following form:

$$(condition, operation) \not\Rightarrow consequence,$$

where *condition* and *consequence* are both events. This form is common, because it is a simplified version of

$$condition \not\Rightarrow (operation \not\Rightarrow consequence)$$

so the *condition* is not really applied on the *operation*, but on its relation with the *consequence*. In complicated situations, the *condition* is typically a conjunction formed by simpler statements as components, and as a result, the *implication* statement looks like a *Horn clause*, which plays a central role in logic programming and theorem proving [Russell and Norvig (2010)].

For an operation to be useful for the system, it needs to have some consequence that is eventually *observable*, so as to provide feedback for the operation in the system's experience. However, the feedback may not be immediately available, and nor is it necessarily in the form of a reward signal, as assumed in reinforcement learning [Sutton and Barto (1998); Hutter (2005)].

As other beliefs, the truth-value of a procedural belief indicates the evidential support for the stated relationship. The system usually has multiple such beliefs for each operation, with different conditions and conclusions included, and each with its truth-value. Under AIKR, in NAL the conditions and consequences of an operation are never exhaustively specified in each belief about it. Instead, each belief only records its (limited) experience on the relation between the operation and the *stated* events.

Such a "statement-based" specification is very different from the "state-based" specification of operations in traditional AI systems, such as General Problem Solver [Newell and Simon (1963)] and various Markov Models studied in reinforcement learning [Sutton and Barto (1998)]. In such a system, a "state" is a *complete* description of (all the the relevant parts of) the environment, and the meaning of an operation is effectively defined as a (deterministic or probabilistic) state transformation function. Though in NARS it is still meaningful to talk about the "state" of the environment or the system, such a complete description is never actually used in the design or the operating of NARS. One of the consequence is that the Frame Problem [McCarthy and Hayes (1969)] does not appear in NARS, since there is no requirement for the consequence of an operation to be fully specified [Xu and Wang (2012)].

As a special type of compound statement, *compound operations* work in NARS like "programs", which organize primitive operations into control structures. The basic compound operations include:

Sequential operation, formed by the *sequential conjunction* connector on operations;

Parallel operation, formed by the *parallel conjunction* connector on operations;

Conditional operation, formed by the *implication* copula from an event and an operation.

Using these control structures repeatedly or recursively, more complicated operations can be specified, such as various types of loop.

Furthermore, the *equivalence* copula allows a compound operation to be identified by an atomic operation, so as to reduce the syntactic complexity of the description. It is just like in a programming language (such as C), where a "function header" (which specifies the abstract relation among the input/output arguments) is associated with a "function body" (which specifies the concrete procedure to get the output from the input). Here a "function" roughly corresponds to a compound operation in Narsese.

These control structures give Narsese the capability of a general-purpose programming language (with the atomic operations as *instructions* and compound operations as *programs*). In this aspect, Narsese, when used in IL-8, is similar to a logic programming language, such as Prolog, except that it is not based on a predicate logic, and nor does it always use the same program to solve a given problem. Instead, the problem-solving process is usually formed by multiple programs at run-time in a context-sensitive manner, as explained in Chapter 5.

12.2.   Goals as Desired Events

At any moment in the system, there usually are many operations whose conditions have been satisfied. Which one is actually executed mainly depends on the system's goals.

Definition 12.3. A *goal* is a sentence containing an event that the system wants to realize.

Here "to realize a goal" actually means "to make the statement in it as close to absolute truth as possible by executing certain operations", since the confidence value of the statement cannot reach its upper bound 1.

Like an operation, in NARS a goal is specified by a "statement", not by a "state". Consequently, a goal is usually specified without revealing all of its presumptions and implications.

Normally the system has multiple goals, and they often conflict with one another (in the sense that the realizing of a goal makes another one harder to be realized), as well as compete for the system's resources (which are insufficient to realize all of them in time). For the system to deal with these conflicts and competitions, a numerical measurement of "desire" is defined on events.

Definition 12.4. The *desire-value* of an event measures the extent to which a desired state is implied by the event, that is, the desire-value of event S is the truth-value of the implication statement "$S \Rightarrow D$", where D is a virtual statement describing the desired state of the system, a summary of its current goals.

Here D is "virtual" in the sense that it is not a concrete statement in Narsese, but a conceptual one in the meta-language, used in the design of the system. By it, the desire-values of the events involved are reduced to truth-values, whose calculations have been specified by the truth-value functions. Here the situation is like in NAL-5 where a "virtual evidence" is introduced so that the truth-value of a statement can be taken as the truth-value for the statement to be implied by the available evidence. In both situations, an evaluation of a statement is interpreted as an evaluation of its relation with a virtual statement, which is coherent with the semantic principle of NARS that the meaning of an item is revealed by its relations with other items, rather than being an intrinsic property of the item itself.[1]

In NARS, a desire-value is not only attached to every *goal*, but to every *event*, because an event may become a goal in the future (if it is not already a goal). This value shows the system's current *attitude* toward the situations in which the statement is true. In the input sentences of the system, the desire-value of a goal can be explicitly expressed by the user or other system providing the goal as a task to NARS, otherwise a default value is assumed.

In this way, operations and goals are integrated into the *term logic* framework. In summary, there is the following hierarchy among terms in NARS:

- a *term* is an internal identifier of the system for a concept;
- a *statement* is a special type of term that has a truth-value;
- an *event* is a special type of statement that has temporal attributes and a desire-value;

---

[1]Intuitively speaking, the truth-value of a statement evaluates its relation with its "source" (where it came from), and the desire-value its "destination" (where it should lead to).

Table 12.1. The new grammar rules of NAL-8.

⟨*sentence*⟩ ::= ⟨*judgment*⟩ | ⟨*goal*⟩ | ⟨*question*⟩
⟨*judgment*⟩ ::= [⟨*tense*⟩]⟨*statement*⟩. ⟨*truth-value*⟩
⟨*goal*⟩ ::= ⟨*statement*⟩! ⟨*desire-value*⟩
⟨*question*⟩ ::= [⟨*tense*⟩]⟨*statement*⟩?
|⟨*statement*⟩¿
⟨*statement*⟩ ::= (⟨*operator*⟩ ⟨*term*⟩*)
⟨*operator*⟩ ::= ⇑⟨*word*⟩

- an *operation* is a special type of event that is realizable by the system;
- a *goal* is a special type of event to be realized by the system.

Now a *question* in NAL can be either about the truth-value of a statement, or about its desire-value (if it is an event).

To separate different types of sentence more clearly, in NAL-8 a punctuation mark is added at the end of each sentence of Narsese: '.' for judgment, '!' for goal, '?' for question on truth-value, and '¿' for *quest*, that is, question on desire-value. The new grammar rules introduced in NAL-8 are summarized in Table 12.1.

A desire-value looks the same as a truth-value, though it is interpreted differently, as explained above. A goal does not have a tense attached, because it is assumed to be realized as soon as possible. If a goal should be achieved in a specific future time, then it should be expressed in Narsese as a conditional statement with the timing requirement as the condition.

12.3. Practical Reasoning

Reasoning on actions is traditionally refereed to as "practical reasoning", which is considered as different from conventional or "theoretical" reasoning, because it is not about "what to believe", but "what to do" [Bratman *et al.* (1988)]. In NAL-8, since operations and goals are events, the previously defined inference rules on events work on them, too, so the system uniformly processes declarative, episodic, and procedural knowledge.

Inference on knowledge about an operation can derive new beliefs about its preconditions and postconditions. For example, the compositional *induction rule* introduced in Table 9.5 can be applied here to carry out classical conditioning with operations [Medin and Ross (1992)]. As mentioned in the previous chapter, if events S_1 and S_2 are observed in succession, "$S_1 /\Rightarrow S_2$" will be derived, and repeated observations of this relation will increase the confidence of the conclusion. After that, any observation of S_1 will trigger an expectation of S_2, as a statement with future tense, "$/\Rightarrow S_2$". When the expectation is confirmed by a following observation, the habit is further strengthened, otherwise (if S_2 does not occur as expected) the habit is weakened (i.e., its *frequency* is decreased by the revision rule). When S_1 is an operation, this process reveals one of its consequences; When S_2 is the form of "*oper* $/\Rightarrow$ *cons*", this process reveals one of its conditions. This is one way for the system's procedural knowledge to be created.

Compound operations are selectively formed from useful combinations of operations, and become "skills" or "routines" of the system that can be executed efficiently, without step-by-step deliberation. For example, if the system has the following beliefs (truth-values omitted):

- $(cond_1, oper_1) /\Rightarrow cons_1$
- $(cond_2, oper_2) /\Rightarrow cons_2$
- $cond_2 \Leftrightarrow cons_1$

then from them the system can derive "$(cond_1, oper_1, oper_2) /\Rightarrow cons_2$", which is effectively a belief about compound operation $(oper_1, oper_2)$ as a whole. Obviously, this step can be repeated to build more complicated operations.

To recursively build "compound" or "macro" operations from simpler ones is an idea that has been used in various forms in AI study. What makes the NAL approach different are:

- The system does not search a program space for all possible combinations [Kaiser (2007)], nor tries random combinations [Koza (1992)]. Instead, it selectively forms compound operations in a data-driven manner. In the above example, $(oper_1, oper_2)$ is built, because its two components are both related to a common term, and the related beliefs happen to be remembered at the time.

- The system does not learn the effect of a compound operation exclusively from rewards and punishments after its execution, as in reinforcement learning [Sutton and Barto (1998)], but uses its reasoning ability to estimate what may happen first, and only executes the promising ones.

- The system can acquire knowledge about (atomic or compound) operations via multiple types of reasoning, and can handle various types of uncertainty in the process. On the contrary, inductive logic programming learns by one type of induction, and does not allow any counter-evidence [Muggleton (1991)].

Inference on knowledge about a goal also derives new beliefs about how it can be realized, as well as reveals its by-products and side-effects. Especially, for a given goal G, the inference engine can find a *plan*, which is a compound operation P that achieves the goal (i.e., "$P \Rightarrow G$" has a high expectation value). By executing the plan, and adjusting it when necessary, the internal or external environment is changed to turn the goal into reality. When repeatedly appearing compound operations are memorized, repeated planning is avoided, and the system learns a new skill. When Narsese is taken as a programming language with atomic operations as instructions, what NARS does in the process can be considered as "self-programming" that produces executable plans, or "programs", for future usage.[2]

When a goal is an operation, it can be directly realized by executing the operator on the arguments. If a goal cannot be directly satisfied in this way, by backward inference it can increase the desire-values of certain events. For a given event, the desire-values coming from different goals are merged together using the revision rule, just like how truth-values from different evidential bases are

---

[2]Please note that NARS does not self-program by modifying its own source code, which remains unchanged at the meta-level, while all the changes happen in the object-level, where "programs" are in Narsese.

merged. Consequently, the desire-value of an event usually depends on multiple existing goals that have be taken into account, rather than a single one.

The *decision-making* rule will turn candidate goals with high desire-value and plausibility into goals being actually pursued by the system. They are "derived goals", but not "subgoals", since a derived goal is not treated as a means for a single goal.

Definition 12.5. The plausibility of candidate goal G is the truth-value of "# $/\!\!\Rightarrow G$" where the variable '#' stands for an anonymous operation.

Intuitively speaking, the plausibility of G is the truth-value of "There is a way to achieve G".

As mentioned previously, the system's procedural knowledge often has the form of "(*condition, operation*) $/\!\!\Rightarrow$ *consequence*". From such a piece of knowledge and a belief about the *condition*, the truth-value of statement "*operation* $/\!\!\Rightarrow$ *consequence*" can be decided, which lead to a version of "# $/\!\!\Rightarrow$ *consequence*" after a variable introduction. When there are multiple versions of this statement, the choice rule will pick one that has high *expectation* and low *complexity* to provide the plausibility for the event *consequence*.

Decision-making Rule. A candidate goal is actually pursued by the system, when its *expected desirability* d and *expected plausibility* p satisfy condition $p(d - 0.5) > t$, where t is a positive constant.

When 0.5 is added to both sides of the formula, the above "decision-making function" has the same form as the *expectation* function defined in Table 4.2, with *desirability* as *frequency* and *plausibility* as *confidence*. Here the "expected desirability" and "expected plausibility" are the output of the expectation function with the desirability and the plausibility of the goal as input, respectively. The threshold t is another "personality parameter" of the system, and measures the system's cautiousness.

The above decision-making rule can be compared with the *Maximum Expected Utility Principle* of decision theory, which asks the system to always choose the alternative that has the largest expected utility value [Savage (1954)]. The NAL decision-making rule is built according to the same intuition, where the *expected desirability* is similar to the *utility* of an event, while the *expected plausibility* is similar to its *probability*. Their differences are that:

- In NAL, it is not assumed that the system knows all the possible alternatives, so can select one of them after comparing with the others. On the contrary, in each decision NAL focuses on whether to realize one event, so the only alternative is not to realize it.
- In NAL, the event's desire-value and plausibility value are usually derived by the system itself, rather than given as constants. Therefore, to make a decision demands more than merely calculating the above function, but often include explorations to decide the desire-value and plausibility values involved. Furthermore, these values can be changed by new experience and further consideration. Therefore, even on the same topic, the decision may change from situation to situation.

If a goal G has been decided to be actively pursued, the system will first check if the desired event has already realized. If there is a matching judgment, the desire-value of the goal will be reduced accordingly, unless something needs to be done to keep the goal satisfied.

Decision making is where the *multi-valued* beliefs and tasks are turned into the *binary* decisions. Though the system usually believes or desires a statement to a degree, it normally cannot execute an operation "to a degree" — it is a matter of "to do or not to do". However, this demand of binary decision cannot be used to justify the usage of binary beliefs and tasks. Due to AIKR, it is preferred to postpone the "binarization" moment of the thinking process to the last moment, that is, right to the point of deciding to actually pursue a goal, which includes the execution of an operation as a special case.

NARS differs from the Belief-Desire-Intention (BDI) model of agents [Rao and Georgeff (1995)] in several key aspects, including its abilities in learning and adaptation, reasoning under uncertainty, real-time decision making, and dealing with the inconsistency among beliefs and goals. All these differences can be traced back to AIKR.

12.4. Sensorimotor Interface

In NAL-8, an atomic operation is defined as a special form of statement such that when it becomes a goal, its satisfaction is achieved by the execution of the operation, rather than through an inference process. Depending on who is responsible for the execution, the operations can be divided into two types: the ones that are executed *outside* NARS and the ones *inside* NARS.

If an operation is executed outside NARS, it is a black-box to the system, and the system can use it as a "tool" that has certain consequences when executed under certain conditions. Such an operator in NARS is similar to a "built-in predicate" in Prolog, except that NARS is not designed with a fixed set of operators, but allow them to be used in a "plug-and-play" manner.

From the viewpoint of NARS, each tool is defined by a set of executable operations in the format of $(\Uparrow op\ a_1 \dots a_n)$, with all the arguments represented as terms in NARS. The system's beliefs about the tool mainly take the form of procedural knowledge, as specified earlier. The feedback of the operations becomes input in the system's experience in two forms:

- **Immediate feedback** of an operation is represented by output values among the arguments, which will be reported to the system right after the execution. It is mainly for sensors. For example, the execution of a *touch* operation will immediately report back the sensory data.
- **Delayed feedback** of an operation is represented by Narsese sentences, which come into the system's experience like other input sentences. They are not explicitly associated with the operation, though the system can learn their causal relations with the responsible operations from experience. It is mainly for actuators. For example, the action of throwing a ball is followed by observations of the ball moving in the air, and movement of the ball is related to the parameters of the throwing operation.

As a reasoning system, NARS communicates with its environments in Narsese, a formal language. In addition to it, NAL-8 introduces an interface between NARS and external devices and programs, each of which can carry out certain operations for NARS. Conceptually speaking, such a device or program can be considered as an "organ" that provides *sensorimotor* function for NARS to directly interact with the outside world.

In NARS, both *sensors* and *actuators* are represented by operations, so sensation and perception are treated as active, rather than passive, processes, as suggested by Noë (2004). Since *operation* is a special type of *term* in Narsese, the system's sensorimotor experience is also described in Narsese, though the vocabulary corresponding to the operators have procedural meaning, which cannot be fully described in the language. Even so, their presence in Narsese allows the concepts of the system to be grounded on these sensorimotor ingredients.

NARS makes no requirements on the granularity or level of description of the terms that go through the sensorimotor interface, and it even allows a device to communicate with it at several levels of description. For example, if NARS is equipped with a visual device, then a term on the interface may correspond to a pixel, a line segment, a surface, and all the way up to a recognized object.

In this way, the meaning of terms in the system becomes richer, since some of them will have "procedural meanings" beyond what can be expressed in Narsese. However, it does not change the semantic principle of NARS. Even when a term corresponds to a mental image, its meaning is not fully determined by the image, but also by its relations with other terms. The mental image only provides partial meaning to the term, like all the other relations of the term. This is the solution of NARS to the "symbol grounding" problem [Harnad (1990)].

This treatment of sensation and perception is a natural extension of the experience-grounded semantics. Unlike in mainstream AI, where perception is taken to be the process through which a "world model" is built within the system, and there is an objective standard for the accuracy of the model [Russell and Norvig (2010)], in NARS perception is taken to be the process for the system to organize its physical (and chemical, etc.) experience, and "objects and events in the world" are nothing but invariant patterns in the experience that are useful in achieving the system's goals. It is further conjectured that "the logic of perception" is basically the same as "the logic of cognition", so that NAL can handle sensorimotor concepts and abstract concepts similarly.

NARS, as a general-purpose "mind", can be embedded within, or connected with, various "bodies", that is, host systems or devices with different sensorimotor mechanisms, either in a physical world or in a virtual world (which also exists in a physical world, though is described abstractly). We will call such a system "NARS+" (NARS plus host/device). For a given host, a special interface module needs to be built, which registers all the relevant commands in the host that are exposed to the control of NARS, so that whenever NARS decides to execute an operation, the corresponding command is sent to the responsible actuator in the host system.

Similarly, the sensors in the host are also formalized as operators, invoked by NARS, and the result of the operations will be received as new experience (input knowledge) to the system. Driven by goals, the system's observation is not a merely passive process which accepts whatever signals coming from the environment, but an active process directed by the system's goal-achieving activities.

NARS leaves the low-level sensorimotor management to host systems or peripheral devices, while still contribute to the perception and action processes, by allowing operations to be defined on multiple levels of abstraction (with different granularity and scope), as well as using anticipations and goals to selectively process incoming information. With a sensorimotor mechanism connected to NARS, the effect of an operation can be anticipated, checked, and confirmed, and the feedback will provide information for various types of learning.

Though a NARS+ as a whole can have experience with multiple modalities, the NARS part of the system remains amodal in design. In this way, the *content* of the system's beliefs and concepts will depend on its "body" (which decides what experience is possible), though the inference process does not (which decide how the experience is processed). NARS is "general-purpose" in the sense that the system allows any software and hardware to be plugged in, though after equipped with a certain body, its experience, and therefore beliefs and concepts, all depend on its body.

One implication of this design is that since a NARS+ normally has a body different from a human body, its beliefs and concepts will not be identical to that of a human being. However, its beliefs and concepts are related to the system's experience in the same way as in a human being. It is in this sense that AI is comparable with human intelligence — in the general principles and functions, rather than in the particular thoughts, behaviors, and capabilities [Wang (2008, 2009c)].

CHAPTER 13

NAL-9: SELF-MONITORING AND
SELF-CONTROL

In a sense, NAL-9 is optional to NAL, since it does not add any new grammar rule or inference rule into the logic, nor does it modify the semantic notions introduced previously. What is added at this layer is a group of operations to be implemented within NARS. These operations enable the system to monitor and control its own internal activities.

13.1. Mental Operations

In NAL-8, an interface is provided for NAL to achieve a goal by invoking an operation registered in the system, though the implementation and execution are not the responsibility of NARS, but that of some other system or device. However, there is nothing to prevent NARS from serving this role itself.

As described in Chapter 5, the working process of NARS consists of a routine of predetermined actions. If some of these actions are represented in Narsese and registered in NARS as *operations*, then the result will be another sensorimotor mechanism, though it is not interacting with the *external* environment of the system, but the *internal* environment of the system. It means a NARS equipped with sensors and actuators that perceive and modify the internal state of the system. These sensors and actuators are invoked by commands issued in NARS, and their results are fedback to the system, represented as Narsese sentences.

Consequently, such a NARS has both an "external experience" and an "internal experience", and the two are represented and processed in similar ways. Like its knowledge of the world, the system's knowledge of itself is also a summary of its experience, and restricted by its sensorimotor and information-processing capability. However, there is an important difference: while its external experience must go through a complicated sensation/perception process to reach the conceptual level, its internal experience is often directly expressed at the conceptual level, so can be processed according to NAL. To stress this difference, the internally implemented operations in NARS are referred to as "mental operations".

Designed as a general-purpose system, NARS does not have a predetermined set of external sensors and actuators, but allows arbitrary hardware and software to be "plugged in" to get various forms of NARS+. On the contrary, the basic mental operations remain the same in all NARS+, so it makes sense to define them as a layer of the logic.

For a given NARS+ (NARS plus sensors and actuators), the sensors and actuators that work on the system itself can be roughly divided into two types, those that are mostly about its "body" and those that are mostly about its "mind". When NARS is implemented in a robot, there will be various sensors to monitor its energy level, status of organs, etc., which do not change the nature of the reasoning/learning process, but provide goals to be achieved and means to achieve them. Though these sensors work on the body of the system, they are not that different from the sensors that work on the outside environment, in that they all need a sensation–perception process to categorize physical signals into internal concepts.

On the other hand, there are also sensors on the reasoning/learning process, which express information about the state of the system in a format (Narsese sentences) that can be directly processed by the system. These sensors are different from the "physical" ones, since they directly produce conceptual-level results, without a perceivable categorization process. Similarly, there are "physical" actuators and "mental" actuators. Though the latter are inevitably carried out by physical processes, they are known to the system only at an abstract level, without their physical details. They are the mental operations we are discussing.

Though the notion of "mental operation" has a long history in psychology, and played a central role in Piaget's theory on intelligence [Piaget (1963)], self-monitoring and self-control only began to get attention in AI research [Anderson and Oates (2007); Cox (2005)], and the results are highly system-specific [Marshall (2006); Shapiro and Bona (2010)]. In this book, I only describe the related ideas accepted in NAL and NARS, and leave the general discussion and comparison to future publications.

Though in principle every internal activity of NARS, no matter at which level and scope it is described, could be treated as an operation in NAL, to actually do that is not a good idea. Not only that it would make the self-monitoring and self-control process too complicated for the system to handle, it is also dangerous — self-modification is not always beneficial to the system, and under AIKR, there is no way for NARS to only carry out the beneficial ones, as assumed in some other models [Schmidhuber (2007)]. Like the situation in the human mind, an intelligent system should have some *voluntary* processes within itself, while leaving most of the jobs to the *autonomic* processes, which do not require deliberation.

Consequently, a major design issue in NAL-9 is to choose the mental operations, that is, to identify certain internal activities, and express them in the required format, so that they can be reasoned on, and invoked by, the inference mechanism. Given this context, what activity should be considered as a "mental operation" in NARS is not decided in the same way as in psychology.

In the current design, the operations are chosen in two main ways. First, the global inference and control routine (introduced in Chapter 5) is divided into major steps, each has a relatively clear and natural function to be treated as an operation. Second, meaningful deviations of the normal routine are added as operations to satisfy special needs. Either way, the obtained mental operations usually resemble certain mental actions in the human mind, though not necessarily in all details.

Table 13.1. Mental operations.

Operator	Function
observe	get an active task from the task buffer
expect	check the input for a given statement
know	find the truth-value of a statement
assess	find the desire-value of a statement
believe	turn a statement into a task containing a judgment
want	turn a statement into a task containing a goal
wonder	turn a statement into a task containing a question
remember	turn a statement into a belief
consider	do inference on a concept
remind	activate a concept
doubt	decrease the confidence of a belief
hesitate	decrease the confidence of a goal
assume	temporarily take a statement as a belief
compile	create a simple internal name for a compound term
wait	pause the system's action for a given number of cycles
repeat	execute an action repeatedly under a given condition
tell	produce an outgoing task containing a judgment
demand	produce an outgoing task containing a goal
ask	produce an outgoing task containing a question
check	produce an outgoing task containing a query
register	let a term be used as an operator

Table 13.1 contains some mental operations that are under consideration. This list is by no means final or complete, since the research on this layer is still going on. Furthermore, each operation does not attempt to capture the full meaning of the English word that names it. Even so, we can still see that many remaining issues in the lower layers can be resolved with certain mental operations in the list:

- The revision rule only increases the confidence of a judgment with new evidence. To disqualify an existing conclusion, a **doubt** operation is needed.
- All direct observations only provide affirmative conclusions. To get denials, it is necessary to compare an observation with an expectation expressed using an **expect** operation — otherwise how can you see "no book" on a table?

- A future goal can be represented as an implication statement with a **want** operation in the consequent.
- As explained previously, the "closed-world assumption" is accepted in IL, but not in NAL. However, there are special situations where "I don't know" does imply "it is not true" with a high confidence level. For example, "Since I don't know I have a brother, I must not" [Elgot-Drapkin and Perlis (1990)]. Such a belief can be established using a **believe** operation, according to the return value of a **know** operation.

Beside the above "reasoning-related" operations, the system can also be equipped with "calculation-related" operations, such as:

- **count** the number of terms in an extensional or intensional set,
- **compare** two numbers to decide their relative rank,
- **calculate** the value of a simple arithmetic expression.

To guarantee that all atomic operations will be finished within a (short) constant time, there are restrictions on the argument range of the above mental operations. More complicated calculations must be carried out by compound operations or external devices under the command of NARS.

The implementation of all these operations is straightforward. Since each mental operation only takes a small constant amount of time to finish, to embed them in Narsese statements does not violate the restriction of AIKR. The meaning of, and the knowledge about, the operations will be mainly acquired from experience, like the other operations, though for efficiency considerations, it will be convenient to "implant" some innate knowledge into the system about their preconditions and consequences.

Before such a self-control mechanism is implemented, the inference control in NARS is purely *autonomic*. In each inference step, the task to be carried out and the belief to be used are selected according to several factors to achieve the highest overall efficiency, as described briefly in Chapter 5, as well as in Wang (2006b). This process is governed by algorithms that are coded in the programming language of the system, and is beyond the reach of the inference rules. With the above self-control mechanism, however, the system can think about its own thinking process, and adjust it as allowed by its internal sensorimotor mechanism. This introduces *voluntary* control (according to knowledge represented declaratively in Narsese) that *supplement* (though does not *replace*) the autonomic control mechanism.

13.2.   Feeling and Emotion

So far, the system's mental operations are discussed mainly with respect to concrete goals. Beside that it is also important for an intelligent system to appraise its overall status, and to take prompt pervasive responses accordingly. This leads to the issue of feeling and emotion.

For NARS, a desire-value of a situation or status *for the system as a whole* can be measured by a global variable *happy*, which can be considered as a degree of happiness or pleasure. It is directly related to the virtual statement D, according to which the desire-values of statements are defined. This variable takes values in $[0, 1]$, with 0 for "unhappy", 0.5 for "neutral", and 1 for "happy", though usually the two extreme values do not occur.

The degree of happiness is adjusted each time a goal is compared with the corresponding belief on the reality. When a goal is (relatively) satisfied, the system becomes happier; when the reality is different from what a goal requires, the system becomes less happy. Of course, the amount of adjustment also depends on the priority of the goal and the difference between the desire and the reality, and the effects of adjustments may last for different durations.

The current value of *happy* can be perceived by a **feel** operation, so as to be expressed as a Narsese judgment, added into the system's beliefs about itself. In this way, the system has a basic *feeling*, which can be positive or negative, reflecting the system's overall evaluation of the current situation.

More complicated feelings can be obtained by further distinguishing this basic feeling into types, along various dimensions: such as self/other, past/present/future, event/entity, cause/effect, and so on.

For example, "joy" and "sorrow" are usually related to the feelings about past *positive* and *negative* events, respectively; "fear" and "anger" are both related to opponent attacks, and the difference is that the former indicates a *more powerful* opponent, and the latter a *less powerful* one. These *compound feelings* can be represented in NARS by compound terms, with the basic feeling and other terms as components. In a complicated situation, different feelings can be mixed — the system may feel "joy" and "sorrow" at the same moment, for different reasons.

Beside the overall situation, feelings can be associated with objects and things. To do that, the definition domain of desire-value is extended from events (as in NAL-8) to all terms, to summarize the desire-values of the related events whenever that term is under consideration. Consequently, if a term usually associates with pleasant events for the system, it will be "liked" by the system; if a term usually associates with unpleasant events, it will be "disliked". Obviously, the system will have "neutral feeling" about some terms, and "mixed feeling" about some others. It will be more natural to say that the system has different feelings for "objects and things", though accurately speaking, the feelings are about the *concepts* representing the "objects and things".

In this way, feeling can be intergated into the experience-grounded semantics of NARS — similar to the "meaning" of a term, the "feeling" associated with a term is also determined by the system's relevant experience about it.

In addition to sensing how much are the goals satisfied, the system may also have self-monitoring sensors on other aspects and processes. For example, for a robot, there can be sensors on the well-being of various parts that can produce feelings that resemble "pain", as well as sensors on the battery or other energy storage that can produce feelings that resemble "hungry". Unlike the mental operations that are mostly universal among NARS implementations, these *somatic feelings* may change from NARS+ to NARS+, and more or less similar to the external sensorimotor mechanism discussed in the previous chapter, so they will not be considered as part of NARS.

The primary function of different feelings is to provoke *emotions*, which are system states that have implications in the behaviors:

- Different emotional states correspond to different (computational) resource allocation policies. For example, when the system is excited, bored, or tired, its attention distribution is very different.
- Changes in emotions lead to adjustments in certain system parameters, such as the threshold for a decision to be made.
- Different emotions prepare the system for different actions, such as "anger" for attack and "fear" for flee.
- By showing different emotions, an intelligent system can influence the behaviors of other systems in various ways, so as to improve cooperation efficiency.

As other concepts in NARS, whether the system is in a certain emotional state is a matter of degree, and different emotions can mix.

Traditionally, "rationality" and "emotion" were widely perceived as opposite of each other, and emotion as a major irrational factor in human thinking, so it is neither necessary nor desired in AI systems. However, in recent years, more and more researchers in AI and cognitive science began to challenge this dogma, and argued for the necessity of emotion in intelligence and cognition [Picard (1997); Fellous and Arbib (2005)]. For example, Ganjoo (2005) wrote that "Behavioral responses to environmental stimuli can be categorized as reflexive, emotional or cognitive. Reflexive responses do not require much analysis or brain power, but are made quickly. Cognitive responses require the most amount of brain power, but are made relatively slowly. Emotional responses fall somewhere between these two in response time and the required brain power."

So "rationality" and "emotion" do not have to be taken as opposite. As argued in Wang (2011), there are different models of rationality, each prescribes "the right thing to do", but under different assumptions. Traditional models of rationality, such as classical logic and probability theory, make highly idealized assumptions about the environment and the system. Especially, they assume the system has consistent goals and sufficient resources to achieve the goals. Since a major effect of emotion is for the system to focus on certain goals and beliefs while ignoring the others, it is considered as unnecessary and undesired in the traditional models.

On the contrary, under AIKR the system does not have the knowledge and resources to behave "rationally" in the traditional sense. However, as has been repeatedly argued in this book, it is still possible to be rational under AIKR, though with a different criterion, which is relative to available knowledge and resources. Now we can add that the advanced form of this *relative rationality* includes emotions in it as a necessary aspect. With insufficient knowledge and resources, the system needs the ability of taking actions based on rough evaluations of the overall situation, as well as giving unequal attention to different objects and events.

It does not mean that emotion is always a good thing in thinking. Though overall it is absolutely necessary for an adaptive system working in a complicated environment, in each individual situations its contributions are different. Especially, for a certain task the system's knowledge and resources may be relatively sufficient, so in that case, the system should take its time to carefully consider what is the desired result and what is the best way to get there, rather than be driven by its emotions to rush responses. That means the system should learn to control its own emotions, by properly carrying out certain operations.

Of course, "systems with emotion" is different from "systems with *human* emotion". Since computers are electronic, not biological, they are not going to have the biochemical and physiological aspects of human emotion. Nevertheless, there will be analogous processes and phenomena that deserve the name of "emotion", since it plays the same functions for the AI systems as emotions for human beings.

13.3.   Consciousness

When a thinking system thinks about its own thinking process, many interesting and challenging issues will inevitably appear [Hofstadter (1979)].

Equipped with external and internal sensorimotor mechanisms, NARS (at the layer of NAL-9) can interact with its external and internal environment. Part of the interactions are expressed as Narsese sentences that come into and out of the system, as the system's *experience* and *behavior*, respectively.

However, not all the experience and behavior can be considered as *conscious*. Consciousness is a notion that has many different interpretations, and to survey the theories is beyond the scope of this book. Here we use the following working definition: NARS is *conscious* of a concept when and only when in a working cycle (as defined in Chapter 5) the concept is selected and processed. Therefore, in any period when the system is running, its train of thought can be partially described as a "stream of consciousness" [James (1890)], in the form of a sequence of terms. This stream can be recorded by, and accessible to, the system itself within a certain period of time. In this sense, the system knows what it is thinking about, and can reason and communicate about it.

This stream of consciousness provides a window for the system to its own thinking process. However, this self-awareness is *limited*, in the following senses:

Subjective: Since some of the sensors are about the internal situation of the system, no other system can get the experience but the system itself. Even the external sensors may produce something unique, due to the system's idiosyncratic position and perspective, so systems in the same environment may not have an identical experience, but similar ones.

Discontinuous: Since the system is working on multiple tasks at the same time, the attention focus of the system will move from concept to concept, and the adjacent concepts in the "stream of consciousness" are not necessarily related to each other in meaning.

Incomplete: Under AIKR, the system's self-knowledge is highly restricted, and at any moment most of its beliefs, goals, feelings, etc. remain unconscious. However, certain parts of the unconscious thought can become conscious, and *vice versa*. The conscious part of NARS is just the part that is expressed in Narsese and is getting enough attention, though it often contains information about the unconscious part.

Because of the above features, in any nontrivial situation, where will the system's stream of consciousness flow is practically unpredictable by an observer or the system itself, even though the system is deterministic by design, without any "purely random" factor.

The system has a concept of *self*, which, like all other concepts in NARS, consists of empirical conceptual relations, such as "who I am", "what I can do", "what I want", and so on. This concept starts with the operations of the system (as mentioned in the previous chapter, every operation implicitly has *self* as an argument), and evolves as the system "lives its life", rather than remaining constant or being fully specified by the designer.

Such a system will surely have various forms of self-reference as discussed by Hofstadter (1979), though it will not be bothered too much by paradoxical statements like "This sentence is false", since it does not have to assign a binary truth-value to each statement.

The existence of self-consciousness plays important roles in the system's cognition and intelligence. For complicated problems, the system needs the ability of introspection, such as to tell itself that "I have spent enough time on that approach, so now is the time to try something different" or to ask itself "Where did that assumption made by me come from?" Systems with or without subjective experience will behave differently, and there is no reason to believe the possibility of having a "zombie" that has no consciousness but shows no difference in behavior [Chalmers (1996)].

After NAL-9 is fully implemented, the system will have two disjoint sets of operations, "mental operations" and "physical operations", that work on its internal and external environments, respectively. Since the operations cannot replace each other, the system will develop two vocabularies for its internal and external experiences, with a "mind-body gap" in between — as far as the system can tell, its mental operations (described using the internal vocabulary) cause physical effects (described using the external vocabulary). My theory accepts this "dualism in description", and does not attempt to reduce one description into another (under the assumption that the latter is "real" or "more accurate", while the former is "approximate" or "illusory"). However, this dualism is not the product of two separate underlying processes (either parallel or interactive), but a single existence and process, which is described in two languages that are not fully reducible to each other.

For the same reason, to consider NARS as having "free will" does not contradict with the claim that it has a "deterministic" design. For an omniscient and omnipotent observer, the behavior of NARS is accurately predictable from its initial design and its lifelong experience; however, since all concrete systems have limited knowledge and experience, NARS (or any similar system) is practically unpredictable, except in trivial situations. Especially, to the system itself, it is its own choices, or free will, that causes most of its behaviors. This is indeed what the system experiences, so cannot be called "an illusion". It is impossible to describe the system "as it is", rather it has to be done from the view point of a certain observer, and different view points lead to different conclusions.

CHAPTER 14

SUMMARY AND BEYOND

The previous chapters have provided a comprehensive description of NAL, with its grammar, semantics, and inference rules. At the current time, a prototype of NARS has implemented all the rules of NAL-1 to NAL-6, plus some rules of NAL-7 to NAL-9, with a highly simplified memory structure and control mechanism. The source code and demonstrating examples can be found at my website.[1] Many of the properties of the system described previously have been verified in the implementation.

In this last chapter, the logic system is discussed as a whole.

14.1. The Nature of NAL

NAL is not designed by following the common practice in the current field of logic, and it is so different from the other logic systems that some researchers have expressed their disagreement on considering it a "logic".

I still consider it a logic, though of a very different type. First, it is because that NAL consists of a symbolic language, a semantics defining meaning and truth, and a set of formally defined inference rules that can be used in various domains, so technically it meets the basic requirements of being a logic. Furthermore, NAL is an attempt to formalize valid inference observed in human thinking

---

[1]Currently at http://sites.google.com/site/narswang/, which is mostly mirrored at http://www.cis.temple.edu/~wangp/.

process. In this sense, I believe it is an even better instance of the category "logic" than mathematical logic, since the latter is primarily about theorem proving in mathematics, rather than about ordinary reasoning in everyday situations.

The fundamental difference between NAL and the other logics is at the definition of *validity*. Since this notion is traditionally defined as "deriving truth from truth", there are two major desired qualities for any logic:

Soundness: All the derived conclusions are true.

Completeness: All the truths can be derived as conclusions.

Together, these two properties guarantee that from a given set of truth as *axioms* in a certain domain, what the system derives as *theorems* precisely coincide with all the truths in the domain, no more and no less.

In these two properties, "truth" is traditionally defined according to model-theoretic semantics, as "corresponding to a fact". Under this definition, NAL is neither sound nor complete. As a logic based on past experience, NAL's conclusions may be revised by new evidence (so the system is not sound in the traditional sense). As an open system, there is always knowledge that the system does not have at a moment (so the system is not complete in the traditional sense). This result directly follows from AIKR. According to the theory of intelligence on which NAL is based [Wang (2010)], no intelligent system *can*, or *should*, be *sound* or *complete*, in the traditional sense of the notions.

However, the above argument does not mean that soundness and completeness cannot be desired in any sense in logics like NAL. For an axiomatic logic, soundness and completeness are requirements *both* on its *object-level* knowledge (such as its axioms) and its *meta-level* knowledge (such as its inference rules). Since NAL by definition has no predetermined object-level knowledge at all, no request can be made there. However, intuitively we can still expect the system to be able to represent and to derive the desired knowledge, no more and no less. Therefore, the qualities can be applied to the meta-level, not the object-level, of NAL.

Since NAL uses an experience-grounded semantics, in which "truth-value" is defined as "degree of evidential support", the desired qualities should be interpreted accordingly:

Soundness: The truth-value of every belief correctly measures the evidential support according to the system's experience.

Completeness: Every possible way of evidential support needed for intelligence is captured by some inference process.

Unlike the situation in axiomatic logics, whether NAL has the above qualities cannot be formally *proved*, because the system's beliefs cannot be checked against a well-specified model, even though the issue can still be meaningfully analyzed.

The *soundness* of NAL is argued as the following: each belief in the system is either an *input* judgment or a *derived* judgment. For an input judgment, its truth-value is provided by a sensor-actuator or by another system, according to the definition of truth-value in NAL; for a derived judgment, its truth-value is calculated by the truth-value function associated with the inference rule from the truth-values of the premises, which are determined recursively, eventually from some input judgments. As far as all the truth-value functions are designed according to the experience-grounded semantics of NAL, the soundness of the whole system is achieved.

This soundness of NAL does not mean that the system never makes mistakes. Since all the conclusions are based on *past* experience, and the system is open to all kinds of *future* experience, it is quite possible for a prediction it makes turns out to be wrong. Instead, what this soundness means is that the system is *reasonable*, in the sense that every conclusion is indeed based on available evidence, rather than obtained randomly or arbitrarily. Even the wrong conclusions have their reasons when produced.

The *completeness* of NAL is a more complicated topic. How do we know there are no missing inference rules in the NAL specified so far? To put it in a more general form: even if all the rules of NAL are properly designed, how can we know that they are powerful enough to carry out what we intuitively call "intelligent reasoning"? This is similar to the Church-Turing Thesis on "computability" — since "intelligent reasoning" is not formally defined, there is no proof that can show its achievability by NAL, or any logic. Even so, the discussion is still important.

The completeness question can be answered by evaluating the *expressing power* of the language and the *inferential power* of the inference rules, separately. It is necessary to take the language into consideration, because if the language is poor, the system will not be very powerful even if the inference rules are "complete" with respect to the language. For instance, the inference rules of NAL-1 are arguably complete, since they cover all possible ways to make new *inheritance statements* from given inheritance statements among existing terms. However, with the introduction of compound terms in the higher layers of NAL, such arguments become less obvious.

Whether Narsese has *complete* expressing capability is a tricky question. As far as a language can express arbitrary relations among its concepts and relations, it can be considered as "complete", because in principle all knowledge can be expressed recursively as relations among concepts. In this sense, all natural languages have the same expressive power, and so are all programming languages. The difference between languages is that certain knowledge may be *easier* to express in one language, compared to another. Compared to the language used in FOPL (the most popular language in reasoning systems), Narsese is more convenient in expressing compound concepts, ill-defined concepts, uncertain beliefs, temporal and procedural knowledge, etc., though may be inferior in expressing well-defined relations among well-defined entities, such as mathematical statements.

As explained in Sec. 10.3, NAL can emulate an arbitrary logic, by representing its inference rules as *implication* or *equivalence* statements, and carrying out its inference steps as deductions with those statements. In this sense, NARS is a *universal* reasoning system, like a "universal Turing Machine" that can emulate any Turing Machine [Hopcroft and Ullman (1979)].

If Narsese is complete in its expressing capability, the completeness of inference rules in NAL can be considered with respect to Narsese. If there is a type of sentence that can be expressed in

Narsese, but cannot be derived by any inference rule, the system is clearly *incomplete*, because knowledge in certain form can be given to the system, but cannot be produced by the system itself via reasoning. In this way, *completeness* in open systems like NARS is no longer defined as the coinciding between "what can be derived" and "what is true", but between "what can be derived" and "what can be expressed". Though different from the traditional notion, this interpretation of completeness still keeps the intuitive meaning of the word, that is, a system is *complete* if its *inferential power* matches its *expressing power*, and is sufficient for the purpose of the system.

In NAL, the completeness of its inference rules to a large extent is provided by the *reversibility* of the rules, especially between the strong inference rules and weak inference rules. In every layer of the logic, each new syntactic structure can be produced by some inference rules, usually in more than one way. Therefore, NAL can be considered as *complete*, in the sense that every sentence expressible in Narsese can be derived by the inference rules of NAL, given proper experience.

Since the semantics of NAL must provide interpretation for every item in the language, as well as justification for every inference rule, its completeness does not need to be addressed separately.

In summary, NAL is *sound* and *complete* according to a reinterpretation of the notions under AIKR, though not according to the conventional interpretation of them in mathematical logic.

Even so, NAL is not claimed to be "perfect" or "fully accomplished" in the sense that no inference rule can be added or modified. We may find that certain inference process happens very often, so it will be more efficient to "compile" the involved rules into a new inference rule. Modifications of the existing rules are also possible after future considerations. After all, the designing of NAL is not carried out within an axiomatic system, so its conclusions are not "final".

14.2.   Comparison with other Logics

In this section, NAL is briefly compared to some other logic systems.

Classical logics

The current logic study is dominated by First-Order Predicate Logic (FOPL) established by Frege (1999) and Whitehead and Russell (1910), which is usually referred to as "classical logic". The differences between NAL and FOPL have been discussed in several previous chapters, and are summarized here:

- NAL is based on AIKR, while FOPL is not.
- NAL uses an experience-grounded semantics, while FOPL is usually used with a model-theoretic semantics.
- NAL has a categorical (subject–predicate) language, while FOPL has a predicate–argument language.
- NAL depends on syllogistic inference rules, while FOPL depends on truth-functional inference rules.
- NAL is multi-valued and allows various types of uncertainty, while FOPL is binary and intolerant to uncertainty.
- NAL has non-deductive rules, while FOPL has deductive rules only.

Many minor differences follow from the above, so as a whole, NAL is very different from FOPL. Even so, the two logics are still related to each other:

- many statements in IL and propositions in FOPL can be mapped into each other approximately;
- in many situations, the inference processes in IL and FOPL draw similar conclusions from similar premises;
- NAL and FOPL can serve as a meta-logic of each other.

In spite of the above relationship, the soundness and completeness of NAL cannot be judged by comparing to FOPL, because the two systems are based on different theoretical foundations, and are suitable for different situations.

As a term logic, NAL is more similar to the Syllogistic of Aristotle (1882) than to FOPL, though Aristotle's logic is also only about binary deduction. Aristotle's Syllogistic was the dominating logic system before FOPL was established, and then was widely judged as inferior to FOPL in expressing and inferential power.

In recent decades, the only noticeable work in the term logic tradition is Sommers' "Term Functor Logic" (TFL) [Sommers (1982); Sommers and Englebretsen (2000)], which shows that a term logic can be as powerful as FOPL. TFL extended Aristotle's Syllogistic in several ways, some of which are similar to the approach taken by NAL, though it remains to be a binary deductive logic.

The practice of TFL and NAL shows that when properly designed, a term logic can have expressing and inferential power comparable to those of predicate logics. With subject–predicate sentences and syllogistic rules, a term logic is closer to natural languages and commonsense reasoning; on the other hand, with predicate–argument sentences and truth-functional rules, a predicate logic is closer to mathematical languages and theorem proving process.

It is obvious that certain key ideas of NAL come from set theory, especially in the representation of compound terms in IL-2, IL-3, and IL-4. Here the key difference is that, while set theory defines a set purely by its extension, in IL (and NAL) a term is defined both by its extension and intension. Furthermore, membership in NAL is not a Yes/No issue.

In NAL, the part that corresponds to Propositional Logic (PL) is mainly in IL-5, which defines the notions of *conjunction, disjunction, negation, implication,* and *equivalence*. Here the difference is that in PL, all the five are defined in the same way (that is, using truth table), while in IL the first three are *statement connectors*, and the latter two are *copulas*. In IL and NAL, only *negation* is purely truth-functional, while the others are used only when the components connected are semantically related. Furthermore, the compositional rules for the copulas only produce weak conclusions.

Overall, the differences between NAL and classical logics can all be traced back to AIKR, and they agree on extreme situations where the assumption can be ignored.

Non-classical logics

A non-classical logic is a logic system that extends or modifies a classical logic [Haack (1996)]. Usually, it is an attempt to capture an aspect or property of human reasoning that is desirable, but missing in the classical logic [McCarthy (1988); Gabbay and Woods (2001)]. In this sense, NAL can also be considered as a non-classical logic. Aimed at fully formalizing human reasoning, NAL is related to many existing non-classical logics. Here I only briefly compare it with some of them:

Multi-valued logic. Such a logic rejects the *Law of Excluded Middle*, and introduces truth-values beyond "true" and "false" [Haack (1996)]. There are many multi-valued logics, each with its own truth-value range and interpretation. NAL belongs to this category since it uses two-dimensional truth-values in $[0, 1] \times [0, 1]$, which is defined according to an *experience-grounded semantics*.

Fuzzy logic. It can be seen as a special type of multi-valued logic, where truth is taken to be a matter of degree, and comes from the graded membership of concepts [Zadeh (1965, 1979)]. NAL is based on similar assumptions, though it explicitly defines the membership measurement as a degree of evidential support, and uses two numbers to measure it [Wang (1996b)].

Modal logic. Modal logics use modals, such as "necessarily true" and "possibly true", to qualify a statement, and define them according to a *possible worlds semantics* [Kleene (2002)]. In NAL, descriptions and qualifications of statements are usually expressed as higher-order statements. In general, statements in NAL are empirical truth (similar to "possibly true"), though NAL-6 has introduced ways to express some statements as "true in a theory" (similar to "necessarily true"). Furthermore, meta-level definitions and theorems of IL also correspond to "necessary truth" in IL, though they are embedded in the inference rules of NAL, rather than explicitly represented as beliefs in the memory of NARS.

Relevance Logic. This type of logic is proposed to solve the "Paradoxes of Material Implication", that is, the counterintuitive results coming from the truth-functional definition of the *implication* relation, where the premises and conclusions lack semantic relevance. It usually takes the form of a modal logic [Anderson and Belnap (1975); Read (1989)]. NAL solves the paradoxes by replacing the truth-functional definition of *implication* by directly linking it to the derivability of a conclusion. Since NAL is a term logic using syllogistic rules, in each inference rule the premises and the conclusion contain shared terms, so they are guaranteed to be semantically related to each other. Here the idea is similar to the "variable sharing principle" of relevance logic, but more general, since the shared term is not limited to propositional variables.

Paraconsistent logic. A paraconsistent logic rejects the *Law of Non-contradiction* by allowing a proposition and its negation to co-existent in the system without deriving an arbitrary conclusion (as a paradox caused by material implication). Paraconsistent logics come in different forms, and some of them are related to relevance logic and modal logic [Priest *et al.* (1989)]. As an open system, NAL allows contradicting beliefs to co-exist, and uses the *revision rule* and the *choice rule* to manage them. Though undesired, a contradiction is a *local* issue among the beliefs, and cannot cause global problems (i.e., by deriving a semantically unrelated conclusion from them), due to the semantic relevance within the syllogistic rules.

Non-monotonic logic. A non-monotonic logic derives tentative conclusions according to default rules, and can change its mind in light of new evidence, as a form of commonsense reasoning [Ginsberg (1987)]. In the broad sense, NAL also belongs to this category. However, most of the non-monotonic logics proposed so far are still binary. Furthermore, though the truth-value of a tentative conclusion can be modified by new evidence in such a system, it cannot modify its "default rules", no matter what evidence has shown up. On the contrary, NAL is "non-axiomatic" in the sense that all of its beliefs (expressed as judgments in Narsese) are multi-values, and revisable by new evidence.

Inductive logic. There have been many attempts to establish formal rules for non-deductive inference, especially induction, both in logic and in AI [Kyburg (1983); Flach and Kakas (2000)]. Such a logic usually treats induction either as "weakened deduction" in the framework of probability theory, or as "reverse deduction" in the framework of classical logic. In NAL, induction is reverse deduction in a sense (and so is abduction, in another sense), though it is formalized in the framework of a multi-valued term logic [Wang (1999)].

Logic programming. By interpreting certain propositions as procedures, logic programming extends the application scope of logic from theorem proving to problem solving [Kowalski (1979)]. A similar approach is taken in NAL-8, though the inference is not limited to binary deduction.

In summary, NAL can be seen as a *radical* instance of non-classical logic — while almost all of the other non-classical logics are designed *conservatively* to only make minimum change in a classical logic to remedy a single issue, NAL is logic rebuilt on the basis of AIKR, as an attempt to provide consistent solutions to many issues that are traditionally perceived as independent of each other. Though this attempt sounds bold, there is a possibility that many of the issues in classical logic happen when a logic designed for mathematics (where AIKR is usually not accepted) is applied outside mathematics (so AIKR has to be accepted) [Wang (2004a)].

Probabilistic models

Probability theory is another widely accepted normative model of valid inference. In recent years, various probabilistic models have becoming more and more popular in AI and CogSci. Though some probabilistic models of reasoning can be considered as non-classical logics [Nilsson (1986)], some others are not presented as a logic [Pearl (1988)]. Either way, probability theory is a major competitor of NAL in modeling valid inference.

NAL and probabilistic models have been compared in several previous publications [Wang (1996a, 2001b, 2004b, 2009d)]. In the following, the major points are summarized.

- The truth-value in NAL is interpreted as a measurement of evidential support, so it is similar to probability under *logical interpretation*, as proposed by Keynes (1921), Carnap (1950), and Kyburg (1994), while different from probability under the *frequency interpretation* or *subjective interpretation* [Kyburg (1970)], though still related to them.

- An evidential probability representation requires the evidence for each statement to be either explicitly specified as the condition of the statement, or implicitly assumed as part of a common background knowledge [Carnap (1950); Kyburg (1994)]. In NAL each statement has its own *evidential base*, which is neither expressed as the condition of the statement, nor shared by every statement, so as to be taken as part of a common background knowledge.

- Because of the above reasons, the truth-values of beliefs in NARS do not necessarily form a consistent probability distribution. It is possible for the system to assign different truth-values to the same statement with different evidential bases. Unlike in probability theory, such an (object-level) inconsistency does not invalidate the system's conclusions, and can be handled by the related inference rules (such as *revision* and *choice*). Though consistency in beliefs is highly desired and actively pursued, it cannot be always achieved or maintained in an open system with insufficient resources.

- In NAL, two numbers (*frequency* and *confidence*) are used to represent a truth-value, by indicating the uncertainty caused by *negative* evidence and *future* evidence, respectively. Though it is possible to combine them into a single measurement (*expectation*) when predicting the future, the two numbers are needed for other types of inferences, specially in *revision*, where the two plays different roles. On the contrary, in usual applications of probability theory, conclusions are based on the same chunk of evidence, and "incremental assimilation of evidence" is not required, so a single number suffices.

- The above conclusion implies that probability does not clearly separate the uncertainty from observed negative evidence and that from future evidence, so cannot be properly used when such a separation is required. Since NAL is based on AIKR, it can assume neither that the system has collected all the relevant evidence, nor that future evidence can be handled by recalculating all truth-values in the system from the raw input data.

- Since the truth-values in NARS do not form a consistent probability distribution, they cannot be legitimately processed using formulas provided by probability theory. Even so, some NAL functions are similar to probabilistic functions. For example, the Triangular norm and co-norm introduced in Sec. 4.2 assign frequency values to conjunctive and disjunctive events in the same way as probability theory under the assumption of independence, though the interpretation and justification are different.

- Probability calculations are normally carried out on a closed sample (or belief) space. On the contrary, the belief space of NAL is open, so the input sentences can contain terms and statements that the system never saw before. Though each input judgment comes with an *initial truth-value*, it is not the same as a *prior probability*, which must belong to a consistent distribution defined on a closed space.

Some extensions of probability theory have moved in similar directions as NAL by extending a probability value from a point to an interval, which solved some problems mentioned above, though there are other issues remaining. For example, see the comparison between NAL and Shafer's Mathematical Theory of Evidence [Shafer (1976)], as well as Walley's Imprecise Probability Theory [Walley (1991)], in [Wang (2009d)].

Once again, the differences between NAL and probabilistic models of reasoning come from AIKR — while NAL is fully based on the assumption, probability theory only partially accepts it. Russell and Norvig (2010) criticized "rule-based methods for uncertain reasoning", which are characterized by the properties of "locality, detachment, and truth-functionality". In certain sense NAL also has these properties. Though some of the issues they raised indeed exist in NAL, these issues have been addressed in the previous chapters, and none of them is fatal. What is important is to realize that if AIKR must be obeyed, this approach becomes inevitable. Russell and Norvig (2010) admits that "we have no idea what BO [Bounded Optimality] programs are like for large, general-purpose computers in complex environments", and a major reason for this, at least to me, is that mainstream AI still has not recognized the fundamental difference between conventional "computational systems" and truly "intelligent systems", but considers the latter as a more advanced form of the former.

14.3. NAL and AI

As stated at the beginning of the book, NAL is designed to serve as a common "logical core" of intelligent systems [Wang (2004c)]. To conclude the book, the role of NAL in AI is further clarified here.

Logic-based AGI

Defined as "adaptation under AIKR", the "intelligence" pursued by this research is general-purpose and domain-independent by nature, and the label "Artificial General Intelligence" stresses this nature in a redundant style, merely because the current mainstream AI community has favored domain-specific and problem-specific approaches for decades, and indefinitely postponed the pursue of its original goal on "thinking machines".

A logic-based approach toward AGI guarantees the general nature of the system. Since the system's knowledge is represented in a *language* specified by a formal grammar, it is normally not restricted to any specific domains or problems. Furthermore, the knowledge and problems of the system are represented as *sentences*, each of which can be interpreted and processed independently, so their usage is modular, versatile, and flexible.

In a reasoning system, a problem-solving process consists of multiple inference steps, each of which follows an inference rule. An inference rule is defined, justified, and applied independently (though consistently), so as to provide sound conclusions no matter how they are combined. On the other hand, different combinations of the rules can handle various situations, even those unanticipated by the designer or the system itself. Especially, in a finite system working in real time, the rules can be used in a "data-driven" manner, triggered by the current goals and available knowledge, without following a predefined order or a problem-specific algorithm [Wang (2009b)].

A logic-based system provides a clear distinction between *object language* and *meta-language*. For NAL, the former is Narsese, and the latter is a natural language (in this book, English) with various formal languages embedded. Similarly, in its computer implementation, there is a clear distinction between the system's *representation language* (which corresponds to the object language of the logic) and *programming language* (such as Java, which is used in the current NARS implementation). Such a distinction provides a natural answer to the "nature versus nurture" problem. Obviously, an AI system cannot have all of its knowledge hard-wired, nor can it starts with a *tabula rasa*. In NARS, everything in Narsese are acquired by the system itself from its experience (though "implanted knowledge" is allowed, for practical purposes). On the contrary, the meta-level knowledge is programmed into the system, and cannot be modified by the system, except in some minor ways. It is the meta-level knowledge that determines the system's "intelligence", though it needs to be displayed in the system's behaviors and capabilities, which are directly produced by is object-level knowledge.

As shown in the previous chapters, the notion of "reasoning" can be extended from its traditional usage to cover many cognitive functions that are commonly treated as separated from *reasoning*, such as *learning, categorizing, perceiving, planning, decision making, problem solving*, and so on. In a general sense (which is accepted in NARS), "reasoning" includes various forms of rule-governed operations on relations among "concepts" that represent stable patterns in the system's experience. In this sense, the reasoning system framework is powerful enough for AGI.

As for the previous criticisms on logic-based AI, most of them can be explained as criticisms on the *specific types of logic* used in traditional AI research. As discussed in several places previously, usually the issues can be traced back to violations of AIKR, and can be resolved within the reasoning system framework.

Memory and control

NAL, as a logic, specifies what knowledge and problems can be represented in a reasoning system, and how to derive new knowledge and problems from given ones. When implemented in a computer, the grammar rules and inference rules become programs that parse the input data and produce new data, respectively.

For a reasoning system to work, the above "logic part" must be accompanied by a "control part" that manages the storage space, and picks premises and rules for each inference step. This relationship is summarized by Kowalski (1979) in the equation "algorithm = logic + control". In the literature, the control part of a reasoning system is related to the study of knowledge base, control algorithm, decision procedure, and inference methodology, in various forms.

The control part of NARS has been introduced briefly in Chapter 5, as well as described with much details in Wang (1995, 1996c, 2006b). Since this book is about NAL, we do not need to evaluate the memory and control mechanism of NARS here, but its fundamental principles, and what it means for the logic.

From a theoretical point of view, what the control part faces is an optimization problem: with insufficient resources, how to allocate them among the tasks and beliefs of the system to achieve the highest (expected) overall efficiency of the system.

Based on AIKR, the memory of NARS is not designed to be able to remember everything the system has been told and has derived by itself, nor is the control strategy designed to explore all possible inference paths. As in heuristic search, NARS usually starts on paths that look promising, according to some evaluation criteria. However, unlike in heuristic search, the evaluation criteria are not formulated in a predetermined heuristic function, but depend on many factors that can only be determined at run time. Consequently, how the system handles an inference task becomes context-sensitive, and the solution and expense cannot be analyzed using notions like "computability" and "computational complexity" [Wang (2009b)].

Consequently, the logic part of NARS (that is, NAL), specifies what is *possible*, while the control part selectively turns some of the *possibilities* into *reality*. Therefore, in the design of NARS, there is a "one-way" dependency between the two parts: NAL can be designed and evaluated without the details of the control part, while the control part must be structed to fully support NAL. This is especially true after NAL-9 introduces self-monitoring and self-control into the system, since certain memory and control operations need to be expressed in Narsese and manipulated by the inference rules. As a result of the self-referential ability of NAL and NARS, the memory and control process of the system is determined both by some *innate* knowledge (that is represented in a programming language and independent of the system's experience) and some *acquired* knowledge (that is represented in Narsese and dependent of the system's experience). The system can learn skills in memory control, attention allocation, problem-solving strategy, and so on, though it cannot fully determine its own reasoning process — there are "built-in routines" that it cannot always control deliberately.

Physical experience

Even after NARS is fully implemented as planned, the system still cannot solve any practical problem, because initially its memory may be empty. The programs that implement NARS only provides meta-level knowledge, and its object-level knowledge all comes from the system's *experience*, that is, the interaction between the system and its environment. For practical purposes (such as efficiency and safety), it is possible to implant certain object-level knowledge into the system when it is "born", but in principle such knowledge still correspond to certain possible experience of the system.

As described previously, in layers NAL-1 to NAL-7, the experience of the system consists of a stream of Narsese sentences as input, and produce another stream of Narsese sentences as output. For practical purposes, it is possible to have multiple input/output channels, though that does not make much fundamental difference.

In NAL-8, the introduction of *operation* into Narsese gives the system the ability to have "physical experience" that is directly provided by sensors and actuators, rather than by another system (human or computer) in Narsese. Such an addition gives the system a set of plug-in operators, which will be used to compose more complicated terms to represent more complex experience of the system, though it does not change the semantic principles of the system [Wang (2005, 2009c)]. The meaning of other terms cannot be completely reduced into the meaning of the operators, though the latter does contribute to the former.

One major conjecture made in NARS is that "the logic of thinking" is basically the same as "the logic of perceiving" and "the logic of acting". Since a term in NARS is not understood as a symbol that denotes an "object" in the outside world, but an identifier that names a stable pattern in the system's experience, it can either correspond to a "high-level" concept, or a "low-level" percept or action. The perception process is often modeled using a conceptual hierarchy, with concepts at each level summarizing patterns of a lower level [Hawkins and Blakeslee (2004); Arel *et al.* (2010)]. Such a hierarchy can be naturally expressed in Narsese, with copulas representing the substitutability among terms, and compound terms representing perceived patterns in experience. Since inference rules in NAL capture the transitivity of substitutability among terms, they are also applicable to percepts and actions.

The theory of intelligence behind NARS [Wang (2010)] does not assume any specific type of sensorimotor mechanism. As far as a system interacts with its environment, it has experience, and the potential to be intelligent. Obviously, if the experience of a system is very simple, it is unlikely to be very capable. Though there are practical reasons for AI systems to have human-like perception (such as vision), there is no reason to require every intelligent system to have the same sensors or actuators. For NARS, various types of sensors and actuators can be plugged into the system, as far as their executable commands can be registered as operations, and their feedback can be reported as Narsese judgments into the system. The only common sensors and actuators in intelligent systems are probably the mental operations used in self-monitoring and self-control.

An implemented NARS within a host system or connected to a group of hardware/software devices forms a NARS+ system. Different NARS+ systems will not only have different capability when interacting with the environment, but also different concepts, due to the difference made by the embedded operators. They will be like computer systems with similar CPU, RAM, and operating systems, but equipped with different peripheral devices and driving programs. When such a system solves a practical problem, it may depend on a technique that is not part of NARS. The situation here is similar to what described in Sec. 10.3, where NAL is used as the meta-logic of an arbitrary logic — in a NARS+ system, the NARS part serves as an "intelligent operating system" that can use various hardware and software as tools. Though the tools contribute to the system's problem-solving capability, it is the NARS part that makes the system "intelligent", that is, makes it possible to use the tools in adaptive, creative, and flexible ways.

Social experience

Though in principle all types of experience are "physical" in the sense that they are carried out by some physical process, some experience should be described in higher levels of description, since the details of the underlying physical processes do not matter when analyzing the consequence of the processes. Among them, "communication" is a process between information systems, which should be analyzed in terms of the *language* used in the communication.

In the current context, "language" can be seen as a system of syntactic, semantic, and pragmatic conventions, by which the systems involved can exchange beliefs and tasks at conceptual level. A message received in a system can be analyzed at the level of *syntax* (how the sentences are structured), *semantics* (how the concepts are related), and *pragmatics* (what goals will be achieved). In NARS, the system's linguistic knowledge at these levels are tangled together, and the processing of a message does not follow the order of syntax, semantics, and pragmatics, as in the common practice of natural language processing.

NARS has a single "native language", Narsese, and can learn other (natural, formal, mathematical, or programming) languages, all using the general-purpose reasoning/learning capability provided by NAL. Once again, here we see that NARS attempts to be "general purpose" by following a *unified* approach, that is, the system is built layer by layer around a constant core, using a single language (which can serve as the meta-language of an arbitrary language), a single logic (which can serve as the meta-logic of an arbitrary logic), and a single problem-solving technique (which can use an arbitrary device as a tool) [Wang (2006a)]. This approach is fundamentally different from the *integrative* or *hybrid* approaches that are popular in AI and AGI research, where a system is formed by coordinating heterogeneous models and techniques directly [Newell (1990); Franklin (2007)].

According to experience-grounded semantics, the meaning of a term in a system is determined by the idiosyncratic experience of the system, so is fundamentally *subjective*. However, communication provides *shared* experience for the involved systems, so it also brings *objectivity* of various extents to the terms used in communication, which in turn also makes communication possible and fruitful. For an advanced AI system, a large part of its knowledge comes from its *social experience* obtained from communication. As a result, its beliefs and goals will be strongly influenced (though not completely determined) by its social environment consisting of the other systems involved in the communication.

Education is a special form of communication, in which a system is put in an environment controlled by an outside authority, so as to get specially arranged experience, and eventually to form a special cognitive structure, with goals, beliefs, and skills desired by the authority. Similar to a human being, a future NARS system also needs to go through an education process to become practically useful, as anticipated by Turing (1950). Such a process will include tutoring, reading, exploring, and so on, like what is experienced by a human student. Most of the knowledge of the system will probably be acquired from existing knowledge bases and the web, via natural language interfaces, or special converters that convert data of various formats into Narsese sentences.

Education is also responsible for the morality of AI systems. Intelligent systems, being adaptive, are *morally neutral* by design, since the content of its initial goals are not restricted, nor can the initial goals fully determine the system's behaviors. Whether a system will become helpful or harmful to human beings will be mainly determined by its *nurture*, rather than its *nature*. "How to raise a good AI" will become an important field of research, though the basics may be the same as human education.

Putting all the above studies together, we can expect the gradual establishing of a "science of intelligence", and NAL is developed to serve as a cornerstone of this enterprise.

APPENDIX A

NARSESE GRAMMAR

The complete list of Narsese grammar rules are in Table A.1.

The grammar rules in this book are written in a variant of the Backus-Naur Form (BNF), specified as the following:

- Each rule has the format "$\langle symbol \rangle ::= expression$", where the *symbol* is a *nonterminal*, and the *expression* consists of a sequence of symbols, as substitution for the symbol.
- Symbols that never appear on a left side are *terminals* that are specified by definitions in the book.
- Symbols without the "$\langle \rangle$" are used literally. Quotation makers are used to avoid confusion if a symbol is also used for other purpose, as in the following.
- Expression "$exp_1|exp_2$" indicates alternative substitutions.
- Expression "$[\langle symbol \rangle]$" indicates an optional symbol.
- Expression "$\langle symbol \rangle^*$" indicates a symbol repeating zero or more times.
- Expression "$\langle symbol \rangle^+$" indicates a symbol repeating one or more times.

Additional notes about the Narsese grammar:

- A $\langle word \rangle$ is a string of characters of a given alphabet.
- A $\langle truth\text{-}value \rangle$ or $\langle desire\text{-}value \rangle$ is a pair of numbers from $[0, 1] \times (0, 1)$, though in communication between the system and its environment, it can be replaced by amounts of evidence or frequency interval, as well as with default values.
- Most prefix operators in compound term and compound statement can also be used in infix form.

Table A.1. The complete grammar of Narsese.

$\langle sentence \rangle ::= \langle judgment \rangle \mid \langle goal \rangle \mid \langle question \rangle$
$\langle judgment \rangle ::= [\langle tense \rangle] \langle statement \rangle . \langle truth\text{-}value \rangle$
$\langle goal \rangle ::= \langle statement \rangle ! \langle desire\text{-}value \rangle$
$\langle question \rangle ::= [\langle tense \rangle] \langle statement \rangle ? \mid \langle statement \rangle \text{¿}$
$\langle statement \rangle ::= (\langle term \rangle \langle copula \rangle \langle term \rangle) \mid \langle term \rangle$
$\mid (\neg \langle statement \rangle)$
$\mid (\wedge \langle statement \rangle \langle statement \rangle^{+})$
$\mid (\vee \langle statement \rangle \langle statement \rangle^{+})$
$\mid (\, , \langle statement \rangle \langle statement \rangle^{+})$
$\mid (\, ; \langle statement \rangle \langle statement \rangle^{+})$
$\mid (\Uparrow \langle word \rangle \langle term \rangle^{*})$
$\langle copula \rangle ::= \rightarrow \mid \leftrightarrow \mid \Rightarrow \mid \Leftrightarrow$
$\mid \circ\!\!\rightarrow \mid \rightarrow\!\!\circ \mid \circ\!\!\rightarrow\!\!\circ$
$\mid /\!\!\Rightarrow \mid \backslash\!\!\Rightarrow \mid \mid\!\!\Rightarrow \mid /\!\!\Leftarrow \mid \mid\!\!\Leftrightarrow$
$\langle tense \rangle ::= /\!\!\Rightarrow \mid \backslash\!\!\Rightarrow \mid \mid\!\!\Rightarrow$
$\langle term \rangle ::= \langle word \rangle \mid \langle variable \rangle \mid \langle statement \rangle$
$\mid \{\langle term \rangle^{+}\} \mid [\langle term \rangle^{+}]$
$\mid (\cap \langle term \rangle \langle term \rangle^{+})$
$\mid (\cup \langle term \rangle \langle term \rangle^{+})$
$\mid (- \langle term \rangle \langle term \rangle)$
$\mid (\ominus \langle term \rangle \langle term \rangle)$
$\mid (\times \langle term \rangle \langle term \rangle^{+})$
$\mid (/ \langle term \rangle \langle term \rangle^{*} \diamond \langle term \rangle^{*})$
$\mid (\backslash \langle term \rangle \langle term \rangle^{*} \diamond \langle term \rangle^{*})$
$\langle variable \rangle ::= \langle independent\text{-}variable \rangle$
$\mid \langle dependent\text{-}variable \rangle$
$\mid \langle query\text{-}variable \rangle$
$\langle independent\text{-}variable \rangle ::= \#\langle word \rangle$
$\langle dependent\text{-}variable \rangle ::= \# [\langle word \rangle (\langle independent\text{-}variable \rangle^{*})]$
$\langle query\text{-}variable \rangle ::= ? [\langle word \rangle]$

- In an (extensional or intensional) image, the two $\langle term \rangle^{*}$ cannot be both empty.
- There are additional restrictions on the meaningful usage of variable introduced in NAL-6.

The symbols appeared in Narsese grammar are listed in Table A.2.

Table A.2. The symbols in Narsese grammar.

Type	Symbol	Name	Layer
Primary copula	→	Inheritance	NAL-1
	↔	Similarity	NAL-2
	⇒	Implication	NAL-5
	⇔	Equivalence	NAL-5
Secondary copula	∘→	Instance	NAL-2
	→∘	Property	NAL-2
	∘→∘	Instance-property	NAL-2
	/⇒	Predictive implication	NAL-7
	\⇒	Retrospective implication	NAL-7
	|⇒	Concurrent implication	NAL-7
	/⇔	Predictive equivalence	NAL-7
	|⇔	Concurrent equivalence	NAL-7
Tense	/⇒	Future	NAL-7
	\⇒	Past	NAL-7
	|⇒	Present	NAL-7
Term connector	{}	Extensional set	NAL-2
	[ ]	Intensional set	NAL-2
	∩	Extensional intersection	NAL-3
	∪	Intensional intersection	NAL-3
	−	Extensional difference	NAL-3
	⊖	Intensional difference	NAL-3
	×	Product	NAL-4
	/	Extensional image	NAL-4
	\	Intensional image	NAL-4
	◇	Image place-holder	NAL-4
Statement connector	¬	Negation	NAL-5
	∧	Conjunction	NAL-5
	∨	Disjunction	NAL-5
	,	Sequential conjunction	NAL-7
	;	Parallel conjunction	NAL-7
Term prefix	#	Variable in judgment	NAL-6
	?	Variable in question	NAL-6
	⇑	Operator	NAL-8
Punctuation	.	Judgment	NAL-8
	!	Goal	NAL-8
	?	Question (on truth-value)	NAL-8
	¿	Query (on desire-value)	NAL-8

APPENDIX B

NAL INFERENCE RULES

The inference rules of NAL are classified into several categories according to their syntactic features.

(1) **Local inference rules:** Each of these rules directly processes a new inference task according to the available information stored locally in the concept representing the content of the task. These rules are applied before the other rules are attempted on the task.

    (1.1) Revision. When the task is a *judgment* and contains neither tense nor dependent variable, the system matches it with the existing judgments on the same statement. If a matching judgment is found and the two judgments have distinct evidential bases, the *revision rule* is applied to produce a new judgment with the same statement and a truth-value calculated by F_{rev}. When the task is a *goal*, the same revision process is done to its desire-value.

    (1.2) Choice. When the task is a *question* (or a *goal*), the system matches it with the existing judgments on the same statement to find candidate answers (or solutions). If the candidates all contain the same statement, the one with the highest *confidence* is chosen; if the candidates suggest different instantiations to the variable(s) in the task, the one with high *expectation* e and low *complexity* n is chosen, using the ranking formula e/n^r (with $r = 1$ as the default).

(1.3) Decision. A candidate goal is accepted by the system as an active goal when its expected desirability d and expected plausibility p satisfy condition $p(d - 0.5) > t$, where t is a positive threshold.

(2) Two-premise inference rules: each of these rules takes two judgments J_1 and J_2 as premises, and derives a judgment J as conclusion, with a truth-value calculated by a function.

(2.1) First-order syllogism, in Table B.1, are defined on copulas *inheritance* and *similarity*.

(2.2) Higher-order syllogism can be obtained by replacing the copulas *inheritance* and *similarity* in Table B.1 with *implication* and *equivalence*, respectively.

(2.3) Conditional syllogism, in Table B.2, are based on the nature of conditional statements.

(2.4) Composition rules, in Table B.3, introduce new compounds in the conclusion.

(2.5) Decomposition rules are the opposite of the composition rules. Each decomposition rule comes from a high-level theorem of the form $(S_1 \wedge S_2) \Longrightarrow S$ (in Table B.4) where S_1 is a statement about a compound, S_2 is a statement about a component of the compound, while S is the statement about the other component.

Table B.1. The first-order syllogistic rules.

$J_2 \backslash J_1$	$M \to P \ \langle f_1, c_1 \rangle$	$P \to M \ \langle f_1, c_1 \rangle$	$M \leftrightarrow P \ \langle f_1, c_1 \rangle$
$S \to M \ \langle f_2, c_2 \rangle$	$S \to P \ \langle F_{\text{ded}} \rangle$ $P \to S \ \langle F'_{\text{exe}} \rangle$	$S \to P \ \langle F_{\text{abd}} \rangle$ $P \to S \ \langle F'_{\text{abd}} \rangle$ $S \leftrightarrow P \ \langle F'_{\text{com}} \rangle$	$S \to P \ \langle F'_{\text{ana}} \rangle$
$M \to S \ \langle f_2, c_2 \rangle$	$S \to P \ \langle F_{\text{ind}} \rangle$ $P \to S \ \langle F'_{\text{ind}} \rangle$ $S \leftrightarrow P \ \langle F_{\text{com}} \rangle$	$S \to P \ \langle F_{\text{exe}} \rangle$ $P \to S \ \langle F'_{\text{ded}} \rangle$	$P \to S \ \langle F'_{\text{ana}} \rangle$
$S \leftrightarrow M \ \langle f_2, c_2 \rangle$	$S \to P \ \langle F_{\text{ana}} \rangle$	$P \to S \ \langle F_{\text{ana}} \rangle$	$S \leftrightarrow P \ \langle F_{\text{res}} \rangle$

Table B.2. The conditional syllogistic rules.

$J_1 \langle f_1, c_1 \rangle$	$J_2 \langle f_2, c_2 \rangle$	J	F
S	$S \Leftrightarrow P$	P	F_{ana}
S	P	$S \Leftrightarrow P$	F_{com}
$S \Rightarrow P$	S	P	F_{ded}
$P \Rightarrow S$	S	P	F_{abd}
P	S	$S \Rightarrow P$	F_{ind}
$(C \wedge S) \Rightarrow P$	S	$C \Rightarrow P$	F_{ded}
$(C \wedge S) \Rightarrow P$	$C \Rightarrow P$	S	F_{abd}
$C \Rightarrow P$	S	$(C \wedge S) \Rightarrow P$	F_{ind}
$(C \wedge S) \Rightarrow P$	$M \Rightarrow S$	$(C \wedge M) \Rightarrow P$	F_{ded}
$(C \wedge S) \Rightarrow P$	$(C \wedge M) \Rightarrow P$	$M \Rightarrow S$	F_{abd}
$(C \wedge M) \Rightarrow P$	$M \Rightarrow S$	$(C \wedge S) \Rightarrow P$	F_{ind}

Table B.3. The composition rules.

$J_1 \langle f_1, c_1 \rangle$	$J_2 \langle f_2, c_2 \rangle$	J	F
$M \to T_1$	$M \to T_2$	$M \to (T_1 \cap T_2)$	F_{int}
		$M \to (T_1 \cup T_2)$	F_{uni}
		$M \to (T_1 - T_2)$	F_{dif}
		$M \to (T_2 - T_1)$	F'_{dif}
$T_1 \to M$	$T_2 \to M$	$(T_1 \cup T_2) \to M$	F_{int}
		$(T_1 \cap T_2) \to M$	F_{uni}
		$(T_1 \ominus T_2) \to M$	F_{dif}
		$(T_2 \ominus T_1) \to M$	F'_{dif}
$M \Rightarrow T_1$	$M \Rightarrow T_2$	$M \Rightarrow (T_1 \wedge T_2)$	F_{int}
		$M \Rightarrow (T_1 \vee T_2)$	F_{uni}
$T_1 \Rightarrow M$	$T_2 \Rightarrow M$	$(T_1 \vee T_2) \Rightarrow M$	F_{int}
		$(T_1 \wedge T_2) \Rightarrow M$	F_{uni}
T_1	T_2	$T_1 \wedge T_2$	F_{int}
		$T_1 \vee T_2$	F_{uni}

(3) **One-premise inference rules:** Each of these rules carries out inference from a judgment J_1 as premise to a judgment J as conclusion, with a truth-value calculated by function F.

(3.1) **Immediate inference**, in Table B.5, are rules with a truth-value function that only takes one truth-value as input.

Table B.4. The decomposition rules.

S_1	S_2	S
$\neg(M \to (T_1 \cap T_2))$	$M \to T_1$	$\neg(M \to T_2)$
$M \to (T_1 \cup T_2)$	$\neg(M \to T_1)$	$M \to T_2$
$\neg(M \to (T_1 - T_2))$	$M \to T_1$	$M \to T_2$
$\neg(M \to (T_2 - T_1))$	$\neg(M \to T_1)$	$\neg(M \to T_2)$
$\neg((T_1 \cup T_2) \to M)$	$T_1 \to M$	$\neg(T_2 \to M)$
$(T_1 \cap T_2) \to M$	$\neg(T_1 \to M)$	$T_2 \to M$
$\neg((T_1 \ominus T_2) \to M)$	$T_1 \to M$	$T_2 \to M$
$\neg((T_2 \ominus T_1) \to M)$	$\neg(T_1 \to M)$	$\neg(T_2 \to M)$
$\neg(T_1 \wedge T_2)$	T_1	$\neg T_2$
$T_1 \vee T_2$	$\neg T_1$	T_2

Table B.5. The immediate inference rules.

J_1	J	F
S	$\neg S$	F_{neg}
$S \to P$	$P \to S$	F_{cnv}
$S \Rightarrow P$	$P \Rightarrow S$	F_{cnv}
$S \Rightarrow P$	$(\neg P) \Rightarrow (\neg S)$	F_{cnt}

Table B.6. The inheritance theorems.

$term_1 \to term_2$	
$(T_1 \cap T_2)$	T_1
T_1	$(T_1 \cup T_2)$
$(T_1 - T_2)$	T_1
T_1	$(T_1 \ominus T_2)$
$((R \,/\, T) \times T)$	R
R	$((R \setminus T) \times T)$

(3.2) Structural inference is carried out according to the literal meaning of compound terms. When a definition or theorem in IL (summarized in Tables B.6–B.9) is used as a Narsese judgment J_2 with truth value $\langle 1, 1 \rangle$, it can be used with an empirical judgment J_1 to derive a conclusion

Table B.7. The similarity theorems.

$term_1 \leftrightarrow term_2$	
$\neg(\neg T)$	T
$(\cup \{T_1\} \cdots \{T_n\})$	$\{T_1, \ldots, T_n\}$
$(\cap [T_1] \cdots [T_n])$	$[T_1, \ldots, T_n]$
$(\{T_1, \ldots, T_n\} - \{T_n\})$	$\{T_1, \ldots, T_{n-1}\}$
$([T_1, \ldots, T_n] \ominus [T_n])$	$[T_1, \ldots, T_{n-1}]$
$((T_1 \times T_2) / T_2)$	T_1
$((T_1 \times T_2) \setminus T_2)$	T_1

Table B.8. The implication theorems.

$statement_1 \Rightarrow statement_2$	
$S \leftrightarrow P$	$S \rightarrow P$
$S \Leftrightarrow P$	$S \Rightarrow P$
$S_1 \wedge S_2$	S_1
S_1	$S_1 \vee S_2$
$S \rightarrow P$	$(S \cup M) \rightarrow (P \cup M)$
$S \rightarrow P$	$(S \cap M) \rightarrow (P \cap M)$
$S \leftrightarrow P$	$(S \cup M) \leftrightarrow (P \cup M)$
$S \leftrightarrow P$	$(S \cap M) \leftrightarrow (P \cap M)$
$S \Rightarrow P$	$(S \vee M) \Rightarrow (P \vee M)$
$S \Rightarrow P$	$(S \wedge M) \Rightarrow (P \wedge M)$
$S \Leftrightarrow P$	$(S \vee M) \Leftrightarrow (P \vee M)$
$S \Leftrightarrow P$	$(S \wedge M) \Leftrightarrow (P \wedge M)$
$S \rightarrow P$	$(S - M) \rightarrow (P - M)$
$S \rightarrow P$	$(M - P) \rightarrow (M - S)$
$S \rightarrow P$	$(S \ominus M) \rightarrow (P \ominus M)$
$S \rightarrow P$	$(M \ominus P) \rightarrow (M \ominus S)$
$S \leftrightarrow P$	$(S - M) \leftrightarrow (P - M)$
$S \leftrightarrow P$	$(M - P) \leftrightarrow (M - S)$
$S \leftrightarrow P$	$(S \ominus M) \leftrightarrow (P \ominus M)$
$S \leftrightarrow P$	$(M \ominus P) \leftrightarrow (M \ominus S)$
$M \rightarrow (T_1 - T_2)$	$\neg(M \rightarrow T_2)$
$(T_1 \ominus T_2) \rightarrow M$	$\neg(T_2 \rightarrow M)$
$S \rightarrow P$	$(S / M) \rightarrow (P / M)$
$S \rightarrow P$	$(S \setminus M) \rightarrow (P \setminus M)$
$S \rightarrow P$	$(M / P) \rightarrow (M / S)$
$S \rightarrow P$	$(M \setminus P) \rightarrow (M \setminus S)$

Table B.9. The equivalence theorems.

$statement_1 \Leftrightarrow statement_2$	
$S \leftrightarrow P$	$(S \to P) \land (P \to S)$
$S \Leftrightarrow P$	$(S \Rightarrow P) \land (P \Rightarrow S)$
$S \leftrightarrow P$	$\{S\} \leftrightarrow \{P\}$
$S \leftrightarrow P$	$[S] \leftrightarrow [P]$
$S \to \{P\}$	$S \leftrightarrow \{P\}$
$[S] \to P$	$[S] \leftrightarrow P$
$(S_1 \times S_2) \to (P_1 \times P_2)$	$(S_1 \to P_1) \land (S_2 \to P_2)$
$(S_1 \times S_2) \leftrightarrow (P_1 \times P_2)$	$(S_1 \leftrightarrow P_1) \land (S_2 \leftrightarrow P_2)$
$S \to P$	$(M \times S) \to (M \times P)$
$S \to P$	$(S \times M) \to (P \times M)$
$S \leftrightarrow P$	$(M \times S) \leftrightarrow (M \times P)$
$S \leftrightarrow P$	$(S \times M) \leftrightarrow (P \times M)$
$(\times\, T_1\, T_2) \to R$	$T_1 \to (/\ R \diamond T_2)$
$(\times\, T_1\, T_2) \to R$	$T_2 \to (/\ R\, T_1 \diamond)$
$R \to (\times\, T_1\, T_2)$	$(\backslash\ R \diamond T_2) \to T_1$
$R \to (\times\, T_1\, T_2)$	$(\backslash\ R\, T_1 \diamond) \to T_2$
$S_1 \Rightarrow (S_2 \Rightarrow S_3)$	$(S_1 \land S_2) \Rightarrow S_3$
$\neg(S_1 \land S_2)$	$(\neg S_1) \lor (\neg S_2)$
$\neg(S_1 \lor S_2)$	$(\neg S_1) \land (\neg S_2)$
$S_1 \Leftrightarrow S_2$	$(\neg S_1) \Leftrightarrow (\neg S_2)$

J by a strong syllogistic rule. Since J_2 is not explicitly represented, this rule effectively derives J from a single premise J_1.

(4) **Meta-level rules:** Each of these rules specifies how to use the other rules defined above for additional functions.

(4.1) **Question derivation.** A question Q and a judgment J produce a derived question Q', if and only if the answer to Q', call it J', can be used with J to derive an answer to Q by a two-premise inference rule; a question Q by itself produces a derived question Q', if and only if the answer to Q', call it J', can be used to derive an answer to Q by a one-premise inference rule.

(4.2) **Goal derivation.** A goal G and a judgment J produce a derived goal G', if and only if the solution to G', call it J', can be used with J to derive a solution to G by a two-premise inference rule; a goal G by itself produces a derived goal G', if and only if the solution to G', call it J', can be used to derive a solution to G by a one-premise inference rule. In both cases, the desire-value of G' is derived as the truth-value of $G' \Rightarrow D$ from the desire-value of G, as the truth-value of $G \Rightarrow D$, as well as the truth-value of J (if it is involved). As mentioned previously, a derived goal needs to go through the decision-making rule to become an actual goal.

(4.3) **Variable substitution.** All occurrences of an independent variable term in a statement can be substituted by another term (constant or variable); all occurrences of a term (constant or variable) in a statement can be substituted by a dependent variable term. The reverse cases of these substitution are limited to the cases discussed in NAL-6. A query variable in a question can be substituted by a constant term in a judgment.

(4.4) **Temporal inference.** Temporal inference is carried out by processing the logical factor and the temporal factor in the premises in parallel. First, temporal variants of IL rules are obtained by turning some statements in the premises into events by adding temporal order among them, and the conclusion must keep the same temporal information. Then these rules are extended into strong NAL rules by using the same truth-value function as in the lower layers. The rules of weak inference are formed as the reverse of the strong rules as in the lower layers.

APPENDIX C

NAL TRUTH-VALUE FUNCTIONS

The relations among the three forms of uncertainty measurements are summarized in Table C.1, which can be extended to include $w^- = w - w^+$ and $i = u - l$.

For independent extended-Boolean variables in $[0, 1]$, the extended Boolean operators are defined in Table C.2.

All truth-value functions are summarized in Table C.3, in their simplest form, so different types of uncertainty measurements are mixed. The functions are classified according to the type of inference.

Table C.1. The relations among uncertainty measurements.

to\from	$\{w^+, w\}$	$\langle f, c \rangle$	$[l, u]$ (and i)
$\{w^+, w\}$		$w^+ = k \times f \times c / (1 - c)$ $w = k \times c / (1 - c)$	$w^+ = k \times l / i$ $w = k \times (1 - i) / i$
$\langle f, c \rangle$	$f = w^+ / w$ $c = w / (w + k)$		$f = l / (1 - i)$ $c = 1 - i$
$[l, u]$	$l = w^+ / (w + k)$ $u = (w^+ + k) / (w + k)$	$l = f \times c$ $u = 1 - c \times (1 - f)$	

Table C.2. The extended Boolean operators.

$$not(x) = 1 - x$$
$$and(x_1, \ldots, x_n) = x_1 \times \cdots \times x_n$$
$$or(x_1, \ldots, x_n) = 1 - (1 - x_1) \times \cdots \times (1 - x_n)$$

Table C.3. The truth-value functions of NAL.

Type	Inference	Name	Function
Local inference	Revision	F_{rev}	$w^+ = w_1^+ + w_2^+$
			$w^- = w_1^- + w_2^-$
	Expectation	F_{exp}	$e = c(f - 0.5) + 0.5$
	Decision	F_{dec}	$g = p(d - 0.5)$
Immediate inference	Negation	F_{neg}	$w^+ = w_1^-$
			$w^- = w_1^+$
	Conversion	F_{cnv}	$w^+ = and(f_1, c_1)$
			$w^- = 0$
	Contraposition	F_{cnt}	$w^+ = 0$
			$w^- = and((not(f_1)), c_1)$
Strong syllogism	Deduction	F_{ded}	$f = and(f_1, f_2)$
			$c = and(f_1, f_2, c_1, c_2)$
	Analogy	F_{ana}	$f = and(f_1, f_2)$
			$c = and(f_2, c_1, c_2)$
	Resemblance	F_{res}	$f = and(f_1, f_2)$
			$c = and(or(f_1, f_2), c_1, c_2)$
Weak syllogism	Abduction	F_{abd}	$w^+ = and(f_1, f_2, c_1, c_2)$
			$w = and(f_1, c_1, c_2)$
	Induction	F_{ind}	$w^+ = and(f_1, f_2, c_1, c_2)$
			$w = and(f_2, c_1, c_2)$
	Exemplification	F_{exe}	$w^+ = and(f_1, f_2, c_1, c_2)$
			$w = and(f_1, f_2, c_1, c_2)$
	Comparison	F_{com}	$w^+ = and(f_1, f_2, c_1, c_2)$
			$w = and(or(f_1, f_2), c_1, c_2)$
Term composition	Intersection	F_{int}	$f = and(f_1, f_2)$
			$c = and(c_1, c_2)$
	Union	F_{uni}	$f = or(f_1, f_2)$
			$c = and(c_1, c_2)$
	Difference	F_{dif}	$f = and(f_1, not(f_2))$
			$c = and(c_1, c_2)$

APPENDIX D

PROOFS OF THEOREMS

Except explicitly specified otherwise, in the following letters S, P, M, and T each represents an arbitrary term in the system's vocabulary, and the T_is are different terms.

Theorem 2.1.

By definition, the copula '$\rightarrow$' is defined among terms, and is *reflexive*. Formally, it means $T \rightarrow T$.

Theorem 2.2.

By definition, the copula '$\rightarrow$' is defined among terms, and is *transitive*. Formally, it means $(S \rightarrow M) \wedge (M \rightarrow P) \Longrightarrow (S \rightarrow P)$.

Theorem 2.3.

By definition, $T^E = \{x \mid (x \in V_K) \wedge (x \rightarrow T)\}$. Since $T \rightarrow T$ is always true, so as far as $T \in V_K$, $T \in T^E$. If T is not in V_K, no x in V_K can make $x \rightarrow T$ true, so $T^E = \{\}$. The T^I part is parallel to the above.

Theorem 2.4.

If both S and P are in V_K, then S^E is not empty. For any T in S^E, by the definition of extension, $T \rightarrow S$ is true. Since $S \rightarrow P$ and '$\rightarrow$' is transitive, $T \rightarrow P$ is true, which means T is also in P^E, and therefore $S^E \subseteq P^E$. The other way around, from $S \in S^E$ and $S^E \subseteq P^E$, it follows that $S \in P^E$. Given the definition of P^E, it means $S \rightarrow P$. The intensional part is parallel to the above.

Theorem 2.5.

$$(S^E = P^E) \Longleftrightarrow (S^E \subseteq P^E) \wedge (P^E \subseteq S^E)$$
$$\Longleftrightarrow (P^I \subseteq S^I) \wedge (S^I \subseteq P^I)$$
$$\Longleftrightarrow (S^I = P^I).$$

Theorem 6.1.

Similarity is a *reflexive* copula, because $T \leftrightarrow T$ is defined as $(T \to T) \wedge (T \to T)$, which is a conjunction of two true propositions.

Similarity is a *symmetric* copula, because $S \leftrightarrow P$ is defined as $(S \to P) \wedge (P \to S)$, which is equivalent to $P \leftrightarrow S$.

Similarity is a *transitive* copula, because $(S \leftrightarrow M) \wedge (M \leftrightarrow P)$ is equivalent to $(S \to M) \wedge (M \to S) \wedge (M \to P) \wedge (P \to M)$. Given the transitivity of inheritance, $(S \to P) \wedge (P \to S)$ follows, and therefore $S \leftrightarrow P$.

Theorem 6.2.

By definition, $S \leftrightarrow P$ is $(S \to P) \wedge (P \to S)$, therefore it implies $S \to P$.

Theorem 6.3.

By definition, $S \leftrightarrow P$ is $(S \to P) \wedge (P \to S)$. Given the definitions of extension and intension, it is equivalent to $(S \in P^E) \wedge (P \in S^I) \wedge (P \in S^E) \wedge (S \in P^I)$, which is the same as $(S \in (P^E \cap P^I))$ and $(P \in (S^E \cap S^I))$.

Theorem 6.4.

By definition, $S \leftrightarrow P$ is $(S \to P) \wedge (P \to S)$. Given Theorem 2.4, it is equivalent to $(S^E \subseteq P^E) \wedge (P^E \subseteq S^E)$, which is the same as $S^E = P^E$. The intensional part is parallel to the above.

Theorem 6.5.

By definition, any M in $\{T\}^E$ is identical to $\{T\}$, which implies $\{T\} \to M$, so M is also in $\{T\}^I$.

Theorem 6.6.

By definition, $S \circ\!\!\rightarrow M$ is equivalent to $\{S\} \rightarrow M$. Given the transitivity of inheritance, it and $M \rightarrow P$ imply $\{S\} \rightarrow P$, that is, $S \circ\!\!\rightarrow P$.

Theorem 6.7.

The proof of this theorem is parallel to the proof of Theorem 6.5.

Theorem 6.8.

The proof of this theorem is parallel to the proof of Theorem 6.6.

Theorem 6.9.

By the definitions of the derived copulas, all the three statements, $S \circ\!\!\rightarrow\!\!\circ P$, $\{S\} \rightarrow\!\!\circ P$, and $S \circ\!\!\rightarrow [P]$, can be rewritten as $\{S\} \rightarrow [P]$.

Theorem 7.1.

This theorem covers two special cases of Definition 7.5.

Theorem 7.2.
$$(S \leftrightarrow P) \Longleftrightarrow (\{S\} \leftrightarrow \{P\})$$
$$\Longleftrightarrow (\{S\} \rightarrow \{P\})$$
$$\Longleftrightarrow (S \circ\!\!\rightarrow \{P\}).$$
$(S \leftrightarrow P) \Longleftrightarrow ([S] \rightarrow\!\!\circ P)$ can be proved in a parallel way.

Theorem 7.3.

Extension:
$$(M \in (T_1 \cap T_2)^E) \Longleftrightarrow (M \rightarrow (T_1 \cap T_2))$$
$$\Longleftrightarrow ((M \rightarrow T_1) \wedge (M \rightarrow T_2))$$
$$\Longleftrightarrow ((M \in T_1^E) \wedge (M \in T_2^E))$$
$$\Longleftrightarrow (M \in (T_1^E \cap T_2^E)).$$

Intension:

$$(M \in (T_1 \cap T_2)^I) \Longleftrightarrow ((T_1 \cap T_2) \to M)$$
$$\Longleftrightarrow ((T_1 \to M) \vee (T_2 \to M))$$
$$\Longleftrightarrow ((M \in T_1^I) \vee (M \in T_2^I))$$
$$\Longleftrightarrow (M \in (T_1^I \cup T_2^I)).$$

In both cases, the compound term is in its own extension and intension, according to Theorem 2.3.

Theorem 7.4.

The proof of this theorem is parallel to the proof of Theorem 7.3.

Theorem 7.5.

In the definitions of *extensional intersection* and *intensional intersection*, the order of the two components can be switched.

Theorem 7.6.

According to Theorem 7.3, $(T_1 \cap T_2)^E = (T_1^E \cap T_2^E)$, so $(T_1 \cap T_2)^E \subseteq T_1^E$. According to Theorem 2.4, it means $(T_1 \cap T_2) \to T_1$. The second conclusion can be proved in a parallel way.

Theorem 7.7.

According to Theorem 7.3, $(T \cap T)^E = (T^E \cap T^E) = T^E$. According to Theorem 6.4, it means $(T \cap T) \leftrightarrow T$. The second conclusion can be proved in a parallel way.

Theorem 7.8.

According to propositional logic, implication of the definition of extensional intersection $((M \to T_1) \wedge (M \to T_2)) \Longrightarrow (M \to (T_1 \cap T_2))$ can be rewritten equivalently into $((M \to T_1) \wedge \neg(M \to (T_1 \cap T_2))) \Longrightarrow \neg(M \to T_2)$, and $((T_1 \cap T_2) \to M) \Longrightarrow ((T_1 \to M) \vee (T_2 \to M))$ into $(\neg(T_1 \to M) \wedge (T_1 \cap T_2) \to M) \Longrightarrow (T_2 \to M)$. The conclusions on intensional intersection can be proved in parallel.

Theorem 7.9.

$(S \to P) \Longrightarrow (S^E \subseteq P^E)$ (Theorem 2.4)
$\qquad \Longrightarrow ((S^E \cap M^E) \subseteq (P^E \cap M^E))$ (set theory)
$\qquad \Longrightarrow ((S \cap M)^E \subseteq (P \cap M)^E)$ (Theorem 7.3)
$\qquad \Longrightarrow ((S \cap M) \to (P \cap M))$ (Theorem 2.4).

The other three conclusions can be proved in a parallel way.

Theorem 7.10.

$(M \in (T_1 - T_2)^E) \Longleftrightarrow (M \to (T_1 - T_2))$
$\qquad \Longleftrightarrow ((M \to T_1) \wedge \neg(M \to T_2))$
$\qquad \Longleftrightarrow ((M \in T_1^E) \wedge \neg(M \in T_2^E))$
$\qquad \Longleftrightarrow (M \in (T_1^E - T_2^E)).$
$(M \in (T_1 - T_2)^I) \Longleftrightarrow ((T_1 - T_2) \to M)$
$\qquad \Longleftrightarrow (T_1 \to M)$
$\qquad \Longleftrightarrow (M \in T_1^I).$

Theorem 7.11.

The proof of this theorem is parallel to the proof of Theorem 7.10.

Theorem 7.12.

This theorem corresponds to the special cases of the definitions of extensional difference (when x is $(T_1 - T_2)$) and intensional difference (when x is $(T_1 \ominus T_2)$), respectively.

Theorem 7.13.

This theorem corresponds to the special cases of the definitions of extensional difference (when M is $(T_1 - T_2)$) and intensional difference (when M is $(T_1 \ominus T_2)$), respectively.

Theorem 7.14.

According to propositional logic, implication of the definition of extensional difference $((M \to T_1) \wedge \neg(M \to T_2)) \Longrightarrow (M \to (T_1 - T_2))$ can be rewritten equivalently into $((M \to T_1) \wedge \neg(M \to (T_1 -$

$T_2))) \Longrightarrow (M \to T_2)$, as well as $(\neg(M \to T_2) \wedge \neg(M \to (T_1 - T_2))) \Longrightarrow \neg(M \to T_1)$. The conclusions on intensional difference can be proved in parallel.

Theorem 7.15.

The proof of this theorem is parallel to the proof of Theorem 7.9, with the role of Theorem 7.3 being played by Theorem 7.10.

Theorem 7.16.

$$
\begin{aligned}
((T \cap M) \cup (T - M))^E &= (T \cap M)^E \cup (T - M)^E \\
&= (T^E \cap M^E) \cup (T^E - M^E) \\
&= T^E.
\end{aligned}
$$
$$
\begin{aligned}
((T \cap M) \cup (T - M))^I &= (T \cap M)^I \cap (T - M)^I \\
&= (T^I \cup M^I) \cap (T^I \cup \{(T - M)\}) \\
&= T^I.
\end{aligned}
$$

According to Theorem 6.4, $T \leftrightarrow ((T \cap M) \cup (T - M))$. The other result can be proved in parallel.

Theorem 7.17.

For any term x,
$$
\begin{aligned}
x \to ((T \cup M) - M) &\Longrightarrow (x \to (T \cup M)) \wedge \neg(x \to M) \\
&\Longrightarrow ((x \to T) \vee (x \to M)) \wedge \neg(x \to M) \Longrightarrow x \to T.
\end{aligned}
$$
$$
\begin{aligned}
x \to T &\Longrightarrow (x \to T) \wedge (\neg(x \to M) \vee (x \to M)) \\
&\Longrightarrow ((x \to T) \wedge \neg(x \to M)) \vee ((x \to T) \wedge (x \to M)) \\
&\Longrightarrow (x \to (T - M)) \vee (x \to M) \Longrightarrow x \to ((T - M) \cup M).
\end{aligned}
$$

The other results can be proved in parallel.

Theorem 7.18.

$$
\begin{aligned}
(M \circ\!\!\to \{T_1, \ldots, T_n\}) \\
\Longleftrightarrow (\{M\} \to \{T_1, \ldots, T_n\}) \\
\Longleftrightarrow (\{M\} \to (\{T_1\} \cup \ldots \cup \{T_n\})) \\
\Longleftrightarrow ((\{M\} \to \{T_1\}) \vee \ldots \vee (\{M\} \to \{T_n\})) \\
\Longleftrightarrow ((M \leftrightarrow T_1) \vee \ldots \vee (M \leftrightarrow T_n)).
\end{aligned}
$$

The conclusion on intensional set can be proved in parallel.

Theorem 7.19.

$$(\{M\} \rightarrow (\{T_1, \ldots, T_n\} - \{T_n\}))$$
$$\Longleftrightarrow ((\{M\} \rightarrow \{T_1, \ldots, T_n\}) \wedge \neg(\{M\} \rightarrow \{T_n\}))$$
$$\Longleftrightarrow (((M \leftrightarrow T_1) \vee \ldots \vee (M \leftrightarrow T_n)) \wedge \neg(M \leftrightarrow T_n))$$
$$\Longleftrightarrow ((M \leftrightarrow T_1) \vee \ldots \vee (M \leftrightarrow T_{n-1}))$$
$$\Longleftrightarrow (\{M\} \rightarrow \{T_1, \ldots, T_{n-1}\}).$$

Since $(\{T_1, \ldots, T_n\} - \{T_n\})$ and $\{T_1, \ldots, T_{n-1}\}$ are extensional sets defined by the same instances, the two terms are identical. The conclusion on intensional set can be proved in parallel.

Theorem 8.1.

$$((S_1 \times S_2) \leftrightarrow (P_1 \times P_2))$$
$$\Longleftrightarrow (((S_1 \times S_2) \rightarrow (P_1 \times P_2)) \wedge ((P_1 \times P_2) \rightarrow (S_1 \times S_2)))$$
$$\Longleftrightarrow ((S_1 \rightarrow P_1) \wedge (S_2 \rightarrow P_2) \wedge (P_1 \rightarrow S_1) \wedge (P_2 \rightarrow S_2))$$
$$\Longleftrightarrow ((S_1 \leftrightarrow P_1) \wedge (S_2 \leftrightarrow P_2)).$$

Theorem 8.2.

This theorem is implied by the definition of product and tautology $M \rightarrow M$.

Theorem 8.3.

$$((x \in T_1^E) \wedge (y \in T_2^E)) \implies ((x \rightarrow T_1) \wedge (y \rightarrow T_2))$$
$$\implies ((x \times y) \rightarrow (T_1 \times T_2))$$
$$\implies ((x \times y) \in (T_1 \times T_2)^E)).$$

The conclusion on intension can be proved in parallel.

Theorem 8.4.

$$(((\times, S_1, S_2) \rightarrow (\times, P_1, P_2)) \wedge ((\times, S_1, S_3) \rightarrow (\times, P_1, P_3)))$$
$$\Longleftrightarrow ((S_1 \rightarrow P_1) \wedge (S_2 \rightarrow P_2) \wedge (S_3 \rightarrow P_3))$$
$$\Longleftrightarrow ((\times, S_1, S_2, S_3) \rightarrow (\times, P_1, P_2, P_3)).$$

Theorem 8.5.

$$((T_1 \times T_2) \rightarrow (T_1 \times T_2)) \implies (T_1 \rightarrow ((T_1 \times T_2) / T_2))$$
$$(x \rightarrow ((T_1 \times T_2) / T_2)) \implies ((x \times T_2) \rightarrow (T_1 \times T_2))$$
$$\implies (x \rightarrow T_1).$$

The conclusion on intensional image can be proved in parallel.

Theorem 8.6.

$((R\,/\,T) \to (R\,/\,T)) \implies (((R\,/\,T) \times T) \to R)$.

The conclusion on intensional image can be proved in parallel.

Theorem 8.7.

$$
\begin{aligned}
& (((S\,/\,M) \times M) \to S) \wedge (S \to P) \\
\implies\ & (((S\,/\,M) \times M) \to P) \\
\implies\ & ((S\,/\,M) \to (P\,/\,M)) \\
& (((M\,/\,P) \times P) \to M) \wedge (S \to P) \\
\implies\ & (P \to (/\,M\,(M\,/\,P)\,\diamond)) \wedge (S \to P) \\
\implies\ & (S \to (/\,M\,(M\,/\,P)\,\diamond)) \\
\implies\ & (M\,/\,P) \to (M\,/\,S).
\end{aligned}
$$

The conclusion on intensional image can be proved in parallel.

Theorem 9.1.

Since $\{S\} \vdash S$, $S \Rightarrow S$ is true. If $S \Rightarrow M$ and $M \Rightarrow P$ are both true, then $\{S\} \vdash M$ and $\{M\} \vdash P$, which means $\{S\} \vdash P$, with M as an intermediate result. Therefore $S \Rightarrow P$ is true.

Theorem 9.2.

The proof of this theorem is parallel to the proof of Theorem 2.4.

Theorem 9.3.

The result directly follows from Definition 9.6, with x substituted by $S_1 \wedge S_2$ and $S_1 \vee S_2$, respectively.

Theorem 9.4.

At the meta-level, $(S_1 \Rightarrow (S_2 \Rightarrow S_3))$ means $(\{S_1\} \vdash (S_2 \Rightarrow S_3))$, therefore $(\{S_1, S_2\} \vdash S_3)$. Rewritten in object-level, it is $((S_1 \wedge S_2) \Rightarrow S_3)$.

Theorem 9.5.

This theorem can be proved using truth table, as in propositional logic.

Theorem 9.6.

This theorem can be proved using truth table, as in propositional logic.

Theorem 9.7.

This theorem can be proved using truth table, as in propositional logic.

Theorem 9.8.

$(S_1 \Leftrightarrow S_2)$ if and only if S_1 and S_2 derive each other, which means $(\neg S_1)$ and $(\neg S_2)$ also derive each other, that is, $((\neg S_1) \Leftrightarrow (\neg S_2))$. Please note that it is not enough if S_1 and S_2 have the same *truth-value*, or the same *amount* of evidence.

BIBLIOGRAPHY

Adams, E. W. [1998] *A Primer of Probability Logic* (CSLI Publications, Stanford, California).

Alchourrón, C. E., Gärdenfors, P. and Makinson, D. [1985] "On the logic of theory change: Partial meet contraction and revision functions," *Journal of Symbolic Logic* **50**, 510–530.

Allen, J. F. [1984] "Towards a general theory of action and time," *Artificial Intelligence* **23**(2), 123–154.

Allen, J. F. [1991] "Time and time again: The many ways to represent time," *International Journal of Intelligent Systems* **6**(4), 341–356.

Allport, G. W. [1937] "The functional autonomy of motives," *American Journal of Psychology* **50**, 141–156.

Allwood, J., Andersson, L.-G. and Dahl, O. (eds.) [1977] *Logic in Linguistics* (Cambridge University Press, Cambridge).

Anderson, A. R. and Belnap, N. D. [1975] *Entailment: The Logic of Relevance and Necessity*, Vol. 1 (Princeton University Press, Princeton, New Jersey).

Anderson, M. L. and Oates, T. [2007] "A review of recent research in metareasoning and metalearning," *AI Magazine* **28**, 7–16.

Arel, I., Rose, D. C. and Karnowski, T. P. [2010] "Deep machine learning — A new frontier in artificial intelligence research [Research Frontier]," *IEEE Computational Intelligence Magazine* **5**(4), 13–18.

Aristotle [1882] *The Organon, or, Logical treatises of Aristotle* Trans. O. F. Owen (George Bell, London).

Barwise, J. and Etchemendy, J. [1989] "Model-theoretic semantics," in *Foundations of Cognitive Science*, ed. Posner, M. I. (MIT Press, Cambridge, Massachusetts), pp. 207–243.

Baum, E. B. [2004] *What is Thought?* (MIT Press, Cambridge, Massachusetts).

Boddy, M. and Dean, T. [1994] "Deliberation scheduling for problem solving in time-constrained environments," *Artificial Intelligence* **67**, 245–285.

241

Bonissone, P. P. [1987] "Summarizing and propagating uncertain information with Triangular Norms," *International Journal of Approximate Reasoning* **1**, 71–101.

Brachman, R. J. [1983] "What is-a is and isn't: An analysis of taxonomic links in semantic networks," *IEEE Computer* **16**, 30–36.

Brachman, R. J. [2006] "(AA)AI — more than the sum of its parts, 2005 AAAI Presidential Address," *AI Magazine* **27**(4), 19–34.

Braine, M. D. S. and O'Brien, D. P. (eds.) [1998] *Mental Logic* (Lawrence Erlbaum Associates, Mahwah, New Jersey).

Bratman, M. E., Israel, D. J. and Pollack, M. E. [1988] "Plans and resource-bounded practical reasoning," *Computational Intelligence* **4**(4), 349–355.

Carnap, R. [1950] *Logical Foundations of Probability* (The University of Chicago Press, Chicago).

Carnap, R. [1952] *The Continuum of Inductive Methods* (The University of Chicago Press, Chicago).

Carroll, L. [1895] "What the tortoise said to Achilles," *Mind* **4**(14), 278–280.

Chalmers, D. J. [1996] *The Conscious Mind: In Search of a Fundamental Theory* (Oxford University Press, New York).

Chong, H.-Q., Tan, A.-H. and Ng, G.-W. [2007] "Integrated cognitive architectures: a survey," *Artificial Intelligence Review* **28**(2), 103–130.

Cox, M. T. [2005] "Metacognition in computation: A selected research review," *Artificial Intelligence* **169**, 104–141.

Dean, T. and Boddy, M. [1988] "An analysis of time-dependent planning," in *Proc. AAAI-88*, pp. 49–54.

Dekking, F. M., Kraaikamp, C., Lopuhaa, H. P. and Meester, L. E. [2007] *A Modern Introduction to Probability and Statistics* (Springer, London).

Dempster, A. P. [1967] "Upper and lower probabilities induced by a multivalued mapping," *Annals of Mathematical Statistics* **38**, 325–339.

Dezert, J., Wang, P. and Tchamova, A. [2012] "On the validity of Dempster–Shafer theory," in *Proc. FUSION 2012*, pp. 655–660.

Donini, F. M., Lenzerini, M., Nardi, D. and Schaerf, A. [1996] "Reasoning in description logics," in *Principles of Knowledge Representation*, ed. Brewka, G. (CSLI Publications, Stanford, California), pp. 191–236.

Doyle, J. [1979] "A truth maintenance system," *Artificial Intelligence* **12**(3), 231–272.

Elgot-Drapkin, J. and Perlis, D. [1990] "Reasoning situated in time I: Basic concepts," *Journal of Experimental & Theoretical Artificial Intelligence* **2**, 75–98.

Enderton, H. B. [2009] "Second-order and higher-order logic," in *The Stanford Encyclopedia of Philosophy*, ed. Zalta, E. N. (Spring, 2009 edn.).

Fellous, J.-M. and Arbib, M. A. (eds.) [2005] *Who Needs Emotions? — The Brain Meets the Robot* (Oxford University Press, US).

Flach, P. A. and Kakas, A. C. [2000] "Abductive and inductive reasoning: Background and issues," in *Abduction and Induction: Essays on their Relation and Integration*, eds. Flach, P. A. and Kakas, A. C. (Kluwer Academic Publishers, Dordrecht), pp. 1–27.

Franklin, S. [2007] "A foundational architecture for artificial general intelligence," in *Advance of Artificial General Intelligence*, eds. Goertzel, B. and Wang, P. (IOS Press, Amsterdam), pp. 36–54.

Frege, G. [1999] "Begriffsschrift, a formula language, modeled upon that of arithmetic, for pure thought," in *Frege and Gödel: Two Fundamental Texts in Mathematical Logic*, ed. van Heijenoort, J. (iUniverse, Lincoln, Nebraska), pp. 1–82.

Gabbay, D. M. [2007] *Logic for Artificial Intelligence and Information Technology* (College Publications, London).

Gabbay, D. M. and Woods, J. [2001] "The new logic," *Logic Journal of the IGPL* **9**(2), 141–174.

Ganjoo, A. [2005] "Designing emotion-capable robots, one emotion at a time," in *Proc. Cognitive Science Society Conf.*, pp. 755–760.

Ginsberg, M. (ed.) [1987] *Readings in Nonmonotonic Reasoning* (Morgan Kaufmann, San Mateo).

Goertzel, B., Iklé, M., Goertzel, I. F. and Heljakka, A. [2008] *Probabilistic Logic Networks: A Comprehensive Framework for Uncertain Inference* (Springer, New York).

Goertzel, B. and Pennachin, C. (eds.) [2007] *Artificial General Intelligence* (Springer, New York).

Goodman, N. [1955] *Fact, Fiction, and Forecast* (Harvard University Press, Cambridge, Massachusetts).

Goodman, N. D., Ullman, T. D. and Tenenbaum, J. B. [2009] "Learning a theory of causality," in *Proc. Thirty-First Annual Conf. Cognitive Science Society*.

Haack, S. [1978] *Philosophy of Logics* (Cambridge University Press, Cambridge).

Haack, S. [1996] *Deviant Logic, Fuzzy Logic: Beyond the Formalism* (University of Chicago Press, Chicago).

Halpern, J. Y., Harper, R., Immerman, N., Kolaitis, P. G., Vardi, M. Y. and Vianu, V. [2001] "On the unusual effectiveness of logic in computer science," *The Bulletin of Symbolic Logic* **7**(2), 213–236.

Halpern, J. Y. and Pearl, J. [2005] "Causes and explanations: A structural-model approach. Part I: Causes," *The British Journal for the Philosophy of Science* **56**(4), 843.

Harnad, S. [1990] "The symbol grounding problem," *Physica D* **42**, 335–346.

Hawkins, J. and Blakeslee, S. [2004] *On Intelligence* (Times Books, New York).

Hayes, P. J. [1977] "In defense of logic," in *Proc. Fifth Int. Joint Conf. Artificial Intelligence*, pp. 559–565.

Hempel, C. G. [1965] "Studies in the logic of confirmation," in *Aspects of Scientific Explanation* (The Free Press, New York), pp. 3–46, Reprinted in *The Concept of Evidence (1983)*, ed. Achinstein, P. (Oxford University Press, Oxford), pp. 11–43.

Hendricks, V. and Symons, J. [2009] "Epistemic logic," in *The Stanford Encyclopedia of Philosophy*, ed. Zalta, E. N. (Spring, 2009 edn.).

Hofstadter, D. R. [1979] *Gödel, Escher, Bach: an Eternal Golden Braid* (Basic Books, New York).

Hofstadter, D. R. [1995] "On seeing A's and seeing As," *Stanford Humanities Review* **4**, 109–121.

Holland, J. H. [1986] "Escaping brittleness: The possibilities of general purpose learning algorithms applied to parallel rule-based systems," in *Machine Learning: An Artificial Intelligence Approach*, eds. Michalski, R. S., Carbonell, J. G. and Mitchell, T. M. Vol. II (Morgan Kaufmann, Los Altos, California), pp. 593–624.

Hopcroft, J. E. and Ullman, J. D. [1979] *Introduction to Automata Theory, Language, and Computation* (Addison-Wesley, Reading, Massachusetts).

Horvitz, E. J. [1989] "Reasoning about beliefs and actions under computational resource constraints," in *Uncertainty in Artificial Intelligence 3*, eds. Kanal, L. N., Levitt, T. S. and Lemmer, J. F. (North-Holland, Amsterdam), pp. 301–324.

Hume, D. [1748] *An Enquiry Concerning Human Understanding* (London).

Hutter, M. [2005] *Universal Artificial Intelligence: Sequential Decisions Based on Algorithmic Probability* (Springer, Berlin).

Ismail, H. O. and Shapiro, S. C. [2000] "Two problems with reasoning and acting in time," in *Principles of Knowledge Representation and Reasoning: Proc. Seventh Int. Conf.*, pp. 355–365.

James, W. [1890] *The Principles of Psychology*.

Jaynes, E. [2003] *Probability Theory: The Logic of Science* (Cambridge University Press).

Kaiser, L. [2007] "Program search as a path to artificial general intelligence," in *Artificial General Intelligence (Cognitive Technologies)*, eds. Goertzel, B. and Pennachin, C. (Springer, New York), pp. 291–327.

Keynes, J. M. [1921] *A Treatise on Probability* (Macmillan, London).

Kleene, S. C. [2002] *Mathematical Logic* (Dover Publications, New York).

Kneale, W. and Kneale, M. [1962] *The Development of Logic* (Clarendon Press, Oxford).

Kolmogorov, A. N. [1950] *Foundations of the Theory of Probability* (Chelsea Publishing Company, New York).

Kowalski, R. [1979] *Logic for Problem Solving* (North Holland, New York).

Koza, J. R. [1992] *Genetic Programming: On the Programming of Computers by Means of Natural Selection* (MIT Press, Cambridge, Massachusetts).

Kyburg, H. E. [1970] *Probability and Inductive Logic* (Macmillan, London).

Kyburg, H. E. [1983] "Recent work in inductive logic," in *Recent Work in Philosophy*, eds. Lucey, K. and Machan, T. (Rowman and Allanfield, Totowa, NJ), pp. 89–150.

Kyburg, H. E. [1994] "Believing on the basis of the evidence," *Computational Intelligence* **10**, 3–20.

Lakoff, G. [1988] "Cognitive semantics," in *Meaning and Mental Representation*, eds. Eco, U., Santambrogio, M. and Violi, P. (Indiana University Press, Bloomington, Indiana), pp. 119–154.

Langacker, R. W. [1999] *Grammar and Conceptualization.* Cognitive Linguistics Research, Vol. 14 (Walter De Gruyter, Berlin).

Lenat, D. B. and Feigenbaum, E. A. [1991] "On the thresholds of knowledge," *Artificial Intelligence* **47**, 185–250.

Lu, S. and Graesser, A. C. [2004] "What is universal in perceiving, remembering, and describing event temporal relations?" in *Proc. 26th Annual Meeting of the Cognitive Science Society.*

Mares, E. [2011] "Relevance logic," in *The Stanford Encyclopedia of Philosophy*, ed. Zalta, E. N. (Winter 2011 edn.).

Marshall, J. B. [2006] "A self-watching model of analogy-making and perception," *Journal of Experimental & Theoretical Artificial Intelligence* **18**(3), 267–307.

McCarthy, J. [1988] "Mathematical logic in artificial intelligence," *Daedalus* **117**(1), 297–311.

McCarthy, J. [1989] "Artificial intelligence, logic and formalizing common sense," in *Philosophical Logic and Artificial Intelligence*, ed. Thomason, R. H. (Kluwer, Dordrecht), pp. 161–190.

McCarthy, J. [1992] "Reminiscences on the history of time-sharing," *IEEE Annals of the History of Computing* **14**(1), 19–24.

McCarthy, J. and Hayes, P. J. [1969] "Some philosophical problems from the standpoint of artificial intelligence," in *Machine Intelligence 4*, eds. Meltzer, B. and Michie, D. (Edinburgh University Press, Edinburgh), pp. 463–502.

McCarthy, J., Minsky, M., Rochester, N. and Shannon, C. [1955] "A Proposal for the Dartmouth Summer Research Project on Artificial Intelligence," Available at http://www-formal.stanford.edu/jmc/history/dartmouth.html.

McKay, T. and Nelson, M. [2010] "Propositional attitude reports," in *The Stanford Encyclopedia of Philosophy*, ed. Zalta, E. N. (Winter 2010 edn.).

Medin, D. L. and Ross, B. H. [1992] *Cognitive Psychology* (Harcourt Brace Jovanovich, Fort Worth).

Mitchell, T. M. [1997] *Machine Learning* (McGraw-Hill, New York).

Muggleton, S. [1991] "Inductive logic programming," *New Generation Computing* **8**(4), 295–318.

Newell, A. [1990] *Unified Theories of Cognition* (Harvard University Press, Cambridge, Massachusetts).

Newell, A. and Simon, H. A. [1963] "GPS, a program that simulates human thought," in *Computers and Thought*, eds. Feigenbaum, E. A. and Feldman, J. (McGraw-Hill, New York), pp. 279–293.

Newell, A. and Simon, H. A. [1976] "Computer science as empirical inquiry: symbols and search," *Communications of the ACM* **19**(3), 113–126.

Nilsson, N. J. [1986] "Probabilistic logic," *Artificial Intelligence* **28**, 71–87.

Nilsson, N. J. [1991] "Logic and artificial intelligence," *Artificial Intelligence* **47**, 31–56.

Noë, A. [2004] *Action in Perception* (MIT Press, Cambridge, Massachusetts).

Pearl, J. [1988] *Probabilistic Reasoning in Intelligent Systems* (Morgan Kaufmann Publishers, San Mateo, California).

Peirce, C. S. [1931] *Collected Papers of Charles Sanders Peirce*, Vol. 2 (Harvard University Press, Cambridge, Massachusetts).

Peregrin, J. [2010] "Inferentializing semantics," *Journal of Philosophical Logic* **39**(3), 255–274.

Piaget, J. [1960] *The Psychology of Intelligence* (Littlefield, Adams & Co., Paterson, New Jersey).

Piaget, J. [1963] *The Origins of Intelligence in Children*, Trans. M. Cook (W.W. Norton & Company, Inc., New York).

Picard, R. W. [1997] *Affective Computing* (MIT Press, Cambridge, Massachusetts).

Popper, K. R. [1959] *The Logic of Scientific Discovery* (Basic Books, New York).

Priest, G., Routley, R. and Norman, J. (eds.) [1989] *Paraconsistent Logic: Essays on the Inconsistent* (Philosophia Verlag, München).

Ramsey, F. P. [1926] "Truth and probability," in *The Foundations of Mathematics and other Logical Essays*, ed. Braithwaite, R. B. (Brace & Co.,), pp. 156–198.

Rao, A. S. and Georgeff, M. P. [1995] "BDI-agents: From theory to practice," in *Proc. First Int. Conf. Multiagent Systems.*

Read, S. [1989] *Relevant Logic: A Philosophical Examination of Inference* (Basil Blackwell, New York).

Rehling, J. and Hostadter, D. [1997] "The parallel terraced scan: An optimization for an agent-oriented architecture," *IEEE Int. Conf. Int. Processing Systems*, pp. 900–904.

Reiter, R. [1987] "Nonmonotonic reasoning," *Annual Review of Computer Science* **2**, 147–186.

Russell, S. and Norvig, P. [2010] *Artificial Intelligence: A Modern Approach*, 3rd edn. (Prentice Hall, Upper Saddle River, New Jersey).

Russell, S. and Wefald, E. H. [1991] *Do the Right Thing: Studies in Limited Rationality* (MIT Press, Cambridge, Massachusetts).

Savage, L. J. [1954] *The Foundations of Statistics* (Wiley, New York).

Schmidhuber, J. [2007] "The new AI: General & sound & relevant for physics," in *Artificial General Intelligence*, eds. Goertzel, B. and Pennachin, C. (Springer, Berlin), pp. 175–198.

Shafer, G. [1976] *A Mathematical Theory of Evidence* (Princeton University Press, Princeton, New Jersey).

Shapiro, S. C. and Bona, J. P. [2010] "The GLAIR cognitive architecture," *International Journal of Machine Consciousness* **2**(2), 307–332.

Simon, H. A. [1957] *Models of Man: Social and Rational* (John Wiley, New York).

Smith, R. [2012] "Aristotle's logic," in *The Stanford Encyclopedia of Philosophy*, ed. Zalta, E. N. (Spring 2012 edn.).

Smolensky, P. [1988] "On the proper treatment of connectionism," *Behavioral and Brain Sciences* **11**, 1–74.

Solomonoff, R. J. [1964] "A formal theory of inductive inference. Part I and II," *Information and Control* **7**(1–2), 1–22, 224–254.

Sommers, F. [1982] *The Logic of Natural Language* (Clarendon Press, Oxford).

Sommers, F. and Englebretsen, G. [2000] *An Invitation to Formal Reasoning: The Logic of terms* (Ashgate, Aldershot).

Stebbing, L. S. [1950] *A Modern Introduction to Logic*, 7th edn. (Harper & Row, New York).

Sutton, R. S. and Barto, A. G. [1990] "Time-derivative models of Pavlovian reinforcement," in *Learning and Computational Neuroscience: Foundations of Adaptive Networks*, eds. Gabriel, M. and Moore, J. (MIT Press, Cambridge, Massachusetts), pp. 497–537.

Sutton, R. S. and Barto, A. G. [1998] *Reinforcement Learning: An Introduction* (MIT Press, Cambridge, Massachusetts).

Turing, A. M. [1950] "Computing machinery and intelligence," *Mind* **LIX**, 433–460.

Tversky, A. and Kahneman, D. [1974] "Judgment under uncertainty: Heuristics and biases," *Science* **185**, 1124–1131.

Tversky, A. and Kahneman, D. [1983] "Extensional versus intuitive reasoning: The conjunction fallacy in probability judgment," *Psychological Review* **90**, 293–315.

Vila, L. [1994] "A survey on temporal reasoning in artificial intelligence," *AI Communications* **7**(1), 4–28.

Walley, P. [1991] *Statistical Reasoning with Imprecise Probabilities* (Chapman and Hall, London).

Wang, P. [1993] "Belief revision in probability theory," in *Proc. Ninth Conf. Uncertainty in Artificial Intelligence* (Morgan Kaufmann Publishers, San Mateo, California), pp. 519–526.

Wang, P. (1994a). "A defect in Dempster–Shafer theory," in *Proc. Tenth Conf. on Uncertainty in Artificial Intelligence* (Morgan Kaufmann Publishers, San Mateo, California), pp. 560–566.

Wang, P. (1994b). "From inheritance relation to nonaxiomatic logic," *International Journal of Approximate Reasoning* **11**(4), 281–319.

Wang, P. (1994c). "On the working definition of intelligence," Tech. Rep. 94, Center for Research on Concepts and Cognition, Indiana University, Bloomington, Indiana.

Wang, P. [1995] *Non-Axiomatic Reasoning System: Exploring the Essence of Intelligence*, Ph. D. thesis, Indiana University.

Wang, P. (1996a). "Heuristics and normative models of judgment under uncertainty," *International Journal of Approximate Reasoning* **14**(4), 221–235.

Wang, P. (1996b). "The interpretation of fuzziness," *IEEE Transactions on Systems, Man, and Cybernetics, Part B: Cybernetics* **26**(4), 321–326.

Wang, P. (1996c). "Problem-solving under insufficient resources," in *Working Notes of the AAAI Fall Symp. Flexible Computation* (Cambridge, Massachusetts), pp. 148–155.

Wang, P. [1999] "A new approach for induction: From a non-axiomatic logical point of view," in *Philosophy, Logic, and Artificial Intelligence*, eds. Ju, S., Liang, Q. and Liang, B. (Zhongshan University Press, Guangzhou), pp. 53–85.

Wang, P. [2000] "The logic of learning," in *Working Notes of the AAAI workshop on New Research Problems for Machine Learning* (Austin, Texas), pp. 37–40.

Wang, P. (2001a). "Abduction in non-axiomatic logic," in *Working Notes of the IJCAI workshop on Abductive Reasoning* (Seattle, Washington), pp. 56–63.

Wang, P. (2001b). "Confidence as higher-order uncertainty," in *Proc. Second Int. Symp. Imprecise Probabilities and Their Applications* (Ithaca, New York), pp. 352–361.

Wang, P. (2004a). "Cognitive logic versus mathematical logic," in *Lecture notes of the Third International Seminar on Logic and Cognition* (Guangzhou), full text available online.

Wang, P. (2004b). "The limitation of Bayesianism," *Artificial Intelligence* **158**(1), 97–106.

Wang, P. (2004c). "Toward a unified artificial intelligence," in *Papers from the 2004 AAAI Fall Symp. Achieving Human-Level Intelligence through Integrated Research and Systems* (Washington, DC), pp. 83–90.

Wang, P. [2005] "Experience-grounded semantics: A theory for intelligent systems," *Cognitive Systems Research* **6**(4), 282–302.

Wang, P. (2006a). "Artificial intelligence: What it is, and what it should be," in *Papers from the AAAI Spring Symp. Between a Rock and a Hard Place: Cognitive Science Principles Meet AI-Hard Problems* (Stanford, California), pp. 97–102.

Wang, P. (2006b). *Rigid Flexibility: The Logic of Intelligence* (Springer, Dordrecht).

Wang, P. [2008] "What do you mean by 'AI'," in *Proc. First Conf. Artificial General Intelligence*, pp. 362–373.

Wang, P. (2009a). "Analogy in a general-purpose reasoning system," *Cognitive Systems Research* **10**(3), 286–296.

Wang, P. (2009b). "Case-by-case problem solving," in *Proc. Second Conf. Artificial General Intelligence*, pp. 180–185.

Wang, P. (2009c). "Embodiment: Does a laptop have a body?" in *Proc. Second Conf. Artificial General Intelligence*, pp. 174–179.

Wang, P. (2009d). "Formalization of evidence: A comparative study," *Journal of Artificial General Intelligence* **1**, 25–53.

Wang, P. [2010] "A General Theory of Intelligence," An on-line book under development. Available at http://sites.google.com/site/narswang/EBook.

Wang, P. [2011] "The assumptions on knowledge and resources in models of rationality," *International Journal of Machine Consciousness* **3**(1), 193–218.

Wang, P. and Goertzel, B. [2007] "Introduction: Aspects of artificial general intelligence," in *Advance of Artificial General Intelligence*, eds. Goertzel, B. and Wang, P. (IOS Press, Amsterdam), pp. 1–16.

Wang, P. and Hofstadter, D. [2006] "A logic of categorization," *Journal of Experimental & Theoretical Artificial Intelligence* **18**(2), 193–213.

Whitehead, A. N. and Russell, B. [1910] *Principia Mathematica* (Cambridge University Press, Cambridge).

Wierzbicka, A. [1996] *Semantics: Primes and Universals* (Oxford University Press, Oxford).

Woods, W. A. [1975] "What's in a link: foundations for semantic networks," in *Representation and Understanding: Studies in Cognitive Science*, eds. Bobrow, D. G. and Collins, A. M. (Academic Press, New York), pp. 35–82.

Xu, Y. and Wang, P. [2012] "The frame problem, the relevance problem, and a package solution to both," *Synthese*, doi:10.1007/s11229-012-0117-8.

Zadeh, L. A. [1965] "Fuzzy sets," *Information and Control* **8**, 338–353.

Zadeh, L. A. [1975] "The concept of a linguistic variable and its application to approximate reasoning," *Information Sciences*, Part I **8**, 199–249; Part II **8**, 301–357; Part III **9**, 43–80.

Zadeh, L. A. [1979] "A theory of approximate reasoning," in *Machine Intelligence*, eds. Hayes, J. E., Michie, D. and Mikulich, L. I. Vol. 9 (Halstead Press, New York), pp. 149–194.

Zadeh, L. A. [1983] "The role of fuzzy logic in the management of uncertainty in expert systems," *Fuzzy Sets and System* **11**, 199–227.

INDEX